In this book, which includes a substantial new introduction and several unpublished essays, Jeffrey Mehlman confronts the politically devastating resonances of the work of several leading French writers. The essays focus on the series of enigmas surrounding the "Blanchot affair" – a scandal provoked by Mehlman's revelation in 1980 that Maurice Blanchot, one of the tutelary figures of contemporary French thought, had in the 1930s been a prominent fascist journalist. Mehlman takes the issue of Blanchot's forgotten political essays deep into the most revered – and misunderstood – of his novels, *L'Arrêt de mort*. Using this affair as a point of departure, Mehlman sheds new light on the question of the usability of psychoanalysis for literary readings (examining, for example, Mallarmé, Valéry, and Proust); he also investigates the ideological and political connotations of similar literary and theoretical material. The volume as a whole provides a consistently provocative meditation on literature, ethics, and the experience of the French in World War II.

CAMBRIDGE STUDIES IN FRENCH 54

GENEALOGIES OF THE TEXT

CAMBRIDGE STUDIES IN FRENCH

Recent titles in this series include

A complete list of books in the series is given at the end of the volume.

GENEALOGIES OF THE TEXT

Literature, psychoanalysis, and politics in modern France

JEFFREY MEHLMAN

Professor of French Literature
Boston University

CAMBRIDGE
UNIVERSITY PRESS

Published by the Press Syndicate of the University of Cambridge
The Pitt Building, Trumpington Street, Cambridge CB2 IRP
40 West 20th Street, New York, NY 10011–4211, USA
10 Stamford Road, Oakleigh, Melbourne 3166, Australia

© Cambridge University Press 1995

First published 1995

Printed in Great Britain at the University Press, Cambridge

A catalogue record for this book is available from the British Library

Library of Congress cataloguing in publication data
Mehlman, Jeffrey.
Genealogies of the text : literature, psychoanalysis, and politics
in modern France / Jeffrey Mehlman.
p.   cm. – (Cambridge studies in French: 54)
Includes bibliographical references and index.
ISBN 0 521 47213 x (hardback)
1. French literature – 20th century – History and criticism.
2. Politics in literature.
3. Psychoanalysis in literature.
I. Title.   II. Series.
PQ307.P64M44   1995
840.9′358 – dc20   95–48082   CIP

ISBN 0 521 47213 x hardback

CE

For Alicia
for Natalia and Ezra

Contents

Acknowledgments

Versions of some of the chapters originally appeared in the following journals: chapter 2, "Craniometry and criticism" in *Boundary 2* (1983); chapter 3, "Literature and hospitality" in *Studies in Romanticism* (1983); chapter 4, "Literature and collaboration" in *MLN* (1983); chapter 5, " 'Pierre Menard, author of *Don Quixote*' again" in *Esprit créateur* (1984); chapter 6, "Iphigenia 38" in *Proceedings of the Northeastern University Center for Literary Studies* (1984); chapter 7, "Writing and deference" in *Representations* (1986); chapter 9, "Prosopopeia revisited" in *Romanic Review* (1990); chapter 10, "The paranoid style in French prose" in *The Oxford Literary Review* (1990). A version of chapter 8, "Perspectives: on Paul de Man and *Le Soir*," appeared in *Responses*, ed. W. Hamacher, N. Hertz, and T. Keenan (Lincoln: University of Nebraska Press, 1989). A version of chapter 11, "The Holocaust comedies of 'Emile Agar,' " appeared in *Auschwitz and After*, ed. L. Kritzman (New York: Routledge, 1995).

I would like to thank Craig Haller, whose computer wizardry greatly facilitated the preparation of this volume.

CHAPTER I

Introduction

Each of the essays here gathered charts and expands an experience of intense readerly surprise. Beyond any methodological considerations, whatever readability they retain lies in the extent to which that surprise continues to permeate them. At a time when "literary theory" often seems bland in the predictability of its outrages, such interest may constitute sufficient justification for their collective publication, but I would not have assembled these papers were it not for the overriding surprise informing my sense of their global coherence – the macro-shock constituting, as it were, the medium within which they were written. These remarks have been compiled toward its delineation.

In the ten years preceding the decade during which these essays were written, in the course of three books,[1] I had been pursuing a dual project: on the one hand, to write an implicit history of the most fruitful phases of that ongoing meditation on textual interpretation in France which had received the journalistic tag(s) of "structuralism" and/or "post-structuralism;" on the other, to do so in the form of a series of readings of canonical texts of French literature. A first book, *A Structural Study of Autobiography*, was intent on bringing Lacan's re-evaluation of Freud to English-speaking academia by showing that that re-evaluation, among other things, had precise and important consequences for any reading of so enshrined a masterwork as *A la recherche du temps perdu*. *Revolution and Repetition*, which followed in 1977, freed the structuralist model of the ballast constituted by its residual investment in the Freudian category of "castration," charted the reversals in Laplanche and Derrida through which it was dismantled, and made the case that there could be no better medium for the optimal functioning (or comprehension) of the entire process than the intertextual field formed by the novels of Victor Hugo. Finally, *Cataract*, I now believe, offered a meditation on the decline of the entire problematic in the form of a reading of Diderot. At a time when "deconstruction" was becoming a byword of American academia, I was struck by how depressingly quickly repetition was winning out over difference in the general field of repetition-as-difference (or deconstruction), and found in the writings of Michel Serres the wherewithal both to propose a new coherence in Diderot's *oeuvre* and to articulate a certain waning of what had previously, in the years prior to its academic respectability, seemed to augur the possibility of a style of reading that might be construed, without inflation, as radical. Serres as the decadence of deconstruction? The suggestion carries conviction both because his thought is a protracted meditation on the diverse valences of "entropy" (or decline) and because the arch perversity with which it posits a virtual equivalence between "literature" and "science" seems a kind of bravura rigidification of the manifold and more credible inter-implications of "literature" and "philosophy" found in Derrida.

Those three books, then, together tell something of a story – a classical narrative of rise and fall, emergence and dissipation – unavailable to a reading of only part of the series, and it is perhaps worth observing that the experience triggering the essays in this volume occurred when that narrative appeared to be drawing to a close.

In 1977, while at the Bibliothèque Nationale, I stumbled on what may be some of the most taboo texts of contemporary French letters: the series of violently anti-democratic, anti-Semitic, and pro-terrorist articles contributed in the 1930s by Maurice Blanchot to the fascist monthly *Combat*. Blanchot, of course, was one of the great tutelary presences of the entire interpretive effort that so fascinated me. My debt to him was amply recorded in my essay of 1974, "Orphée scripteur."[2] Moreover, one of the more intriguing aspects of his writing was the constant strain toward Judaic metaphor in his delineation of a crucial realm of textual dispersion. Here, then, in the transition from the pre-War anti-

Semitic journalism to the post-War philo-Semitic meditation on "literary space" lay an enigma I set myself to pondering. The result was "Of Literature and Terror: Blanchot at *Combat*," which became the first chapter of my *Legacies: Of Anti-Semitism in France.*[3] But it is in the prehistory of that publication that the overriding surprise referred to in the inception of these remarks is to be found.

The essay situated Blanchot's former anti-Semitism against the strange backdrop of France's pre-World War II tradition of anti-Jewish thought and its precipitous liquidation once Hitler in effect made of anti-Semitism an untenable option for the vast majority of French intellectuals. Perhaps the (Möbian) context against which the Blanchot enigma might best be encapsulated and situated is the lineage moving from Edouard Drumont to Georges Bernanos to Maurice Clavel. Drumont, in *La France juive* (1886), wrote a thousand pages intent on promoting left-wing anti-capitalist anti-Semitism as *the* political philosophy of modern times. It was one of the two best-selling works in France in the latter half of the nineteenth century. The Catholic novelist and polemicist Bernanos, in his influential *La Grande Peur des bien-pensants* (1931), wrote a lengthy biography in praise of Drumont. By the end of the decade, Bernanos' politics had taken a militantly anti-Fascist (i.e., anti-Francoist) turn, but he was careful to maintain that even then he had not broken with the values of his beloved "master," Drumont. Finally, there came in the 1970s the Catholic *gauchiste* patron of the resolutely philo-Semitic "new philosophers," Maurice Clavel. For Clavel was careful to maintain that *his* "master" remained Bernanos, and even the unassimilable Bernanos of *La Grande Peur*. From Drumont to Bernanos to Clavel, in brief, there was no break, but a paradoxical twist bringing a fundamentally anti-Semitic configuration into alignment with a later philo-Semitic one. Such, in summary, was the perverse progress against which I assayed the enigma I had located in Blanchot.

The essay first appeared in 1980 in a special issue of *Modern Language Notes* dedicated to the 1930s in France.[4] Meanwhile, Philippe Sollers, who had heard a version of the paper (in improvised French) at Columbia University, confirmed that he was eager to publish a French translation (which he would commission) in *Tel quel.* When that translation finally did appear, in 1982, it was riddled with misrenderings in French, but nonetheless provoked considerable interest *pro* and *con* in the French press. All without my knowledge. It was not until a number of months later that I saw the botched translation and the two principal articles devoted to my own. The first, in *Le Matin,* hailed a major and barely believable revelation and declared it particularly significant that France would have had to wait for an American to reveal matters of such import about French intellectual life.[5] The second, in *La Quinzaine littéraire,* simply denied the premise of my piece, refused to credit the existence of any anti-Semitic writings in Blanchot's past, and more or less implied that only a foreigner would stoop to such slander against the great French monument.[6] Given the opportunity for ridicule opened up by some of the more ludicrous errors in the translation of my essay, I confess that I was relieved to see the attack focusing on the article's premise, and dashed off a letter to Maurice Nadeau, the editor of the *Quinzaine,* in which I dissociated myself from the translation, nonetheless responded to the denial by quoting at some length two particularly hair-raising passages of anti-Jewish polemic by Blanchot in the 1930s, took the liberty of connecting the refusal to acknowledge the existence of such passages with the manifestly xenophobic tenor of the attack, and had the pleasure of ending my letter by paraphrasing a well-known Bernanos title: "Français, si vous saviez ... l'anglais par exemple."

When a month passed without word from the *Quinzaine,* I called up Nadeau and was told to my surprise that he had received the letter, but could not publish the two passages I had quoted because they were just too violent, Blanchot was now too old – and a friend of the house to boot. I reminded him that I had been attacked in his journal for claiming that such passages existed, specified that their existence could (and should) be carefully circumscribed in the *Quinzaine* by documenting Blanchot's activities during the War in the Resistance, but insisted that he publish my letter as written. At which point he pleaded a faulty (overseas) connection and I hung up – in astonishment. When Sollers discovered the existence of my letter, he was all too happy to publish it in the first issue of *L'Infini* (as the newly relocated *Tel quel* has since been called).[7] What measure of Parisian resentment dictated the relish with which Nadeau's refusal to publish the letter was announced in *L'Infini* is, of course, open to speculation.

Now at the time all this was transpiring, my teaching in Boston brought me to review comments I had made years earlier in a preface to Jean Laplanche's *Life and Death in Psychoanalysis*.[8] In that piece, I saw myself (ten years after the fact) brandishing the thousand presumably unreadable pages of Lacan's *Ecrits* and telling my American readership that what was remarkable about the French reading of Freud was not simply that it was an alternative interpretation, different from the going American one, but that what it mediated was nothing so much as an elaborate theory of the inevitability of the error entailed by the American reading. Laplanche's book, I maintained, would offer superlative access to that insight. Of a sudden, it dawned on me that that very scenario was being perversely re-enacted ten years later in the controversy surrounding my essay on Blanchot. For I saw myself again brandishing a thousand presumably "unreadable" pages, Drumont's *La France juive*, only to find myself this time – or so the *Quinzaine* would have it – in the position of the "American" who could not but be wrong. The seal provided by the twin motifs of the "inevitability of American error" and the thousand-page "unreadable" Gallic masterpiece was unmistakable. As in Lacan's "Seminar on 'The Purloined Letter,'" an identical structure was being mobilized, but with a change of sign.[9] As though the discursive dilemma into which I had been written in the recent polemic had always already been scripted in the somewhat triumphant heralding of the accomplishments of French thought found in the earlier essays.

The essays in this book are attempts to dwell within that unsettling insight in the hope of seeing where it might lead. Some return to texts I had analyzed earlier to view them as though my previous readings had been *at best* virtuoso renditions of the treble part of works for which I could now supply a rather rich, though sinister, bass. The return to the Valéry of my 1970s speculation "On Tear-Work"[10] in "Craniometry and criticism," the opening essay of this volume, is, in this regard, exemplary, but the resurfacing of the Proust of *A Structural Study of Autobiography* in "Litera-

ture and Collaboration," and of the Blanchot of "Orphée scripteur" in "Iphigenia 38" (which takes the enigma of Blanchot's political journalism of the 1930s deep into the most revered – and
misread – of his novels) may be viewed in the same perspective.
As may the return of the Mallarmé of "Mallarmé/Maxwell,"[11] in
the (anti-Dreyfusard) anticipation of the future of Mallarmé criticism in " 'Pierre Menard, author of *Don Quixote*' again." Even the
Lacan of "Poe *pourri*"[12] emerges in uncomfortable, if illuminating, proximity to the wildly reactionary Léon Bloy in "The
paranoid style in French prose."

The Blanchot controversy of the early 1980s was, in fact, the first
of several in which I was to be embroiled. Convinced as I was of
the centrality of the 1930s journalism to any understanding of
Blanchot, I could not but be disappointed to find Derrida publishing an entire volume on Blanchot without referring to the tell-
tale articles.[13] That disappointment is registered in "Writing and
deference: the politics of literary adulation" (chapter 7), an essay
in which what I took to be an evasion is interpreted as sympto-
matic of a general waning of the intellectual energy (or audacity)
of deconstruction in the age of its academic respectability. My
sense was that Derrida would eventually – I did not realize how
soon – have to confront the whole vexed matter of the War, the
Collaboration, the Resistance, etc. I compared him to Jean
Paulhan, in his last years something of a mystic of language, a
man of impeccable credentials in the Resistance, but who, as soon
as the War was over, began arguing with some stridency that
there were no ethical grounds for condemning any intellectual
who had collaborated with the Nazis. Why? The great paradox of
World War II, according to Paulhan, was that the national Resistance to foreign occupation was to a considerable extent the
achievement of an ideological group that had long been denigrating all national values with a view toward future collaboration
– with Moscow. In addition, the Collaborators with the Germans
were a group that had long been training as Resistance fighters –
against the Russians. I endeavored to show that that constitutive
chiasmus (between Resistance and Collaboration) was also the
configuration informing what Paulhan as meditator on the con-

undra of language was to call a principle of "counteridentity." The political upshot of his position was to call for a general amnesty. Yet he felt inadequate to the task. "Ah! je voudrais être juif, pour dire – avec plus d'autorité que je n'en puis avoir [and yet he was a leader of the Resistance] – que j'ai pardonné à la France, une fois pour toutes, son impuissance à me défendre."[14] Let the chiasmus survive, but let its painful political crux be voided.

It was at this point in my speculative scenario that I had Derrida enter the scene – his *différance* taking over for Paulhan's principle of counteridentity, his "dissemination" for the more radical polysemy Paulhan envisaged. And above all, I suggested, in what I called a "speculative genealogy," Derrida separating the later Paulhan's problematic from the political chiasmus that seemed to underpin it.

When "Writing and deference" appeared in *Representations* in 1986, the reaction was unexpectedly intense (although, once again, as in the case of the Blanchot polemic in France, it was not until months later that I learned the details). J. Hillis Miller drew up a list of four or five left-wing enemies of literary theory to denounce in his 1986 Presidential address to the Modern Language Association. The list included myself as well as the editors of *Representations* for having published my piece. Derrida, I'm told, refused to lecture at Berkeley because of it, and Stephen Greenblatt has told me that it changed the history of the journal.

In retrospect, the commotion over "Writing and deference" strikes me as justified less by the extremeness of what was presented as a speculative argument – Derrida, it should be repeated, was compared to Paulhan, a hero of the Resistance – than by the essay's premonition of what would soon submerge the literary-theoretical community under the name of the "de Man affair." My own favorite comment on the controversy – which was born of the discovery that the eminent Yale critic, recently deceased, had written numerous articles in the Brussels collaborationist press – is that of Howard Bloch, an editor of *Representations*, whom I ran into one evening in San Francisco and who asked me straightaway: "who would have believed you were right?" The present volume contains two essays (chapters 8 and 9) on the de

Man affair – which, because of an ill conceived defense, very soon became a "de Man-Derrida affair." Ultimately less interested in the (undeniable and precise) repercussions of de Man's past in his later work than in the structure of Derrida's apology, I have, I confess, observed with some fascination Derrida, in his writings on de Man, all but acting out, as it were, the scenario scripted for him in "Writing and deference."

Finally, note should be taken of the public reception of the pe-nultimate essay in this volume: "*Pour Sainte-Beuve*: Maurice Blan-chot, 10 March 1942." It was originally presented to a symposium on Blanchot at the University of London in January 1993, and deals with the author's front-page article (on Sainte-Beuve's poli-tics) in the collaborationist newspaper *Le Journal des débats*. My ar-gument ultimately has Blanchot misreading his subject in order to avoid the trap set for him (in 1942) by his collaborationist editors. Its subject, that is, is the political honor of Maurice Blanchot. Now in the course of the London symposium, Roger Laporte, a friend of the author's, announced to general surprise that Blan-chot, queried about the date in my title, drew a blank, but that upon being confronted with his own text of 1942, he had written a letter, which he had agreed to have read (by Laporte) at the end of my lecture. That letter, a rather violent act of self-criticism, does not see much beyond the egregiousness of the author's en-dorsement of an argument by the royalist leader Charles Maurras. And yet it is a remarkable document, in some ways the letter many would have wished de Man had written, in others a rehearsal of Derrida's own apology for de Man. Upon receiving the text of the letter, after my presentation, from Laporte, it was unclear to me whether it constituted a perverse sort of diploma or the epistolary equivalent of a pound of flesh. I have included it in an appendix.

"Writing and deference," the two de Man articles, and "*Pour Sainte-Beuve*," whatever polemical prominence they may have achieved, remain – or record – after-shocks, speculations carried out in the wake of my surprise, mentioned above, at rediscovering the contours of the polemic over Blanchot in the earlier proble-matic of my preface to Laplanche. And it is to that enigma, which furnishes the very medium within which these essays were written, that I shall now return. For the surprise implied, of course, that an unwitting anti-Semitic counterpoint was perhaps a dimension not simply of the texts I was *championing* (or explicating) but of those I was writing as well. The point might be sustained by considering that whereas the "method" of textual superimposition, first elaborated by Charles Mauron, is implicitly at work throughout my essays, "Craniometry and criticism" situates that most fruitful technique of "literary psychoanalysis" genealogically as part of the arsenal of social Darwinism, and " 'Pierre Menard' again" details the role it played in the theory used to pin the incriminating text in 1894 on Captain Dreyfus in the celebrated Affair bearing his name.[15] The general dilemma of the "status of my discourse" (as critical jargon would put it) – the un-ease with which one cannot but attend to the apparent enrichment of texts through a delineation of their anti-Semitic underpinnings – is the subject of the conclusion to my *Legacies*. I situate my recent efforts there within the context of Gershom Scholem's remarks on the afterlife of Sabbatian antinomianism and their contribution to an understanding of the criticism of his friend Walter Benjamin.[16] Within the present volume, that link   between Kabbalism and contemporary French letters – will be found in the discussion of Klossowski's edition of Hamann in "Literature and hospitality" as well – more obliquely – as in the remarks on Bernard Lazare, anti-Jewish "Symbolist of Nîmes" and future hero of the Dreyfus Affair, in " 'Pierre Menard' again." If Scholem is right in suggesting that Jewish secularist culture, the whole of the Jewish Enlightenment, has its deepest roots not in a flight from religious mysticism, but in its desperate exacerbation, then a Jew's deepest achievements in secular culture will tend to join up, however tangentially, with that will to violence against the Law which was Sabbatian antinomianism's most characteristic tendency. As though at a certain pitch of intensity the fascination with the secular were less a forgetting of classical Judaism than an oblique remembering or unwitting re-enactment of a major Jewish heresy.

That heresy, of course, might be read reductively in terms of "anti-Semitism," even "Jewish anti-Semitism." Indeed, to entertain that proposition is to be reminded (first) that Jewish self-hatred historically was a matter of Eastern European Jews trying to work their way into German by sounding more Western than the Germans, that is: by sounding French; and (second) that a detour via French to the core of alien German texts is in many ways a precise and economical description of what has been called "literary theory" in this country. A tempting superimposition indeed: the "theoretical" or aesthetic dream and the nightmare it may always already have been.[17] Yet whatever the seductions of such literary sociology, I prefer to remain with Scholem, reviving that deep historical fracture – the legacy of Sabbatianism, the perilous, even *erroneous* business of pretending to defeat evil from within – whose persistence may well be the enabling condition of these pages. Enlightenment and catastrophe, then: for it is within their conjunction and its repercussions that these essays, not quite *flowers of evil* all, have been culled.

CHAPTER 2

Craniometry and criticism: notes on a Valéryan criss-cross

Un homme d'esprit *(lato et stricto sensu)* est un homme qui a de bonnes séries. Gagne souvent. On ne sait pas pourquoi. Il ne sait pas pourquoi.

Paul Valéry, *Mauvaises Pensées et autres*

First series, Poetry. Valéry, during World War I, undertakes, at Gide's suggestion, to consolidate his farewell to poetry by preparing an edition of the *vers anciens* of his youth, the remains of a vocation he had abandoned during his crisis of 1892 as ultimately deleterious to mind. That farewell, in one of the hoariest episodes of modern literary history, turned into a paradoxical return. Valéry soon found himself embarked in spite of himself on his major poem, "La Jeune Parque," the "involuntary *Aeneid*" he completed in 1917.[1] A virgin awakens to find her virginity threatened by the tear she can no longer quite remember having shed during a dream: who indeed could be crying, she asks, beside(s) herself ("Mais qui pleure, / Si proche de moi-même au moment de pleurer?") (*Oeuvres*, p. 96).[2] As the tear writes (or "marks") its way through the Parque's body, provoking its host to flight, it comes to figure the poem itself, the apparently unwanted issue of Valéry's reawakening to poetry. For the subsequent volume *Charmes*, I have attempted to demonstrate elsewhere, is readable as a transformation of the complex "tear-work" of "La Jeune Parque."[3] From which demonstration, two examples: "Le Cimetière marin" begins with a meditation on the sparkling surface of the sea ("La mer, la mer toujours recommencée"), and modulates into an evocation of the sea as a retentive eye:

Stable trésor, temple simple à Minerve,
Masse de calme, et visible réserve

Eau sourcilleuse, Oeil qui gardes en toi
Tant de sommeil sous un voile de flamme,
O mon silence! . . .   (*O*, p. 148)

Valéry's "silence," the cult of Intelligence (Minerva), the eye closed with slumber . . . A minimal solicitation of the text, and we find the awakening of the Jeune Parque and the scintillation of the Mediterranean surface (LA MER, LA MER) begun anew, anagramatically, as LARME. A redistribution to which we shall return.

A second recurrence of the tear, in summary of my earlier demonstration, is afforded by "Le Vin perdu." The poet finds himself gratuitously casting a bit of wine ("tout un peu de vin précieux") into the ocean. The sea resumes its transparency, but the poet becomes witness thereafter to a kind of intoxication of the waves as "les figures les plus profondes" spring into the air. Now the poem's second quatrain begins by asking who desired that loss or waste ("Qui voulut ta perte, ô liqueur?") (*O*, p. 146). It repeats, that is, the Jeune Parque's mystification concerning her tear: "Qui pleure là . . . ?" True, the (transformed) tear here is emitted unimaginably *into* the "eye" (i.e., the sea of our previous example, "Le Cimetière marin"). But it is precisely the threat to both visual imagination and the distinction within/without that is at stake in Valéry's tear-work. A final line we shall quote from "Le Vin perdu" ("Songeant au sang, versant le vin") has the poet dreaming – un-Eucharistically – blood for wine. Let us retain it as an index of the extent to which the repetition of the tear is inseparable from its transformation as difference.

Second series, Politics. Toward the end of World War I, then, Valéry emerged with his poetic "maturity," but as well with a political formula, which he himself was inclined to repeat as a kind of short-hand for his own presumably profound sense of the political state of the world: "Nous autres, civilisations, nous savons maintenant que nous sommes mortelles" (*O*, p. 988).[4] The line served as something of a signature for Valéry after its initial appearance in "La Crise de l'esprit" (1919), to which we shall presently turn. From that text, consider first Valéry's evocation of Europe during the years of the War, the period, that is, during

which he was composing "La Jeune Parque": "Un frisson extraordinaire a couru la moelle de l'Europe. Elle a senti, par tous ses
noyaux pensants, qu'elle ne se reconnaissait plus, qu'elle cessait
de se ressembler, qu'elle allait perdre conscience ... Alors, –
comme par une défense désespérée de son être et de son avoir
physiologiques, toute sa mémoire lui est revenue confusément ...
Et dans le même désordre mental, à l'appel de la même angoisse,
l'Europe a subi la reviviscence rapide de ses innombrables
pensées" (*O*, p. 989). Above and beyond the accuracy of Valéry's
suggestions about the intellectual intoxication of the war years,
one is hard put not to relate the threateningly intense return of
Europe's intellectual memory to the return of Valéry's abandoned
poetic vocation in the near-convulsions of "La Jeune Parque."
Whence, moreover, the interest of Valéry's meditation on Europe
in the second "letter" of his essay, for it culminates in an elaborate recurrence of an image we have already encountered. The
poet argues that the crisis of European intelligence is less a function of the havoc wreaked by the War than of the random diffusion of the treasure of European inventiveness into areas of the
world more populated than itself. The inequality among regions
of the globe, the improbable superiority of Europe, will thus disappear, or rather superiority will henceforth be based no longer
on intelligence but on the "statistical" realities of population,
area, raw materials, etc. Whereupon Valéry, forgetting the national argument, poses a class analogy: the current crisis of
Europe recalls the effects of the diffusion of culture within each
nation amidst progressively larger sections of the population. Is
there a fated degradation of mental life concomitant with such
diffusion? He comments:

Le charme de ce problème, pour l'esprit spéculatif, provient d'abord de
sa ressemblance avec le fait physique de la diffusion, – et ensuite du
changement brusque de cette ressemblance en différence profonde, dès
que le penseur revient à son premier objet, qui est *hommes* et non *molécules*.

Une goutte de vin tombée dans l'eau la colore à peine et tend à
disparaître, après une rose fumée. Voilà le fait physique. Mais supposez
maintenant que, quelque temps après cet évanouissement et ce retour à
la limpidité, nous voyions, ça et là, dans ce vase qui semblait redevenu

eau *pure*, se former des gouttes de vin sombre et *pur*, – quel étonnement ...

Ce phénomène de Cana n'est pas impossible dans la physique intellectuelle et sociale. On parle alors du *génie* et on l'oppose à la diffusion. (*O*, p. 999)

Not the least of the problem's incipient "charms," it will be seen, is that it is centered on an image that will appear three years later in *Charmes* as "Le Vin perdu." We are, then, to all appearances, at one of those crossroads – between poetry and politics – with which thought, in Monsieur Teste's phrase, is paved.[5] For the expenditure of wine in the poem is part of the tear-work series. The intersection, moreover, is sufficiently ample to accommodate an entire line of verse: "Après une rose fumée." An interpretation? Let us first underscore the dimensions of the parallel. From 1913 to 1917, Valéry re-emerges, in spite of himself, as a poet in the figure of the awakening Jeune Parque, traumatized to observe what is no longer quite her own substance, a tear, spent in the world. During the same years, Valéry's Europe knows a comparably intense reactivation of its intellectual capital only to see it spent – as a liquid emission – outside itself. The political problem of the essay is the retrieval of that initial inequality, in the precise form of the return of that emission. But the poetry – as tear-work – is thinkable as nothing so much as the logic – or graphics – of that return ...

Third series, Physics. The image which Valéry uses in "Le Vin perdu" and "La Crise de l'esprit" was borrowed from Henri Poincaré's discussion of the second principle of thermodynamics ("Carnot's Principle") in *La Valeur de la science:* "Qu'une goutte de vin tombe dans un verre d'eau; quelle que soit la loi du mouvement interne du liquide, nous le verrons bientôt se colorer d'une teinte rosée uniforme et à partir de ce moment on aura beau agiter le vase, le vin et l'eau ne paraîtront plus pouvoir se séparer."[6] It is precisely the irreversibility of such processes – ultimately of physical time itself – which is posited by Carnot: in Poincaré's formulation: "la chaleur peut passer du corps chaud sur le corps froid, et il est impossible ensuite de lui faire reprendre le chemin inverse et de rétablir des différences de température qui se sont effacées."[7] Time is the obliteration of difference. But Valéry's excursion into "intellectual physics" was predicated on the suddenly perceived possibility of a "différence profonde," the reconstitution of the wine-drops. Such was the task assigned in Poincaré's text to Maxwell's imaginary demon, "qui peut trier les molécules une à une, [et] saurait bien contraindre le monde à revenir en arrière."[8] The dilemma of the tear, then, is the condition of (im)possibility of re-establishing European superiority.

J. C. Maxwell introduced the demon in his *Theory of Heat* (1871). Observing that the second law of thermodynamics posits the impossibility of producing "any inequality of temperature or of pressure without the expenditure of work," he continued:

Now let us suppose that . . . a vessel is divided into two portions, A and B, by a division in which there is a small hole, and that a being, who can see the individual molecules, opens and closes this hole, so as to allow only the swifter molecules to pass from A to B, and only the slower ones to pass from B to A. He will thus without expenditure of work raise the temperature of B and lower that of A, in contradiction to the second law of thermodynamics.[9]

The demon, thus, in producing difference, reduces entropy and eliminates the disorder of chance.

Jean Hyppolite, toward the end of his life, read Mallarmé's *Un coup de dés* in conjunction with Norbert Wiener on cybernetics, and assimilated the old man of that poem ("cadavre par le bras écarté du secret qu'il détient"), his fist clenched around the dice he will – perhaps – never throw, to Maxwell's demon . . . in the process of going under.[10] The poem would affirm the irreducibility of the informational equivalent of entropy – noise – against any effort to thwart that universal and transmit a message entire: "Un coup de dés jamais n'abolira le hasard." Mallarmé's text, however, was, curiously enough, a palinode: the culmination of a poetic career dedicated to the proposition that poetry would allow one to eliminate chance, *le hasard*, word by word. And the body of that poetry, I have demonstrated elsewhere, finds its locus in the infinitesimal partition or window separating a mass of white from a mass of red.[11] The poems, that is, are superimposable as a virtually abstract design, or as the action of Maxwell's chance-eradicating demon: a perpetual-motion machine endlessly, uncannily repeating the difference of its partition.

Mallarmé's ultimate legacy, then, *Un coup* de *dés*, proposed the impossibility of eradicating chance or noise, the demise, in Hyppolite's terms, of Maxwell's demon. The performance or legitimation of that legacy, its transmission, however, would paradoxically entail its partial obliteration (by noise). In 1920, Valéry, the privileged legatee, defended the legacy of *Un coup de dés* (against efforts to set it to music) in these terms: "cette gloire [de Mallarmé] n'est pas une gloire *statistique*. Elle ne dépend pas du nombre d'un public indistinct. Elle est composée de solitaires qui ne se ressemblent pas. Son possesseur l'a acquise tête par tête, comme il a 'vaincu le hasard,' mot par mot" (*O*, p. 628). Thus does he simultaneously receive, protect, and obliterate the heritage of Mallarmé. But *"les éléments de statistique, les nombres, – population, superficie, matières premières"* were precisely those forces now triumphant at the expense of Europe and/as Intelligence, the infinitely *probable* or random reality which Maxwell's demon – borrowed from Poincaré – was to eradicate in "La Crise de l'esprit" and, by implication in "Le Vin perdu" (*O*, p. 998). The detour from the tear-work of Valéry's poetry – through politics and physics – has brought us to Mallarmé and the poetic tradition Valéry would perpetuate.

A curious junction between Mallarmé and politics occurs even earlier in Valéry's writings, in the first of his "quasi-political essays," "Une conquête méthodique."[12] The young Valéry, vacationing in London in 1896, visits, upon recommendation from Mallarmé, the British poet William Henley. Henley requests a curiously assigned article of his guest for a journal he is currently editing, *The New Review*. The journal has been running a series of statistically informative articles on the danger which German industrial competition poses for English commerce.[13] Henley requests of Valéry a philosophical conclusion "in the French manner."[14] The Frenchman, recipient of copious good wishes "for the good Stéphane," at first laughs off the assignment, but ends up writing an essay to which we shall presently turn.[15] The reality Valéry was invited to speculate on was essentially one of interstitial expropriation. Here, for instance, is the author of "Made in Germany" in a characteristic passage:

Take observation, Gentle Reader, to your own surroundings: the mental exercise is recommended as an antidote to that form of self-sufficiency which our candid friends regard as indigenous to the British climate. Your investigations will work out somewhat in this fashion. You will find that the material of some of your own clothes was woven in Germany. Still more probable is it that some of your wife's garments are German importations; while it is practically beyond a doubt that the magnificent mantles and jackets wherein her maids array themselves on their Sundays out are German-made and German sold, for only so could they be done at the figure. Your governess's *fiancé is* a clerk in the City; but he also was made in Germany.

By day's end:

If you are imaginative and dyspeptic, you drop off to sleep only to dream that St. Peter (with a duly stamped halo around his head and a bunch of keys from Eison) has refused your admission into Paradise, because you bear not the Mark of the Beast upon your forehead, and are not of German make. But you console youself with the thought that it was only a Bierhaus Paradise anyway; and you are awakened in the morning by the sonorous brass of a German band.[16]

Thus E. Williams in the pre-text of Valéry's meditation, quoted at some length on the assumption of the usefulness – at the inception of the political writing of an author who has contributed as much as any to the contemporary esthetics of expropriation – of evoking the primal (political) shock informing that discourse, the privileged status of "made-in-Germany" as a floating signifier.[17]

Valéry's essay is characterized above all by the desire to relegate "national bitterness" to a secondary status and indulge in a "special admiration" for an accomplishment as perfect as German industrial "method." He claims that the German achievement lay in organizing the economy with the same strategic awareness that had been employed in building Prussia's army. Two principal – and italicized – slogans motivate the German effort in Valéry's view: "*Il faut organiser l'inégalité*" and "*le véritable ennemi, c'est le hasard*" (*O*, pp. 978, 981). Although the essay, that is, is ultimately about the refinements of German marketing, its principal motifs are of a piece with those present at the intersection of poetry, politics, and physics with which we began. The hero of the new impersonal order, moreover, is neither Poe nor Leonardo, but Count von Moltke, the Prussian field marshal, who is said to "personify" the system. In fact, though, his greatest accomplishment is the achievement of his own superfluity in the German success; "Il semble que le plus profond de ses desseins ait été de ne pas mourir indispensable" (*O*, p. 980). Transposed into esthetics, the sentence yields Valéry's later pronouncements: "Toute oeuvre est l'oeuvre de bien d'autres choses qu'un auteur" and "le véritable ouvrier d'un bel ouvrage ... n'est positivement *personne*."[18] The author seems intent on affirming the mediocrity of his exemplary figure. The gifts of Moltke – like those of Maxwell's demon – are those of the second-rate: patience and attention. And yet it is precisely the intensity to which those banal aptitudes are brought which fascinates Valéry. By the essay's end, the author, in fact, extrapolates from the case of Moltke to a kind of incipient "method" no longer opposed to but at the heart of the great achievements of civilization: "Supposons, si l'on veut, que plusieurs de ces grands esprits dont j'ai parlé, après avoir usé de méthodes intimes, soient arrivés à la conscience de ces méthodes" (*O*, p. 987). The case of "Moltke," then, would bring us to an understanding of the esthetic unconscious: the phenomena of choice, substitution, and association that remain so "obscure." And nowhere more so, we would suggest, than in the case of Valéry. For the essay on the "German conquest" has, in fact, brought us back to the Maxwellian program of organizing inequalities and eradicating chance which has been the focus of these notes from the beginning.

Return to "La Crise de l'esprit." One figure of the poet in that text is an "intellectual Hamlet" pondering the skulls of a host of illustrious men in Europe's imaginary graveyard: "S'il saisit un crâne, c'est un crâne illustre. – *Whose was it?* – Celui-ci fut *Leonardo* ... Hamlet ne sait trop que faire de tous ces crânes. Mais s'il les abandonne! ... Va-t-il cesser d'être lui-même?" (*O*, p. 993). Now

that image of the Valéryan surrogate pondering the skulls of the
great serves to remind us that in his youth Valéry, during an apprenticeship served under the anthropologist and craniometer
Georges Vacher de Lapouge, measured 600 skulls exhumed from
a disused cemetery.[19] Indeed one of the editors of Valéry's correspondence dubs him an "anthropological Hamlet" on that occasion.[20] As we approach Valéry's relation to Montpellier's most
prestigious intellectual of the 1890s, probably its sole aspirant to
world renown, it should first be observed that the culmination of
their relation appears to have been in 1892, the year Valéry – in
Genoa – would deem poetry deleterious to intelligence and consequently unworthy of being pursued.[21] Valéry, that year, not only
attended the – packed – courses of the city's premier theoretician
of intelligence, but lectured on Villiers de l'Isle-Adam at a session
presided by him. Vacher subsequently published the following
evocation of the evening:

Pendant que l'on jouait le *Lohengrin* de Wagner, l'Association faisait lire
les *Contes cruels*, de Villiers de l'Isle-Adam, son ami et le premier qui l'ait
compris en France. Coïncidence voulue, car l'oeuvre profonde, étrange
et mystique de Villiers, c'est ce wagnérisme de la littérature. M. Valéry
a su rendre, par un art infini de la parole et de mise en oeuvre, les *Contes*
accessibles au public. L'étude littéraire a été impeccable de fond,
sculpturale de forme. Quand on a lu l'apparition d'Asraël, l'ange de la
mort, le souffle de l'effroi est passé sur la salle. Toute l'horreur mystique
du temple de Siva, aux rets homicides, s'est abattue ensuite sur
l'auditoire. L'impression laissée par cette seconde réunion a été
profonde et durable.[22]

Valéry's relation with Vacher, then, was of sufficient depth as to
have attained a measure of mutuality.

And yet the name of Vacher is absent from Valéry's *oeuvre*, unmentioned in the *Cahiers*, appearing a single time in the published correspondence. That letter – to Gide, 13 January 1899 –
is alluded to on the final page of Derrida's essay on the poet's
"sources écartées" (Freud, Nietzsche), and is indeed worthy of
reinvoking in the context of that topos.[23] The bulk of the letter
consists of two *post-scripta* relating Valéry's difficult relation to
Nietzsche's "contradictions." In the first entry, the poet sorts out
two incompatible strands in the philosopher's work: "Donc, dans

son ensemble, il y a des choses admirables ou naïves ou inutiles; donc, il faut choisir ce qui convient et revenir soit à Stendhal, soit à Descartes, car il n'y a guère de milieu possible."[24] Energy or Mind, Stendhal or Descartes, impossible to reconcile. The second *post-scriptum*, however, offers a possible articulation of the two:

Tu dis qu'il prônait l'inconscience. Je ne crois pas. Il y a même des phrases nettement contraires. Mais tout simplement son *Uebermensch* chéri *doit* avoir toute conscience *avec tous* les "avantages" de l'INCON-SCIENCE. Cela est clair, sans cela ce ne serait pas un *Uebermensch*, ce serait dans un sens ou dans l'autre un simple agrandissement d'un type quelconque, choisi, soit inconscient, soit conscient. Vacher ou Poe, démesurés.

C'est ainsi que j'aurais personnellement procédé à faire un person-nage. (Cf. *Teste*)[25]

The suggestion here is that the Stendhal/Descartes gap that Nietzsche was unable to close was bridged – if only virtually – by Valéry in *Monsieur Teste*. But that articulation is imagined no longer in terms of Stendhal and Descartes, but of Vacher and Poe, respectively *"inconscience"* and *"conscience."* As though the cra-niometer Vacher were at some level the unconscious of Valéry's hero of intelligence, Monsieur Teste.

Consider the context of that virtuality. "Monsieur Teste," more than a character, was the consolidation of an option to abandon poetry as deleterious to intelligence. That poetry, more-over, is conceivable as the tear-work which re-emerges – from re-pression – in "La Jeune Parque," and that we evoked at the beginning of these pages. In Valéry's phantasmagoria, then, it is as though Intelligence were to Poetry as Consciousness is to the Unconscious. But the tear-work, we have seen, had a funda-mental political coefficient. It embraced the threat to European superiority posed by the diffusion of its Intelligence outside itself. As Valéry puts it in the "Avant-Propos" to *Regards sur le monde actuel*, "L'Europe n'aura pas eu la politique de sa pensée" (*O* II, p. 926).[26] Poetry and Politics are deleterious to Mind, and the threat they together pose and that Monsieur Teste would repress is fig-urable as tear-work. But the menace to mind is above all a threat to European superiority, or rather to the pre-eminence of what

Valéry, at the conclusion of "La Crise de l'esprit" calls "*Homo europaeus*" (*O*, p. 1014).

Which returns us to Vacher, the virtual "unconscious" of "Monsieur Teste." For *Homo europaeus* was the Linnaean term that Vacher had revived to designate what popular usage still obliged him to call the Aryan race. Indeed the major set of lectures that Vacher delivered at Montpellier, later published as *L'Aryen: son rôle social*, begin (in book-form): "Ce livre est la monographie de l'*Homo Europaeus*, c'est-à-dire de la variété à laquelle on a donné les noms divers de race dolichocéphale blonde, kymrique, galatique, germanique et aryenne."[27] It is therefore all the more significant that Valéry, immediately after concluding his essay with an encomium to the "astonishing inequality" enjoyed by *Homo europaeus*, should tack on the following denial: "Il est remarquable que l'homme d'Europe n'est pas défini par la race, ni par la langue, ni par les coutumes, mais par les désirs et par l'amplitude de la volonté ... Etc." For the choice of the technical racial term exempted from any reference to race is a further index of Vacher's role as "rejected source."

Monsieur Teste's "unconscious"? Perhaps the closest we come to a text figurable as such is the extraordinary and unfinished short piece entitled alternately "Agathe" and "Manuscrit trouvé dans une cervelle."[28] For Valéry would later write to Gide that it constituted "l'*intérieur* de la nuit de M. Teste."[29] It relates the degenerating dream of a woman asleep for several years: "Or, depuis deux, trois ... dix ans, il n'y a pas eu de sensations pour elle; donc étudier l'appauvrissement (ou autre chose) du donné avec lequel elle s'est endormie ... Les zones successives d'altération des images, etc., la variation de la pensée devenue peu à peu vide seraient curieuse à faire." The several pages that Valéry wrote but never published are probably as close as anything in the nineteenth century to the novelistic prose of Maurice Blanchot. Concerning them, several observations:

1. The figure who will sleep and dream in Monsieur Teste's night is plainly a version of the Jeune Parque. In her disorientation, she loses all sense of identity, asks: "QUI interroge? Le même répond. Le même écrit, efface une même ligne. Ce ne sont que des écritures sur des eaux" (*O* II, p. 1389). Her future lies in a fas-

cination with some internal vitiation of thought, an anticipation, I would suggest, of the Parque's tear: "une perle abstraite roulerait future dans le repli de la pensée ordinaire: une loi étonnante, confondue à celui qui la cherche, habiterait ceci: un instant livrerait cette perle ... Extérieure à tout chemin, inconnue à toute violence, elle est gisant hors de toute figure et de toute ressemblance ... J'ai d'elle le désir ... mais j'en découvre infiniment le manque, et déjà, de ce manque, je me suis fait un signe utile" (*O* II, p. 1391). The night of Monsieur Teste is literally that of poetry, twenty years dormant.

2. The awakening of the Parque, we have seen from "Crise de l'esprit," was at some level the awakening of the threatened European in Valéry, *Homo europaeus.* The point of departure for the body of his political writings proper, *Regards sur le monde actuel,* moreover, was the newly acquired sense of being a European ... endangered in his essence by those two estranged manifestations of European might, the Japanese incursion against China (1895) and the American war with Spain (1898): "Ce coup indirect en Extrême-Orient, et ce coup direct dans les Antilles me firent donc percevoir confusément l'existence de quelque chose qui pouvait être atteinte et inquiétée par de tels événements. Je me trouvai 'sensibilisé' à des conjonctures qui affectaient une sorte d'idée virtuelle de l'Europe que j'ignorais jusqu'alors porter en moi" (*O* II, p. 914). *La Jeune Parque* as *Homo europaeus?*

3. The title "Manuscrit trouvé dans une cervelle" links up Poe, author of "MS. Found in a Bottle," with Vacher, technician of skull measurement, brain capacity, and cephalic indices.[30] But Poe and Vacher, we have seen in the letter to Gide, were the two sides tendentially united in Teste. The Valéry text relates a dreamed obliteration of thought, born of sensory deprivation, in a seemingly endless night. The Poe tale, of course, imagines a ship drawn wildly through the white ice into a polar maelstrom. Valéryan thought, by (intertextual) implication, is whitened out. And Vacher's *Homo europaeus?* The most enigmatic trait of "European man," and the subject treated at greatest length in the chapter of Vacher's treatise on "L'Origine des Aryens," is depigmentation. The "superior race," in fact, is characterized first of all by a "kind of degeneration" of the normal "chromoblastic"

capacity of its skin: "[La coloration] de *H. Europaeus* est un phénomène unique, anormal et pour ainsi dire pathologique ... un
phénomène d'étiolement" (*L'Origine des Aryens*, p. 74). And it is a
phenomenon attributable above all to a climate deprived of sun.
Indeed much of Vacher's chapter situates its humanity somewhere between the random patterns of meteorology and the
"Brownian movement" of protoplasmic "granulations of
melanin" which color the skin (*L*, p. 51). In between the two, a
photographic technology for calibrating degrees of pigmentation
is invoked. In some cases, the subject's extremities are registered
at the expense of the rest of the body: "le reste n'est exprimé que
par une nébulosité sur le papier. C'est la fille sans corps." In
others, "le cliché est tel que la tête et les mains viennent trop vite,
et si l'on donne l'exposition nécessaire pour le corps, le reste est
perdu ... C'est la fille-tronc" (*L*, p. 54). Consider, then, that in
Valéry (with Poe), we have a girl all but disarticulated by a
whitening out of thought in the long night of her slumber. In
Vacher we find a girl scattered or dismembered as part of the
analysis of a unique and pathological depigmentation of skin, the
result of a prolonged absence of sun. Valéry's heroine will awaken
from M. Teste's night during the War as Poetry homologous to a
Europe threatened – by diffusion – in its superiority. As for Vacher's *Homo europaeus*, he emerged in the Montpellier lectures as
the protagonist of a racial tragedy whose outline was later
sketched by the author in "Lois de la vie et de la mort des
nations":

Mais de même que dans une pile il y a l'élément zinc et un autre, et que
le zinc s'use bientôt, de même dans cette société à deux termes l'élément
actif ne tarde pas à s'affaiblir. Les croisements d'abord que la nature
humaine ne permet pas d'éviter, altèrent la race des conquérants.
Goutte à goutte le sang de la race supérieure s'en va dans la classe
inférieure, et le sang servile s'infiltre dans les familles des vainqueurs.[31]

This drama of racial decline, of the victory – already in France
– of the servile, dark (brachycephalic) round-heads over the
Aryan, blond (dolichocephalic) long-heads is the core of Vacher's
version of social Darwinism. What is striking in the present
context is the extent to which it reproduces the poetico-politico-

physical node with which we began these notes: the decline of
European man as a diffusion of wine into water; (but) the wine
imaginable originally as blood ("songeant au sang, versant le
vin"); the merging of "race" with "class" analysis; the scientific
analogy invoked to convey decline as an erosion of difference ...
The only missing element in the homology is Maxwell's demon,
for which Vacher would substitute a particularly grisly program
of eugenics.[32]

The figure of Vacher as "rejected source," *source écartée*, in Valéry's
phantasia of intelligence receives some sustenance from a consideration of the role of craniology – the science of skull measurement – in a still broader phantasmagoria of intelligence and/as
inequality. Indeed the most recent inquiry into the history of craniology, S. J. Gould's *The Mismeasure of Man*, has succeeded in demonstrating that the ultimate legacy of that pseudo-science was
the American IQ test.[33] And since the name of Vacher figures on
both sides of the divide, we shall do well to digress briefly to a
consideration of that account. At the beginning of the sequence,
we find Paul Broca leading the French scientific community in
debate as to the proper correlations among cranial conformation,
brain capacity, level of intelligence, and hierarchy of race. It was
an odd debate, in which etiquette all but demanded that one be
willing to submit one's brain to dissection and measurement after
death, and in which the suspicion lingered that the ultimate
worth of one's arguments would be determined in the course of
that posthumous exercise (*MM*, pp. 92–94). The transition from
"cranial" to "psychological" measurement of intelligence was the
achievement of Alfred Binet early in the century, but it was in the
United States that the twin legacies of craniology – reification and
hereditarianism – were made to inflect the study of intelligence
and the interpretation of the Binet scale. The stages of the Ameri-
canization of Binet's efforts to study, in their plurality, varieties of
intelligence, though they will not detain us, are worth recalling:
H. H. Goddard's importation of the Binet scale to America, his
reification of its scores as innate intelligence and invention of the
– omnipresent – "moron"; L. M. Terman's dream of a rational
society allocating professions in accordance with IQ scores; R. M.

Yerkes' success in convincing the Army to test almost two million men in World War I, thus laying the "objective" basis for the hereditarian perspective that led to the Immigration Restriction Act of 1924, "with its low ceiling for lands suffering from the blight of poor genes" (*MM*, p. 157). Now in one of the "classic" texts of the tradition, A *Study of American Intelligence (1923)*, C. C. Brigham was faced with an apparent threat to the thesis of essentially innate intelligence. For the results of Yerkes' mass-testing seemed to indicate that the immigrant groups that had been in the United States longer did better in proportion to the length of their stay. Environment, that is, and not heredity, would appear to be the key factor. It was at this juncture that the work of Vacher was adduced in order to save the hereditarian thesis. For what the test results demonstrated, it was argued, was not the priority of environment in the development of intelligence, but rather the historical circumstance that the innate intelligence of the various racial pools of immigrants the United States had been tapping had been gradually declining over the past twenty years. And it was Vacher's racial categories that were invoked to substantiate the thesis. The corrective Immigration Restriction Act would follow a year later, attempting to reverse the demographic impact of inferior immigrations. And shortly thereafter, Brigham would become Secretary of the College Entrance Examination Board, and develop the Scholastic Aptitude Tests on the model of the Army IQ Tests (*MM*, p. 199). All of which is to suggest that the impediments to a perception of the subliminal insistence of Vacher in the writings of Valéry may not be unrelated to the role played by the legacy of Vacher in the enabling conditions of academic discourse itself . . .[34]

Return to the poetry: "Le Cimetière marin." Earlier we evoked the nodal figure of a tear (LARME) not quite lost in the retentive eye of the sea (LA MER). Whereby the poem enters into contact with the crisis of "Le Vin perdu" and "La Crise de l'esprit." That figure of randomness, however, is pitted against the stable and specular dualism of sun and cemetery. The cemetery: "Pères profonds, têtes inhabitées." The sun: "Tête complète et parfait diadème." The complex that emerges links up ideal intelligence, a fantasy of power, and the presence of the potentially perfect skull. A bracing communion with the poet's deceased father?[35] Perhaps. Yet the complex would seem as well to refer us to Valéry's apprenticeship in craniometry, unearthing and measuring skulls – for their index of perfection – under Vacher. The general air of exaltation would bespeak the set of values destined to enter into an acute phase of crisis in that section of the poem we have read in terms of tear-work.[36]

"Le Cimetière marin" as a poem of *Homo europaeus* threatened in his essence … That interpretation may be sustained by a reading of a short text that is in many ways a prose rehearsal of the major poem of 1920. The piece is entitled "Le Yalou," dates from 1895, in all probability originated as the fragment of *Monsieur Teste* alluded to in the correspondence as "Teste en Chine," and finally found its place in *Regards sur le monde actuel*.[37] "Yalou" is the French name of the river running between Korea and Manchuria, in whose delta the Chinese suffered a devastating defeat at the hands of the Japanese on 17 September 1894. Our text, in fact, is in large part a dialogue, overlooking the delta, between a European visitor and a Chinese sage prior to – and in anticipation of – that conflict. But it will be recalled from the "Avant-propos" to *Regards* that the Japanese attack on China lay at the inception of Valéry's sense of himself as European: "Je me trouvai 'sensibilisé' à des conjectures qui affectaient une sorte d'idée virtuelle de l'Europe que j'ignorais jusqu'alors porter en moi" (*O* II, p. 914). For it was a Europeanized Japan that now attacked European interests in China. We approach here the motif of "La Crise de l'esprit": the diffusion of Europe's intellectual substance as a kind of entropy. Or as Valéry himself put it, in his *Cahier* of 1896: "Les hommes de génie servent à tout mettre aux mains des imbéciles. Les nations civilisées cultivent les Japons."[38] Valéry, that is, awakened as a European much as the Jeune Parque would later come to consciousness: threatened – and constituted – by the return of an estranged fragment of his own substance even as she would ponder the menacing strangeness of her tear.

"Le Cimetière marin," it has been suggested, may be read in terms of the relations among three poles: sun, cemetery, and sea.

Between "sun" and "cemetery," "tête complète" and "têtes in-habitées," there is a specular relation of interdependence. The two registers have opposite affective charges (of immobility: *Midi sans mouvement*, and flight: *Allez! tout fuit!*), but are perceived by Valéry as oddly complicitous. Thus does the Poet address the sun at high noon:

> Mais dans leur nuit toute lourde de marbres,
> Un peuple vague aux racines des arbres
> A pris déjà ton parti lentement.

The interdependence of sun and skull, then, fueling a fantasy of intellectual power, is opposed to the sea. Or rather less to the sea *per se* than to the play of tear-work – that crisis of (European) mind – which we have seen (through "La Jeune Parque," "Le Vin perdu," and "La Crise de l'esprit") take the tranquil sea as its deceptive scene. Consider now that in "Le Yalou," we find a precise homology with the system I have sketched in "Le Cime-tière marin." A European intellectual is in dialogue with a Chinese sage in front of the body of water from which they both sense the Japanese will soon attack. The European views himself as a characteristic articulation of light, intellectual potency, and the immobility of immediacy: "car le groupe de lumière et pensée qui dans ce moment me constitue, demeure encore iden-tique. Alors, le changement est nul. Le temps ne marche plus. Ma vie se pose" (*O* II, p. 1020). Transposed to the cemetery in Sète, we find:

> Midi là-haut, Midi sans mouvement
> En soi se pense et convient à soi-même . . .
> Tête complète et parfait diadème.

The other – Chinese – voice in the dialogue offers a radical cri-tique of the violence of Western intelligence in the name of that solidarity with ancestry and earth which is the wisdom of China. Thus: "L'Intelligence, pour vous, n'est pas une chose comme les autres . . . vous l'adorez comme une bête prépondérante. Chaque jour elle dévore ce qui existe" (*O* II, p. 1018). Better that capacity to feel one's almost passive solidarity with one's predecessors and the earth to which they have returned: "Chaque homme d'ici se sent fils et père … et se voit saisi … dans le peuple mort au-dessous de lui … Chaque homme d'ici sait qu'il n'est rien sans cette terre pleine, et hors de la merveilleuse construction d'ancêtres … Ici, tout est historique" (*O* ii, p. 1018).

In our tripartite construct, then, the Chinese sage incarnates the cemetery even as the European may be superimposed on the sun. And just as our analysis of the poem posed a complicity between the two, so, in Valéry's political statement, was China the representative of Western interests. What then of the sea? It would appear in the two cases to be a source of infinite calm. "Le Yalou": "la douce égalité du mouvement, du calme nous saisit" (*O* ii, p. 1016). "Le Cimetière": "O récompense après une pensée / Qu'un long regard sur le calme des dieux!" Yet already our reading of the poem had detected the threatening tear at the surface of the sea's retentive eye. Consider in that light the following sentence of "Le Yalou": "Et je baissai mes paupières, ne voyant plus de la brillante mer que ce qu'on voit d'un petit verre de liqueur dorée, portée aux yeux" (*O* ii, p. 1017). Almost gratuitously, we find an image midway between the tear-drop of "La Jeune Parque" and the image of diffusion in "Le Vin perdu": a tiny receptacle of liquid against the eye, in or of the sea. The tear-work, then, is once again emergent in a political context. But the politics of the circumstance are the same as those of "La Crise de l'esprit": the destruction of Europe through the diffusion of its intelligence outside itself. For the Japanese strike against China is an "indirect blow" against Europe. The Chinese sage comments: "Nippon … nous fait la guerre. Ses grands bateaux blancs fument dans nos mauvais rêves. Ils vont troubler nos golfes" (*O* ii, p. 1017). The threat of war is indeed coming from the white boats on the water, and it is uncanny that Valéry in 1920 should have chosen the dove (of peace) as his metaphor of the white sails off the coast of the graveyard: "Ce toit tranquille où marchent les colombes." For he even invites us to doubt that peace in the line: "Et quelle paix *semble* se concevoir!" In an earlier analysis, I have interpreted that semblance of peace as opening the way to a reading in terms of the violence of tear-work.[39] But the logic of the present superimposition, while confirming that reading, also reveals the extent to which the historical reality of that "tear" was war.

From superimposition to superimposition, we have arrived at a Valéry whose poetry – at its most intense – is in perpetual – meta-phorical – contact with a political concern: the crisis of inegalitar-ianism-cum-intelligence. To engage that poetry, moreover, is perhaps to encounter the texture of "Valéry's politics" more tell-ingly than in any inventory of his political options, be they disas-trous (against Dreyfus in 1898, for Salazar in the 1930s) or commendable (the eulogy of Bergson in occupied Paris).[40] Indeed a final series of methodological observations plays some havoc with the metalinguistic distance from which such options might be judged.

From superimposition to superimposition ... The technique of superimposing texts, first formulated explicitly by Charles Mauron, is intended to provide analytic access to that register of uncanny repetition amid extreme difference that is a touchstone of the effects of what Freud called "the unconscious."[41] Thus the reading of "Le Yalou" with "Le Cimetière marin" has detected the complex repetition of the sun-skull-tear series in two otherwise unrelated texts. My initial delineation of Valéry's tear-work, moreover, in the essay already alluded to, was an effort to save Mauron's own remarkable superimpositions of Valéry's poems from regressing beneath their own most liberating potential. It ended with a reading of Mauron on an early poem, "Baignée," that takes up the series we have just encountered once again. The poem begins:

> Un fruit de chair se baigne en quelque jeune vasque,
> (Azur dans les jardins tremblants) mais hors de l'eau,
> Isolant la torsade aux puissances de casque,
> Luit ce chef d'or que tranche à la nuque un tombeau.
>
> (*O*, p. 78)

In the luminous head ("chef d'or") above the grave ("tombeau"), we find the decor of "Le Cimetière marin." The poem ends, moreover, with the bather's arm brushing away an insect in orbit around her head:

> Si l'autre [bras], courbé sous le beau firmament
> Parmi la chevelure immense qu'il humecte,
> Capture dans l'or simple un vol ivre d'insecte.

The gesture is essentially that of the Parque at the beginning of her poem ("Cette main, sur mes traits qu'elle rêve effleurer"). The insect, that is, corresponds to the tear. Now in Mauron's interpretation that insect figures a "fascinated lucidity" spying on – and ultimately repressing – a "fascinating image." "Désormais le témoin s'opposera à la dormeuse comme le soleil au crâne ... Une telle dualité est caractéristique des poèmes de cette période."[42] The tripartite system (sun-skull-tear) has been reduced to a dualism, and the insect-tear has been absorbed centripetally by the solar head. That obliteration of the poem's disruptive tear-work by Mauron, I have argued, is a falling short – in the name of psychoanalysis – of the poet's own affinity with Freud at his most virulent. In absorbing the insect-tear back into the luminous head, Mauron has effaced the rudiments of a theory of the unconscious (dis)articulated by the poetry itself.

In the present poetico-political context, however, it seems worth observing a significant link between that act of absorption and the practice of superimposition itself. Mauron regarded that technique as the beginning of literary analysis, the necessary surrogate of the psychoanalyst's "free associations." It was to be a more radical procedure than "comparison," in which the individuality of texts was maintained: "La superposition brouille, au contraire, [chaque texte] et l'attention doit y consentir, pour ne s'attacher qu'aux seules coïncidences énigmatiques."[43] Whence the effect of uncanniness. Now Mauron's acknowledged "source" for the technique of superimposition was Francis Galton and his efforts at "composite portraiture."[44] Galton managed to project simultaneously the photographs of several members of an actual or alleged family and derive therefrom a generic image. But the knowledge gained thereby had a rather precise political coefficient. Thus Galton, discoursing on one series of his composite portraits: "I have also various criminal types, composed from the photographs of men convicted of heinous crimes. They are instructive as showing the type of face that is apt to accompany criminal tendencies *before* (if I may be allowed the expression) the features have become brutalized by crime. The brands of Cain are varied; therefore the special expressions of different criminals do not reinforce one another in the composite, but disappear. What remains are types of faces on which some one of the many brands of Cain is frequently to be set."[45] The original object of "superimposition," then, is skull-type, sought in an effort to determine the innate and inherited inferiority – or superiority – of various racial types. Which is to suggest that the most characteristic technique of "literary Freudianism" was borrowed from the arsenal of "social Darwinism." It is a fact to which Mauron, in effacing Valéry's tearwork and the historical crisis in European self-confidence it mediates, pays unwitting and oblique homage.

The extent, in fact, to which composite portraiture was to find in skull-type its ideal subject is revealed by the fact that it was introduced in France by Vacher de Lapouge. Indeed the first text of "anthroposociologie" proper to appear in his annotated bibliography begins with a summary of Galton's inquiries into heredity and ends with the description of an apparatus developed by Vacher "for the photographic production of images composed with the help of negatives."[46] "Composite portraiture," the basis of "superimposition of texts," was to figure as a minor technique in the new science of "eugenics," which received its appellation from Galton and would form the core of Vacher's practical politics.[47] Here, in conclusion, we allude but briefly to the horizon of this inquiry. Consider, on the one hand, Galton, at the end of his treatise on *Probability, the Foundation of Eugenics:* "When the desired fullness of information shall have been acquired, then, and not till then, will be the fit moment to proclaim a 'Jehad' or Holy War against customs and prejudices that impair the physical and moral faculties of our race."[48] On the other hand, Vacher: "Je suis convaincu qu'au siècle prochain, on s'égorgera par millions pour un ou deux degrés en plus ou en moins dans l'indice céphalique … les derniers sentimentaux pourront assister à de copieuses exterminations de peuples."[49] Somewhere between those two cries to race war, we find Mauron, heir to Galton's technique, (mis)encountering Valéry, Vacher's student, in the privileged medium of a human skull. That the near-sublimity of their exchange should figure so profoundly *within* the dialogue of our two craniometers, a virtual

silence at the heart of their shrillness, is a circumstance sufficiently engaging in its distribution of political and esthetic values
to sustain some hope of its usefulness, beyond the idiosyncratic
case of Valéry, in future articulations of literature and/as history
in general.

CHAPTER 3

Literature and hospitality: Klossowski's Hamann

On several occasions, Walter Benjamin, in his letters of 1936, acknowledges his delight at the talent of Pierre Klossowski, then embarked on a translation of his essay, "The Work of Art in the Age of Mechanical Reproduction."[1] It was a task that was to leave its mark on the Frenchman's later work. For Benjamin's celebrated meditation on the "revolutionary" esthetic import of photography, an art whose very mode of production is inseparable from a technique of reproduction, furnishes several motifs of the almost Baudelairean prose poem on photography in *La Révocation de l'Edit de Nantes*. Octave, in his journal (in that novel), praises the blessed days when Daguerre "fixait la vie quotidienne d'alors sur le point d'être atteinte par l'austérité enlaidissante des premières industries ..." (p. 47).[2] The nostalgic phase, however, is eclipsed by a rhetorical explosion attempting to convey the energy unleashed by the new technique ("centuplant les intentions agressives de la pensée ... désarticulant les structures") and whose upshot is that painting itself (in the figure of van Gogh) is no longer the same. That retroactive effect of photography on all of art, the "primary question" of Benjamin's essay, furnishes the conclusion of Klossowski's prose poem: "La photographie a libéré la peinture du besoin d'imiter la nature ..." (p. 47). The essential relation to presence, in Klossowski as in Benjamin, is the principal casualty of photographic technique.

Painting/photography: the split around which Benjamin's article is organized reproduces a crucial division between the first and second volumes of Klossowski's novelistic trilogy, *Les Lois de l'hospitalité*. For if Octave's obsession in *La Révocation de l'Edit de Nantes* is his collection of paintings, *Roberte, ce soir*, the quasi-play that follows, is centered on a humiliating photograph he has taken of his wife as her dress catches fire and she is saved by her ravisher: *Roberte, ce soir-là*. Moreover, it is the originary reproducibility of the photograph, its essential relation to repetition, which perhaps offers us our best guide to the final volume of the series, *Le Souffleur*. For its subject is the proliferation of Roberte in a series of women her bewildered spouse can no longer distinguish. Indeed he himself, in the course of the volume, finds himself first plagiarized, then an instance of plagiarism, in a sequence of repetitive simulacra. As though the film to which Roberte, in Klossowski's mind, was always destined, should inflict its essential perturbation on the play (*Roberte, ce soir*) *Le Souffleur* would rehearse. "Octave" – become "Théodore" – resists, insists on remaining faithful to Roberte in his rituals of humiliation, but is ultimately forced to the realization that he has never known which woman he has loved. For Roberte is a fixture of the state-run orgy of Longchamp. In Benjamin's terms, the loss of the aura effected by film opens onto the politics of fascism.[3] Klossowski-Benjamin, then, or rather Benjamin-Octave, theorist of the advent of photography, poised ambivalently between the auratic realm of painting and its essential disarticulation in the mechanics of reproduction. It is a posture which finds the strangest of resonances in Octave's politics. For in a eulogy of Pétain ("mon vieux Philippe"), he sings of the uncanny beauties of the Occupation, the wiles of collaborating with the Germans in their own destruction: allowing them to deport every impulse toward modernity out of France, the better, thinks Octave, to choke on them. Paris would again be a royal city, awakened from the "long winter of the infamous Third Republic" (p. 75). France, in a sense we have yet to gauge, would once more be a "manual" civilization ... Now, by the final volume of the trilogy, Octave has found his probable prototype in Doctor Rodin, whose name identifies him as a cast-off from the novels of Sade: "maurrassien enragé, [il] fut nommé par le gouvernement de Vichy au contrôle médical des gens en partance pour le Service obligatoire du Travail ... Ce vieux fou était alors au mieux avec l'administration de Sauckel" (p. 272). Rodin's wife, Roberte, a member of the Resistance, makes a deal with the perverse doctor: she will give herself under their conjugal roof to any man designated for deportation in exchange for a certificate of exemption to be delivered by the doctor in each case. Therein, it will be perceived, lay one "origin" of the laws of hospitality, the transgressive complex elaborated by the trilogy. As Guy de Savigny suggests in his crucial debate with the narrator: "Si K. a substitué sa femme à la vôtre, je finirai par croire que Rodin a été le modèle du vieux 'professeur Octave,' le personnage de votre livre" (p. 303). The esthetic distinction between authorial and narrative voice – i.e., between K. (the "Slavic consonances" of whose name would seem to designate Klossowski) and the protagonist of *Le Souffleur*, "Théodore" – is exceeded and overwhelmed by a broader oscillation between history and fiction: Rodin and Octave.

What would it mean for Klossowski to grant Benjamin's esthetic concern – from the essay he himself had translated – to Octave, to cast the Jew who died in flight from Nazi deportation from France in the role of the character whose "prototype" is a devious and fanatical French bureaucrat of Nazi deportation? Our path to an answer brings us first to Benjamin's strange text, "Agesilaus Santander," written in 1933 in Ibiza.[4] The author evokes the circumstance whereby his parents, fearful that he might one day have to conceal being a Jew, bestowed upon him "two further exceptional names" which he might reveal in some future extremity. He compares them, curiously, to the additional Hebrew names Jews secretly bestow on their children. We are dealing, then, with a name which is by analogy Hebrew-non-Jewish: non-Jewish, that is, as Jewish. A reference to the angelology of Kabbalah prepares us for the subsequent realization, first advanced by Gershom Scholem, that the name Agesilaus Santander is an anagram of *Der Angelus Satanas*.[5] Benjamin's "other name," the Angel Satan, is a legacy of antinomian theology.[6] Whereby we approach the scandal of Klossowski's text: Benjamin-Octave or, worse yet, Benjamin-Rodin: the Jew as para-Nazi functionary in France. Benjamin's "Angel" possessed a special relation to the writer's esthetic of melancholy: he would take advantage, we read, of "the circumstance that I came into the world under the sign of Saturn – the star of the slowest revolution, the planet of detours and delays ..."[7] Such melancholy, moreover, crops up in a related context at a key juncture of one of Benjamin's more theological texts, "On Language as Such and on the Language of Man." Upon engaging the necessity of locating the concept of translation "at the deepest level of linguistic theory," Benjamin speaks of "overnaming as the linguistic being of melancholy."[8] That phrase is available to a more or less profound interpretation as a reflection on the multiplicity of languages, but it bears a more precise and more superficial link with the plight of the Jew in "Agesilaus Santander." For it is precisely overnaming – the assignment of a second (Hebrew-non-Jewish) name – that is at stake in that text. The theory of language as always already subordinate to the Satanic Angel.

We approach our subject. For the author guiding Benjamin's speculations in the essay "On Language as Such" is Johann-Georg Hamann: "Language, the mother of reason and revelation, its alpha and omega," in Benjamin's quotation from the Magus of the North.[9] Scholem, of course, wrote that it was Benjamin's thwarted destiny to be the "legitimate continuer of the most fruitful and most genuine traditions of a Hamann or a Humboldt."[10] And Paul de Man has recently suggested that Hamann is the great forerunner of Benjamin in his treatment of allegory.[11] Now it happens that a few years after translating Benjamin's essay on "Mechanical Reproduction," Klossowski was drawn to Henri Corbin's "brilliant translation" of Hamann's "rhapsody in Kabbalistic prose," "Aesthetica in Nuce."[12] He would subsequently lament that a text offering so many affinities with the "most ardent endeavors of [his] generation" should have had so little impact.[13] Hamann was not, however, a completely unknown name in pre-War France. In the Maurrassian milieu of Octave and Dr. Rodin, one could read – in Léon Daudet's *Le Stupide Dix-neuvième Siècle* – that "derrière Kant, il y a le juif Hamann." Benjamin quotes that sentence in dismay and offers it as a "bizarre and venomous flower" culled for Horkheimer's perusal in a letter of 16 April 1938.[14] When, he wonders, will the German blend of ignorance and baseness toward the Jews enter into action in France? Behind the Hebrew-non-Jew Benjamin, we find, then, the "Jew" (non-Jew) Hamann. Such is the horizon against which our reading of

Klossowski's post-War volume of translations of Hamann will
be conducted.

Klossowski's selection of texts is preceded by two lengthy introductory essays. The first is the editor's attempt to delineate the
German's thought, and the second Hegel's article – translated, introduced, and critically annotated by Klossowski – on Hamann's
inability to achieve the measure of universality that would conse-
crate his writing as philosophy.[15] The volume begins, that is, with
a curious criss-cross: the French novelist offers a quasi-philoso-
phical essay, and the German philosopher is constrained by the
allegedly sub-philosophical "particularism" and "bizarreness" of
his subject to the genre of narrative prose. It is to the comedy of
Hegel's narrative, the Molièresque turn that finds the philosopher
all but imagining the "Magus of the North" as a latter-day composite of Tartuffe and the Misanthrope, that we shall presently
turn. For beyond the role Klossowski assigns it as an anticipation
of the response Hegel never gave Kierkegaard, the German's
essay on Hamann, in the contour of its plot, opens a stranger
path still to the novels of *Les Lois de l'hospitalité*.[16]

The "point of departure" for a comprehension of Hamann's
writing, according to Hegel, and the core of his own essay, is a
delineation of the German's protracted and stormy relations
with a family of Prussian merchants, the Berens of Riga (p. 79).[17]
Indeed, "les intrigues avec cet ami [Berens] et sa famille sont
bien ce qui a le plus marqué le destin de Hamann" (p. 73).
Hegel's chronicle of their relations begins with an initial meeting
between the young preceptor and Berens in Koenigsberg.
Hamann soon came to live for a brief period with the Berens
family, where he was treated royally, but reacted to every
gesture of generosity with surly distrust. He was, Hegel writes in
French, "un homme mal élevé," given to a "savage passion for
intellectual dissipation without object." He then left the Berens
to resume his work as a preceptor, but shortly thereafter, in
1756, on his own admission, cheated his way out of his contract
to return to the Berens household. It was decided that for his
amusement and for the Berens' commercial benefit he would be
sent on a mission to London, with the specific aim of collecting
on a debt owed the family. From Hamann's point of view, the

London journey, begun on 1 October 1756, was to prove a providential disaster. An initial awareness of his total inadequacy for the mission came with his discovery that he stuttered. Significantly, Hegel records that his first endeavor upon arriving in London (18 April 1757) was to contact an alleged expert in correcting speech defects in the hope of remedying that shortcoming. The treatment, however, proved ineffective. There follows an evocation of Hamann's depression at being smiled at in disbelief by Berens' debtors at any mention of the possibility of payment. That disappointment in turn led to a season of utter dissipation ("dévergondage") in London, followed by a reading of the Bible *de profundis*. Whereupon Hamann underwent the climactic conversion during which he recognized himself as a sinner, deemed the failure of his mission providential, and vowed to return to Prussia to inflict the consequences of his revelation on his benefactors. As Klossowski puts it, Hegel views the conversion as "le simulacre cynique ... d'une génialité qui n'aurait pu parvenir à son accomplissement qu'à la faveur du simulacre" (p. 60).[18] Hamann returned to Riga, and woke up on the morning of 15 December 1758 with the idea that the next step in his spiritual progress must be to marry the sister of the Berens family. That strain on the family's hospitality was, however, too great to be accommodated, and Hegel's Hamann at this point comes closest to resembling Tartuffe. The last day of 1758 was filled with "extraordinary incidents," as Hamann was cast out of the house: "toutes relations sont rompues entre lui et les Berens" (p. 79) Now the idiosyncrasy of Hamann's career lay in the circumstance that this crisis of hospitality was never resolved. His hosts remained sufficiently taken with him to attempt to bring him back on their own terms, even after the explosion following the marriage proposal. Their principal mediators in the project were the pastor Johann Lindner and their Koenigsberg associate Immanuel Kant. So that Hamann's radical-Lutheran attacks against *Aufklärung* and Kant were always inscribed within the idiosyncratic circumstance of the fury of the parasite expelled. It was indeed the interposition of Kant in the debate that allows Hegel's text to work its transition from Hamann-as-hypocrite to Hamann-as misanthrope, from Tartuffe to Alceste in our imagined subtext.

We shall return to Hegel's extrapolation of the role of Kant in Hamann's career as parasite. First, an indication of the durability of the structure of hospitality in Hegel's perception of Hamann. The essay ends by evoking Hamann's "sublime" relations with Jonathan Jacobi in his final years, the "roman de l'amitié" which replaced the Molièresque comedy of his relation with the Berens. Now after a long stay in the home of Jacobi, Hamann was suddenly to take flight, leaving little more than the following written explanation:

Pauvre Jonathan, tu as fort mal agi à l'égard de tes deux soeurs comme à l'égard de moi-même, pauvre Lazare, en infligeant le dur joug, le lourd fardeau d'une amitié aussi virile, d'une passion aussi sainte que celle qui règne entre nous, à leur sexe que la nature a fait plus tendre et plus docile. N'as-tu pas remarqué, cher Jonathan, que les deux Amazones ne visaient qu'à me faire perdre, à moi, vieil homme, l'honneur de toute ma philosophie et de tous les préjugés favorables à cette dernière et à nous jeter l'un par rapport à l'autre dans une perplexité telle que nous serions l'un pour l'autre non moins ridicules qu'un couple de spectres philosophiques. (p. 115)

Hegel agrees that the two aging speculators would be hard put indeed to win any indulgence for their pseudo-conceptual shenanigans from two sharp-witted young women. He does not remark, however, that the structure of male hospitality suddenly interrupted by a female (sisterly) presence repeats that of the Berens episode. Yet in searching for some sub-philosophical term to evoke the matter of Hamann's thought, he happens, in Klossowski's rendering, on "phantomalisme scintillant." Now that phantasmal insistence links up with the stuff of Hamann's thought, but even more – in this context – with its practitioner(s): the "philosophical spectres" of Hamann and Jacobi, the ghosts of a relation born of the "simulacrum" of a conversion. With this phantom-return of the simulacrum, however, we engage the very core of Hamann's thought, the prophetic structure of reality. For the *Méditations bibliques*, the written journal of his conversion, begin: "Chaque histoire biblique est une prophétie qui s'accomplit à travers les siècles et dans l'âme de chaque homme" (p. 125). Now Hegel's essay makes reference to a Biblical tale invoked by Hamann as the prototext of his crises of hospitality (p. 82).

Indeed, the allusion to two Amazons in the letter to Jacobi just cited renders the passage referred to by Hegel particularly illuminating. Here, then, is a page of a long letter to Lindner (27 April 1759) translated by Klossowski:

Jean était violent, il oubliait le respect que l'on doit à la richesse, à la société, aux princes. La prison était un châtiment gracieux qu'il s'était attiré lui-même et le sort de sa tête, l'effet d'une loi de l'hospitalité, d'une trop large promesse, d'un naturel emportement, de l'ordinaire égard d'un maître de céans accompli qui veut recommander son caractère à ses hôtes, et enfin la conséquence d'un rare scrupule envers la religion d'un serment. Est-il concevable qu'un monstre tel Hérodias ait pu mettre au jour une fille aussi vertueuse? Où trouverions-nous à présent son exemple, une fille qui, ayant les mérites d'une bonne danseuse, n'en demanderait pas moins conseil à sa mère et serait prête à sacrifier la moitié d'un royaume à un mets tel que l'était la tête d'un prisonnier d'Etat aussi aventureux? Son père songeait: qu'en dira-t-on? Sa fille n'avait-elle pas plus de raison de se le demander? Que de coeur ne faut-il pas pour faire une prière aussi absurde et aussi cruelle que le fut celle-là: donne-moi dans un plat la tête du Baptiste. Et cependant, elle le fit comme une enfant obéissante et aimable. (p. 189)

The passage, as excerpted by Klossowski, is enigmatic, but receives its proper interpretation in Hegel's essay. The ironically conceived miracle of Salome's comportment lies in her willingness to be the passive vehicle of Herodias' will. The application to Hamann's situation would have Berens playing Herod, his sister Katharina Herodias, Hamann John the Baptist, and Lindner, the addressee of the letter, Salome. For Hamann's outrage is in reaction to the disingenuousness with which Lindner – and Kant – pretend to the role of neutral intermediaries in his dispute with his former benefactor. How, in particular, could Lindner serve as "messenger" for Berens, the unbiased medium of his thoughts: "With what kind of heart can you assure me you are neutral?"[19] Lindner's Salomaic sin lay in the neat integrity of the text he had conveyed. For were Hamann himself asked to deliver to Lindner a letter as abusive as the one he himself had just received, the results would have been quite different: "so would I at least have taken the liberty against the letter's author, were he the Pope himself, of underscoring all the lies therein, leaving without judgment whatever I was ignorant of, but whatever I was convinced I had different information about I would have annotated with crosses and I know not what other signs or have registered exceptions and protestations against it."[20] Hamann, that is, would have delivered a text which in its baroque, annotated, self-contradictory, and fragmented cast would have resembled nothing so much as a text by Hamann himself. Note that by this juncture, Herod-Berens has been imagined as the Pope, and that the desperate task of Protestantism lies in a savage refusal to transmit a text whole. Protestantism's battle with the Enlightenment (Lindner, Kant) should lie, according to Hamann, in its refusal to admit any critical "purification" of language as medium of communication into the "transparency" or "neutrality" denounced in the letter to Lindner. For it is that will, he claims, which ultimately makes *Aufklärung* as much the docile heir of Catholic rationalism as it does Lindner the obedient vehicle of Berens in Hamann's domestic drama. Now at this crux between Hamann's life (as narrated by Hegel) and his thought, we should do well to take stock of the elements in suspense. From the letter to Lindner, it may be observed that "loi de l'hospitalité," before serving – in the plural – as the title of Klossowski's trilogy, was a translation from the German (*Gastgebot*) of Hamann. Now this fact takes on importance in the context of the crisis of hospitality which was in its inassimilability the very medium (in Hegel's reading) of Hamann's thought. For Klossowski's laws of hospitality, which entail a yielding of the woman of the house to the exemplary guest, read like an exacerbated fulfillment of the fantasy informing the scandal joining (asunder) Hamann and Berens. As we observed in our consideration of the letter to Lindner, it was a wish whose ramifications were lived by Hamann as the martyrization of the Protestant by the ultimately Catholic forces of the Enlightenment. The first volume of Klossowski's trilogy bears the name of the epic of Protestant persecution in France, *La Révocation de l'Edit de Nantes*.

As Klossowski's Hamann begins to take on the form of a matrix for (a reading of) *Les Lois de l'hospitalité*, the relation to Kant, we shall see, takes on added importance. In anticipation of that discussion, several remarks may be helpful at this juncture. In Hamann's private drama, Kant and Lindner, according to Hegel, play identical roles. Their thankless task is to keep alive the virtuality of Hamann's parasitism (or Berens' hospitality) as the medium within which Hamann can engage his polemic. Hegel: "il [Hamann] provoque Kant à le repousser et à résister à ses préjugés avec autant de violence que lui, Hamann, en met pour attaquer les préjugés de Kant" (p. 86). The adversary, that is, is Kant. Now that reality takes on added interest in the context of the most incisive writing on Klossowski, the essay Deleuze appended to his *Logique du sens*.[21] For Deleuze reads Klossowski as a reaction against the ontological interpretation of the disjunctive syllogism in the *Critique of Pure Reason*. God, the sum of all possibilities, is the ground of the disjunctive genesis of all that is (in its substance) through a series of delimiting exclusions. Klossowski, in Deleuze's reading, retains the *either/or* disjunction, but interprets it affirmatively as *and* – with all the debilitating effects on ontology that ensue. "Le *ou bien* ne cesse pas d'être *ou bien*. Mais, au lieu que la disjonction signifie qu'un certain nombre de prédicats sont exclus d'une chose en vertu de l'identité du concept correspondant, elle signifie que chaque chose s'ouvre à l'infini des prédicats par lesquels elle passe, à condition de perdre son identité comme concept et comme moi."[22] The disjunctive syllogism is delivered over to Klossowski's Anti-Christ, and ceases to be a (Kantian) principle of identity through exclusion to become an affirmation of difference or divergence *per se*. Such is the horizon of Deleuze's reading of Klossowski. We shall have occasion to refer to it again when we engage Hamann's own reading of Kant's *Critique* in terms of a coincidence of opposites. Yet it should not be forgotten that Kant was part of the cast of Hamann's intimate drama. The letter to Lindner we quoted has many counterparts in Hamann's correspondence with Kant. Here, for example, in Klossowski's translation, is a fragment of a letter of 27 July 1759 quoted by Hegel: "Je dois rire du choix d'un philosophe en vue de provoquer en moi un changement d'esprit; je lis la meilleure démonstration comme une jeune fille lirait une lettre d'amour" (p. 83). Now that quotation opens up another avenue in Hamann's thought that brings it into the proximity of a related contemporary meditation on interpretation. For Hamann's statement can be found all but rewritten in R. Rorty's essay on Derrida, "Philosophy as a Kind of Writing": "The twentieth century attempt to purify Kant's general theory into the relation between representations and their objects by turning it into a philosophy of language is, for Derrida, to be countered by making philosophy even more impure – more unprofessional, funnier, more allusive, sexier, and above all more 'written.' "[23] The statement is the most original and accurate in Rorty's essay and is virtually a transcription of Hamann's message to Kant. Which is to suggest that the humorist Hamann, beyond even the matrix of Klossowski's fiction, may offer the elements for constructing a genealogy of a particularly far-reaching analysis of textuality *per se*.

In a region between the narrative (fiction) of Hamann's life and the rigors of philosophical thought, we thus encounter Derrida eroticizing, in Rorty's terms, the legacy of Kant. The circumstance takes on importance in view of the fact that Hamann's most explicit defence of the sacred parasite, his role in the scenario of hospitality, took the form of an onslaught against phonocentrism. I refer to Hamann's contribution to the eighteenth-century debate on phonetic spelling, and specifically his defence of the silent letter *h* against efforts to rationalize it out of existence. The text is not included in Klossowski's anthology, but can serve as an introduction to the questions raised in his introductory essay.[24] A Wolffian scholar, C. T. Damm, had undertaken a campaign to eliminate the silent *h* from German on the grounds that its existence was an irrationality that could only be regarded as barbaric by men of reason.[25] Hamann's response is ultimately that anything figuring as a thorn in Reason's side should no doubt be defended rather than eradicated. Indeed his identification with the cause of the parasitic letter was such that he eventually wrote "A New Apology of the Letter *h* by Itself" (1773).[26] In it the mute letter is allowed to speak: "You little prophets of Böhmisch-Breda," the text begins, with an apostrophaic allusion to a Grimm character and, by extension, to the Encyclopedia, "do not be surprised that I speak to you with a human voice like that dumb beast of burden [Balaam's mule] in order to punish your trespass. Your life is what I am – a breath [*Hauch, souffle*]. So do not think that I should crawl before you, whine to be retained, or lament at being banished or eradicated from your writings. I regard it as an honor and benefit to be less subject to the service of your vanity than my fellow vowels and consonants."[27] Here then is a writing more written, more mute, than usual, an *archiécriture*, which escapes the "service [*Dienst*]" of voice (as reason) only to speak miraculously with a new voice born of the exacerbation of script. For the dumb beast of burden is the mute letter – and Balaam's mule, which speaks in 2 Peter, as well. Lindner, in the letter quoted, was seen as the mute vehicle of the message consolidating the expulsion of the parasite (Hamann), and was denounced for it. In the "New Apology," the mute vehicle (*h*) is the parasite, but manages to complicate its muteness (or parasitism) to the point of speaking the case against its own expulsion. And that process – or miracle – of the talking text, silent *h* voicing its own defence, is identical with the cause of authentic religion.

But with the disfigured text, its dream of phonetic spelling, *Rechtschreiben*, right-writing, marred by a proliferation of silent letters or *souffles*, we approach the core of Klossowski's essay on Hamann: the world as faulty transcription, solecism as the dialect of God. "All of my Christianity," he would write to Lavater, "is but a predilection for signs" (p. 20). But it was in fact a passion for the inadequacy of signs. The implicit armature of Klossowski's essay is the following homology: signifier is to signified as flesh is to soul as the Jews are to the divine scheme.[28] And it is the inadequacy of the former term in each pair to serve as the vehicle of the latter, the radical discontinuity between sign and sense, which is the ground on which all understanding must rest. Klossowski: "Le choix même de cette race la plus réfractaire et la plus opiniâtre, en même temps que l'une des plus maltraitées et des plus méprisées parmi les peuples de l'antiquité, race aussi la plus humble, avant qu'il s'incarnât dans l'un des fils de celle-ci, ce choix insensé constitue le scandale de la raison et de la science, des philosophes et des Juifs" (p. 18). The Protestantism of Klossowski's Hamann is Judeo-centric or, better, Judeo-eccentric: it is the Hebrews' way of straying from the divinity they were given to incarnate which is the reality to be affirmed, and all of philosophy is viewed as an effort (to deny that breach) which is ultimately no less deluded than Kant's efforts to mediate between Hamann and Berens. Indeed in reaction to the incursions of Reason, the constitutive inadequacy of the (Jewish) sign can modulate to an affirmation of the principle of *coincidentia oppositorum*. In the face of philosophy's will toward adequate representation, the cause of authenticity is served by exacerbating the gap: Spirit is best approached through the passions of the flesh; the exemplary Old Testament figure is Noah "drunk with the fruit of his own vineyard, plunged into sleep after the orgy" (p. 31); mute letters are given to speak ... against the myriad lies of *Menschenvernunft* (p. 196). Whereby we again encounter the affirmative or non-exclusive use of the "disjunctive syllogism," which is, in Deleuze's reading, Klossowski's signal and anti-Kantian innovation.

Turn now to Hamann's "Metacritique of the Purism of Reason," published posthumously in 1800. It is an effort to introduce language-as-solecism, or even the coincidence of opposites, as the impure medium within which Kant is unwilling to admit he has constructed the mirage of pure reason:

Reste encore une question capitale: Comment la faculté de penser est-elle possible? La faculté de penser à droite, à gauche, avant et sans, avec et par-delà l'expérience. Guère n'est besoin de prouver la primauté généalogique du langage sur les sept fonctions sacrées de propositions et de conclusions logiques ni pour établir son héraldique. Non seulement la faculté toute entière de penser réside dans le langage, conformément aux prédictions et aux miracles de Samuel Heinecke [a teacher of deaf-mutes], si riches en mérites; mais le langage est aussi le foyer des malentendus de la raison par rapport à elle-même, en partie à cause de la fréquente coïncidence de la notion la plus grande avec la plus petite, de leur vide et de leur plénitude dans les propositions idéales, en partie à cause de l'infini du discours – avant les péroraisons, etc. (p. 254)

The inherently self-contradictory texture of language as the ground of reason ... Now, as Hamann presses his case, that language becomes increasingly a differential mode of writing: sounds and letters reveal their source in the "palpable rhythm of pulse and nasal respiration," the matrix of "every measure of time" (p. 255). Writing is traced back to a style of design generative of an "economy of space" (p. 255). There follows an ironic meditation on the matter of the written word *Vernunft*, the impossibility of deriving the concept of reason from it, or it from its concept. Whereafter, Hamann's conclusion:

Ce que la philosophie métagrabolise [*metagrabolosirt*], moi, pour en faciliter la compréhension au lecteur non averti, je l'ai interprété selon le sacrement du langage, la lettre de ses éléments et l'esprit de son institution; libre à chacun de faire du poing fermé une main largement ouverte. (p. 259)

The burlesque neologism *métagraboliser* is adapted from Rabelais, and may be transcribed as to plumb beyond writing. Against the logocentric depth of philosophy, then, the writing of Hamann. The hand that closes the paragraph all but hints as much.[29]

Dei dialectus solecismus (p. 19).[30] That affirmation of the world as a faulty transcription of divine discourse, a solecism, opens a path back to *Les Lois de l'hospitalité*. For the opening notation in Octave's journal in *La Révocation de l'Edit de Nantes* is a translation of a passage from Quintilian: "Certains pensent qu'il y a solécisme dans le geste également, toutes les fois que par un mouvement de la tête ou de la main on doit entendre le contraire de ce que l'on dit" (p. 15). The quotation, in fact, is the epigraph of the *catalogue raisonné* of Octave's art collection and takes on major importance in the novel. For the ritual of the laws of hospitality – yielding Roberte to others – is carried on in implicit counterpoint with a series of rape scenes (by the imaginary Tonnerre) featured in Octave's collection and described at length in the novel. And the principal gesture of the women painted is precisely a solecism: a lost movement of the hand which conveys the opposite of the resistance they act out in each tableau and which Tonnerre succeeds in affirming in its positivity. It is a gesture that infects and inflects the hospitality of Roberte as well. Here, for instance, is Tonnerre's Lucrèce: "cette autre main, plus bas, qui, loin d'interdire l'accès au trésor, le dirai-je maintenant, dresse, allonge les doigts ..." (p. 24). And here, at the other end of the painted series, is a passage describing the reaction of the Belle Versaillaise violently accosted by two "Communards": "mais la main gantée offrant la paume dont la chair apparaît dans l'échancrure du gant, les doigts repliés sur le creux de la main, le pouce appuyé sur la phalange de l'index, exprimant de la vaine résistance, tandis que la main gauche, que l'on voit à revers, tous doigts dressés, forme un geste d'effroi où le pathétique le cède à la provocation" (p. 81). And now, in summary of the rituals of Roberte's hospitality, we shall merely evoke the conclusion of the bravura episode that finds Roberte, *en route* to her parliamentary duties, accosted by two young lycée students:

Alors cette main de Roberte qu'il n'avait osé déganter lui-même ni seulement toucher, se renversa, allongeant ses longs doigts vers X. Lui-même, debout d'un mouvement qu'il ne prévoyait plus, s'était à peine avancé; cette main gantée le dégageait lentement et sûrement, lui frayait la voie si lentement et sûrement que X. put retrousser le gant sur la paume de Roberte et tirer à son tour: la naissance du pouce apparut et tout l'épiderme satiné de la paume, et enfin les longs doigts souples qui pour lors se repliaient sur l'audace étonnée du jeune garçon, la recouvrant de leurs ongles étincelants. Et quand le gras du pouce de Roberte l'effleura – était-ce l'éclair des ongles nacrés? – X. ne distinguait plus la raison de son plaisir, tandis que Roberte, les cuisses et les fesses ruisselantes de l'impertinence de nos deux néophytes, s'abandonnait à ses ultimes secousses, ahanant et vouant à tous les diables ses obligations à la Chambre, et de députée devenant pute entre Condorcet et Saint Lazare ..." (p. 60)

Roberte's eroticism lies in coinciding with that phantasm of the hand opened – here ungloved – which is the recurrent motif of Tonnerre's art and Octave's collection. It is an affirmation of what the epigraph to Octave's catalogue calls solecism. But at this juncture we may modulate back to the end of Hamann's "Meta-critique of the Purism of Reason," the image of a fist clenched around the solecistic core of reality itself ("des fantômes de mots, des non-mots, des impossibilités de mots"), with its invitation to force that hand open: "libre à chacun de faire du poing fermé une main largement ouverte" (p. 259). Now that image is expanded teleologically by Hegel in his essay on Hamann. Philosophy's task, he writes, is precisely to develop the germ of truth in Hamann's thought until it matures as Hegelian philosophy, a hand with fingers outstretched: "mais que s'il n'a tendu qu'un poing fermé, il laisse au lecteur le soin de 'le déplier en une main ouverte,' c'est-à-dire d'en tirer ce qui serait utile à la science. Hamann, pour sa part ne s'est point donné la peine que Dieu, en un sens supérieur, s'est donnée Lui-même: développer dans la réalité le noyau compact de la Vérité qu'il est Lui-même (d'anciens philosophes disaient de Dieu qu'il est une sphère) en un système de la nature, en un système de l'Etat, de la légalité et de la moralité, en un système de l'histoire universelle, en une main ouverte aux doigts tendus ..." (p. 100). The future of Hamann's thought, that is, was to be its progressive and corrective irradiation into the generality of philosophy as conceived by Hegel.

We are faced then with two reinscriptions of Hamann's clenched fist. On the one hand, we have seen Hegel's effort to force it open, to correct the inhibited development of what he took, in Klossowski's formula, to be an "aborted" prefiguration of his own genius (p. 59). But on the other, consider the strangely incorrect relation between Hamann's fist, clenched on the secret of the solecistic texture of reality, ready to open, and the repetitive solecism of the female hand inadvertently stretched open, the erotic-esthetic focus of Octave's collection of art and the rituals of hospitality to which he drives Roberte. It is as though from crisis of hospitality to crisis of hospitality, from the text (or translation) of Hamann to the novel of Roberte, from an image for solecism (in the "Metacritique") to the solecism of an image (in *La Révocation*), an identical formation were insistent. Unless, of course, that repetition in (or as) reversal were a case of (Hamann's? Klossowski's?) solecism itself ...

From crisis of hospitality to crisis of hospitality ... Octave offered a wife (Roberte), principally to the preceptor Vittorio. Hamann (sometime preceptor) requested a sister (Katharina) of his host Berens. Somewhere in between, we find Octave speculating in *La Révocation* on the pleasure he takes in his rituals of hospitality at seeing Roberte virtually depersonalized beneath the gaze of another: "l'inciter à détacher ses gestes de ce sentiment de soi sans jamais se perdre de vue ... Mais les lui faire attribuer à son reflet jusqu'à se mimer en quelque sorte elle-même sous la dictée de l'autre sans se douter jamais pour autant qu'elle obéissait à une volonté étrangère ..." (p. 38). For that reflection – on Roberte and her reflection – develops into a consideration that

Roberte's secret propensity, rather than motherhood, is sisterhood: "Ce quelque chose d'autre que j'entends ici, c'est une aspiration sororale, sans doute virile à l'intérieur de la féminité . . ." (p. 39). Hamann's fantasy is here all but granted.

But the passage just quoted from *La Révocation* leads us back to our initial comments about Klossowski and Benjamin. For if the evocation of Roberte mimicking herself prepares a discussion of her "sororal tendency," it also anticipates the replication of Roberte in *Le Souffleur*. We had seen Octave meditating amidst his paintings on the explosive implications – for painting itself – of the invention of photography and had posited the readability of the trilogy in terms of the pivotal moment of "The Work of Art in the Age of Mechanical Reproduction": from painting (*La Révocation*) to a humiliating photograph (*Roberte, ce soir*) to the originary reproducibility of Roberte (*Le Souffleur*). With Roberte as "sister," Klossowski's text is poised between the writings of the two para-Kabbalists (Hamann, Benjamin) he had translated. A step further . . . Our reference to Gershom Scholem on Benjamin's relation to Kabbalah was prompted by the odd circumstance that Octave, even as he voices thoughts previously translated from Benjamin, communicates a nostalgia for the German occupation of Paris and eventually finds his prototype (in *Le Souffleur*) in a zealot of Nazi collaboration. Kabbalah as the (imperative to) plunge into evil . . . Klossowski's Hamann, on the other hand, finds his "cabbala" (p. 36) in an identification with the Jews: "il a lu l'histoire des Hébreux comme l'histoire de sa propre vie" (p. 21). But with the Jews as evil. Whence the important letter to Kant (27 July 1759) in which he writes: "la loi de Moïse fut donnée aux Juifs non pour les rendre justes, mais pour rendre leurs péchés plus criminels" (p. 204). After the Jew (Benjamin) identifying with the German, the German (Hamann) identifying with the Jew, cabbalistically, in Klossowski's French.

But there is an explicitly German-Jewish nexus in *La Révocation de l'Edit de Nantes*. For the volume is framed by a crucial series of "Impressions romaines" recounting an episode of Roberte's life at the end of the Second World War. It will be seen that the scenario of hospitality finds therein a prototype as well. At the end of the novel, we learn that Roberte had served in Nazi-occupied

Rome as an agent of the Red Cross. A young Protestant woman free among the convalescing Germans of the Vatican, she flourishes in an ambience of flirtation-cum-religious-transgression. All the while, she is charged with the mission of retrieving Jewish children who had been hidden throughout Rome to avoid Nazi deportation (p. 89). Now Roberte's Roman Impressions are concerned principally with an encounter with a handsome German convalescent named von A. He first draws Roberte into his complicity by imagining her deliriously as his incestuous sister, Malwyda. He asks her ("Schwester") to retrieve their incestuous correspondence from its hiding place in the tabernacle of a church in Anzio. Of Malwyda, moreover, we learn that Roberte's future lover Vittorio had designs on her: "Très amoureux de Malwyda, Vittorio espérait la partager avec lui, qui s'y était opposé, naturellement" (p. 98). Consider, then, that for Roberte to enter the phantasm of "Impressions romaines" is to do so as a sister (Schwester), the motif we have retained from Hamann. (Indeed the incestuous relation even brings us to the Biblical prototype of Herod and Herodias evoked by Hamann in the letter to Lindner.) Note in addition that the Catholic persecution of Protestants, the revocation of the Edict of Nantes, which gives its title to Klossowski's grim historical carnival, is here transformed into the Nazi persecution of the Jews. Now as von A. proceeds in his delirium, he reveals that he had been charged with the deportation of Jews to Germany, but found himself emotionally incapable of sending the children of the affected families to their death. As the baroque sequence proliferates, moreover, we learn that the list of the Jewish children saved is to be found in the tabernacle of the church in Anzio von A. has already referred to, that the incestuous correspondence with his sister never existed, and that Vittorio, his accomplice in thwarting the official policy of deportation, has proved himself a swindler, extorting a payment for each of the children saved. All of this information excites Roberte erotically, but her dalliance with von A. is interrupted by the arrival of American military police agents. They take away von A., whose last words are: "Nous qui ne regrettons rien, nous aussi nous aurons notre heure" (p. 102). How far have these "Roman Impressions" – conceived by Roberte as something of a "dress rehearsal [*répétition générale*]" – taken us? We should do well at this point to take stock. Our reflections began with Benjamin on the advent of photography, translated by Klossowski, and voiced at a revealing juncture by Octave. But behind Octave, we have found first Rodin, French technician of deportation under the Nazis, and now von A., Nazi officer charged with deporting Jews. From the para-Kabbalist Jew, Benjamin, sacrificed by the Germans, to the Nazi: *coincidentia oppositorum*, in Hamann's terms.

Now the Revocation of the Edict of Nantes is reinscribed in the novel as the German deportation of the Jews, but also as the series of humiliations which the Catholic theologian Octave inflicts – as hospitality – on his Protestant wife Roberte. Roberte's sororal essence, however, is liberated in her assimilation (in the "Roman Impressions") to the (incestuous) sister Malwyda. But the record of Malwyda's love, as we have seen, is superimposed on the list of Jewish victims. The Protestant as Jew: the central conceit of Hamann's "Kabbalistic rhapsody," "Aesthetica in Nuce."

And finally, Vittorio, the parasite-swindler-trickster-rapist, who decides gratuitously to pass himself off as Binsnicht, a Nazi war criminal. Vittorio? "Car enfin," asks Roberte, "que voulez-vous que je pense d'un individu qui entre le Vatican et la rue de la Paix éprouve le besoin de jouer au 'criminel de guerre'?" (p. 163).[31] But Binsnicht was the roar of Luther – "Ich bin's nit! – Ich bin's nit!" – in that "fit in the choir" which his biographers have placed at the heart of his spiritual development, and Catholic tradition has interpreted as a yielding to the Evil One.[32] Klossowski: "A ses contemporains wolffiens, Hamann déclare: 'Je luthérise . . .'" (p. 17).

The Evil One . . . As our two para-Kabbalists – German and Jew – circulate through every member (host, hostess, guest) of the phantasm of hospitality, we are reminded of Klossowski's own Evil One, Baphomet, "prince of every modification."[33] Deleuze evokes the world of Klossowski's last novel as the horizon of his accomplishment: "Nous touchons au point où le mythe klossows-kien des souffles devient aussi une philosophie . . . Le moi dissous s'ouvre à des séries de rôles, parce qu'il fait monter une intensité qui comprend déjà la différence en soi, et qui pénètre toutes les autres, à travers et dans les corps multiples."[34] But the endless traversal of "self" by multiple insufflations and fluctuations was already the project sketched in Klossowski's introduction to Hamann: " 'Exposé à l'influence perpétuelle d'autres esprits, notre âme est en connexion avec ces derniers. C'est ce qui rend notre propre soi si indiscutablement problématique que nous ne pouvons guère le reconnaître ni le discerner, ni non plus le déterminer nous-mêmes.' Si Hamann n'a pas développé davantage cette théorie de l'influence des esprits sur l'âme qu'il évoque dans ses *Miettes* au début de sa carrière ... (p. 34). "To speak is to translate," wrote Hamann in his rhapsody. In translating Klossowski's – translations of – Hamann and Benjamin through every modification of his para-historical fiction, I have hoped to bring the project of the introduction to Hamann to a measure of rhapsodic fulfillment.

CHAPTER 4

Literature and collaboration: Benoist-Méchin's return to Proust

I always think of Swann's story as Proust's equivalent of
Wagner's Prize Song from *Die Meistersinger.*

M. Hindus, *A Reader's Guide to Marcel Proust*

Might psychoanalysis itself, it has recently been asked, be *une histoire juive* – a fragment of Jewish history or, even more, an elaborate Jewish anecdote?[1] In the course of the colloquium – in
Montpellier – which pondered that question, D. Sibony chose to
accord one Jewish joke emblematic status: Katzmann, intent on
Gallicizing his name, translates *Katz (=chat)* and *mann (=l'homme),*
and ends up as Monsieur Chalom.[2] The onomastic malaise, the
interlinguistic inventiveness mediating a blind and self-defeating
aggression against the (name of the) father invite one to conclude
that if indeed psychoanalysis may be construed as *une histoire juive,*
it is in the sense of the anecdote just related. Call it the case of the
Cat Man.

Sibony's joke may be found, in a curious transformation.
toward the end of *A la recherche du temps perdu.* The narrator encounters Bloch, Proust's prototypal assimilated Jew, in the Guermantes salon: "J'eus de la peine à reconnaître mon camarade
Bloch, lequel d'ailleurs maintenant avait pris non seulement le
pseudonyme, mais le nom de Jacques du Rozier, sous lequel il eût
fallu le flair de mon grand-père pour reconnaître la 'douce vallée'
de l'Hébron et les 'chaînes d'Israël' que mon ami semblait avoir
définitivement rompues."[3] The attentive reader realizes that in
his flight from Jewishness, Bloch has inadvertently taken on the
name of the *Judengasse* – *la rue des Rosiers* – which Charlus, a thousand pages earlier, had deemed the only address fit for him.[4]
Here, then, is an exemplary version of the vacuity of snobbery in

Proust: even as Madame Verdurin is recognized in the Princess de Guermantes, so does one detect the Jewish ghetto in the pseudonymous French aristocrat. Jacques du Rozier is the butt of the same joke as Monsieur Chalom. We may call the episode for short Proust's *S/Z*.

In a first approximation, the much vexed question of "psychoanalysis and literature" (or "psychoanalysis and narration") might be transcribed as (Freud's) *Cat Man* vs. (Proust's) *S/Z* – with the psychoanalytic traditionalist affirming Monsieur Chalom's (sympathetic) understanding of Jacques du Rozier's plight and his (more advanced?) adversary contending that on the contrary, *S/Z* is a far more insightful rendering of matters than the *Cat Man*. And yet it is precisely the refusal of that mirror-like stand-off (between snobs), the intuition that new understanding can emerge only in a rigorous disruption of such symmetry, that constitutes a principal contribution of Lacan to textual interpretation. It is the effects of such a disruption which structure the remarks on Proust – and one of his readers – that follow.

Our social existence, Proustian orthodoxy has it, is a long lesson in the vanity and illusions of snobbery. We are all ultimately Jacques du Rozier, and can evade his fate only if genius and good fortune allow us to abandon social life entirely for the realm of art. Here, then, is an evocation of Proust – forsaking social intercourse for esthetic contemplation – on the path to that realization:

"Le jour de mon arrivée," raconte Reynaldo Hahn, en évoquant le souvenir d'un séjour qu'il fit chez des amis avec l'auteur des *Jeunes Filles en fleur*, "nous allâmes ensemble nous promener dans le jardin. Nous passâmes devant une bordure de rosiers du Bengale, quand, soudain, il se tut et s'arrêta. Je m'arrêtai aussi, mais il se remit alors à marcher et je fis de même. Bientôt il m'arrêta et me dit avec cette douceur enfantine et un peu triste qu'il conserva toujours dans le ton et dans la voix: 'Est-ce que cela vous fâcherait que je reste un peu en arrière? Je voudrais revoir les petits rosiers.' Je le quittai. Au tournant de l'allée, je regardai derrière moi. Proust avait rebroussé chemin jusqu'aux rosiers. Ayant fait le tour du château, je le retrouvai à la même place, regardant fixement les roses..."

In this anecdote, quoted from Jacques Benoist-Méchin's *Avec Marcel Proust*, we find our author pondering in isolation the hidden essence of a rosebush, speculating on the mystery of which the bush formed but a "lid" *(couvercle).*[5] That development, in fact, serves as Benoist-Méchin's introduction to the esthetically crucial episode of the *madeleine,* an "experience of the same order."[6] Consider, then, in the fragments of Proust we have assembled, that in order to evade the disillusionment attendant on perceiving the rue des Rosiers in du Rozier, one flees society for art – and the hidden essence of a *rosier.* What is striking, that is, is not so much the street name behind the pseudonym, which is but a witty exemplification of Proust's orthodoxy about Society, but the recurrence of the same term *(rosier)* at the core of a fantasy of Art. For that repetition constitutes an implicit violation of his philosophy. As though the opposition between Art and Society, thematized in Proust under the rubric *contre Sainte-Beuve,* in this case would not hold. In Proust? It should be acknowledged at this point that the link between the *madeleine* episode and Hahn's anecdote about the rosebush is established not by Proust, but by Benoist-Méchin. It is to his reading, then, that we shall turn.

Jacques Benoist-Méchin is a name rarely quoted in Proust scholarship. In literary history, he perhaps merits a footnote as the musician-friend of Joyce who transcribed into music for him (and his printer in Dijon) the ballad – of the Jew's daughter – in the "Ithaca" section of *Ulysses.*[7] It is not as a footnote to English literature, however, but as an appendix to French history that he is no doubt best known. For he is the principal protagonist of the appendix – on "The War Question of January 1942" – to R. O. Paxton's *Vichy France: Old Guard and New Order, 1940–1944.*[8] And if indeed collaboration with the Nazis "was not a German demand to which some Frenchmen acceded," but "a French proposal that Hitler ultimately rejected," then Benoist-Méchin was without doubt France's exemplary collaborator.[9] For it was he, as Darlan's roving negotiator with the Germans and Secrétaire-général à la vice-présidence du conseil, who attempted to negotiate with Hitler's ambassador Abetz a more favorable peace settlement in exchange for a French declaration of war against Britain and the United States. That venture failed and Benoist-Méchin was soon to lose his power in Vichy, but it was precisely the nature of his project which branded him a collaborator *par excellence* and resulted in a death sentence – from which he was eventually pardoned – after the Liberation.[10] Benoist-Méchin would live out the rest of his years – until 1983 – as a historian, and it is within that context that his anomalous volume *Avec Marcel Proust* was to appear: first in 1957, then in 1977.[11] The book is in part an early essay (1922) on music in Proust, the author's "first completed text," and in part a memoir (from 1957) of his brief but decisive encounter with Proust in 1922. One wonders what it meant for the would-be architect of collaboration with Hitler to imagine his life in terms of the legacy of a Jewish (or half-Jewish) novelist. One suspects that *Avec Marcel Proust* was written out of a profound sympathy with the Proustian thesis of the ultimate incommensurability of art and life – as though, if indeed there were a "Proustian" dimension to his existence, it would be permanently secure from contamination by, say, his book of 1939, *Eclaircissements sur 'Mein Kampf'* and all that ensued thereafter.[12] In Benoist-Méchin's words: "Quel rapport y a-t-il, me demandais-je, entre mes préoccupations d'aujourd'hui, entre *La Musique du temps perdu* et les *Soixante Jours qui ébranlèrent l'Occident?* Se peut-il que je sois l'auteur de l'un et de l'autre? . . . Je leur trouvais si peu de traits communs qu'ils me paraissent appartenir moins à deux époques d'une même vie qu'à deux vies différentes, n'ayant aucun rapport entre elles . . ."[13]

According to his memoir, reading Proust was for Benoist-Méchin an illumination: "il projetait un faisceau de lumière sur la zone d'ombres où je me débattais encore. D'où l'impression que certaines de ses analyses venaient à ma rencontre pour me tendre la main."[14] Retain *the faisceau*, but even more the quality of the light. Here is the scenario of the encounter. Benoist-Méchin, stationed in the Rhineland in 1922, dreams of Franco-German friendship, visits the Francophile scholar E. R. Curtius, and persuades him to allow him to intervene in securing Proust's permission for a German edition of excerpts from *La Recherche*. Benoist-Méchin writes to Proust, who agrees to the project in a courtly letter to which we shall return. The novelist even agrees to receive his young admirer several weeks later (during his leave) at 1 A.M. in the Ritz, as was his wont. Benoist-Méchin arrives, is struck first by the pink taffeta shade of the lamp in Proust's room, the sole source of light in an otherwise dark chamber, then by the long-suffering "Assyrian" physiognomy of Proust in what was to be the last year of his life. They talk, mostly about music, for two hours before Proust pleads fatigue and bids his guest farewell. Benoist-Méchin returns to the Rhineland, witnesses the further decline of Franco-German relations, and is too obsessed with his political tasks to assimilate the news of Proust's death in November. As the Germans lag in reparations payments, the French, to Benoist-Méchin's chagrin, decide to occupy the Ruhr. The night before that surprise military action, he finds himself at the opera in Wiesbaden, the only Frenchman in an audience tense with anticipation of bad times for Germany. The performance: *Die Meistersinger von Nürnberg*. As the lights dim, he is suddenly struck by the quality of the light in his box: "Les lumières s'éteignirent progressivement et, dans mon alvéole faiblement éclairée par une applique dont les ampoules étaient masquées par de petits abat-jour roses, s'établit une pénombre étrangement semblable à celle où s'était déroulé mon entretien avec Proust."[15] Whereupon he realizes the full import of Proust – and his death – for him. This will be Proust's night even as the chance resurrection of the ambience of their past encounter will mark Benoist-Méchin's consecration as a writer. The pink-shaded light, that is, is at some level his *madeleine*.

The political tension of the evening results in a second surprise. In act III of the opera, as Hans Sachs intones his hymn to holy German art, affirms its virtue as consolation for every political humiliation, a febrile woman rises in the audience, her head erect; several rows away another strikes a similar pose. Soon the entire audience, group by group, row by row, has risen and remains standing in silent solidarity until the end of the performance. Whereupon, instead of the expected applause: "durant un long moment, la foule garda le silence, un silence enivré, total, vertigineux, comme si elle avait peine à retrouver le chemin de la terre. Et puis, un à un, les groupes se défirent et les assistants quittèrent le théâtre sans proférer un mot."[16] Benoist-Méchin is overcome with emotion, concludes that this is what Proust had in mind when he spoke of music in terms of a "communication of souls." He leaves the theatre determined to be a writer, and composes his first "complete piece" on "La Musique et l'Immortalité dans l'Oeuvre de Marcel Proust."

Consider, then, that for Benoist-Méchin to recount this sequence in 1957 was virtually to claim that Proust – French literature – was his path to collaboration. For whether or not he rose – with "les deux milles personnes de l'assistance" – the almost religious solidarity with the German community at the outbreak of a new phase of Franco-German hostility is read here as a scenario scripted by Proust.[17] As though it were the novelist's "faisceau de lumière" which would bring Benoist-Méchin, in the fullness of time, to the light of that earliest of French symbols of fascism, *le faisceau* ...[18]

A "fascist" Proust? The most memorable pages of Benoist-Méchin's essay of 1922 are in the chapter, "La Communication des âmes." They elaborate as a vast metaphor for Proust's novel the glass wall of the entrance hall of the Gare d'Orsay. Through its semi-transparency one could see superimposed and subdivided into rooms the floors of the Palais d'Orsay: "Des grappes superposées [d'individus] se nouent, puis se dissolvent, séparées par la ligne horizontale d'un plancher invisible le long duquel défilent des processions de fantômes qui semblent avancer dans le vide ... On croirait assister à quelque rite obscur, à quelque sacrifice inhumain où chacun serait à la fois officiant et victime ..."[19] Benoist-Méchin's intuition is that the glass wall, with its magisterial clock, is the esthetic medium within which a new sociality is forged. As in the music of Proust, the compartmentalized existences of the denizens of the Palais can here unconsciously commune. Now Benoist-Méchin's preferred metaphor for Proust's novel is, of course, at a great remove from the reality of collaboration. Yet to seek out the specificity of Proust ("un changement de régime au sein de notre subconscient") in an idealist affirmation of the primacy of the collectivity over the individual is both to depart sharply from Proustian orthodoxy (what P. Sollers has called "le triomphalisme esthético-subjectif") and to link up with that spiritualist dream of a "socialism" shorn of specifically proletarian aspirations which was a crucial juncture on the path to fascism.[20]

The pinkish light at the Opera in Wiesbaden was the element through which the Proustian effect *took*, Benoist-Méchin's graft of the *madeleine*. But this is not the first occasion in his book in which a *rose* motif leads to the *madeleine*. We have already quoted Reynaldo Hahn's recollection of Proust pondering the hidden essence of a *rosier* and seen Benoist-Méchin's use of it to introduce a discussion of the *madeleine*. But rosier/Rozier brings us back to the Jewish *parvenu* Bloch and the rue des Rosiers, the anecdote – *S/Z* – with which we began. Even as the pinkish light in Wiesbaden returns us to the *taffetas rose* of the Ritz shading Proust's distinctly Oriental ("Assyrian") face. As the associations in our intertext proliferate, they will be seen to converge with devastating rigor on a single historical eventuality: had Proust lived long enough, he would have been slated for annihilation as a Jew by the very collectivity – the New Europe – he was being enlisted (in Wiesbaden) to underwrite.

But at this juncture Benoist-Méchin begins sounding less like a reader than a character of Proust. Music in Proust? Consider that after Vinteuil, Proust's exemplary composer, dies, the narrator finds himself transfixed at a spectacle – or theatre – as well. Outside the window of the house where Vinteuil used to compose, Marcel peers in to see his daughter and her friend desecrating Vinteuil's portrait in a highly charged ritual of evil.[21] The humiliation, that is, which would in strict logic befall the deceased Jew Proust, mentor in music, at some level *repeats* the desecration of the dead father and musician Vinteuil.

Benoist-Méchin as a character out of Proust? The more one reads his account, the more one suspects that if the young man was searching for a mentor, the dying novelist was looking for materials for his book. It is in that light, perhaps, that Proust's letter to him should be read. After authorizing the German translation, Proust appends a curious request:

Je me souviens d'avoir vu jadis Madame votre Mère. Je ne la connaissais pas, mais me la rappelle très bien. Elle était superbe et très grande. Est-ce que vous lui ressemblez? Comme je ne vous verrai probablement jamais, si vous pouviez me faire envoyer par la poste une photo de vous, je vous la renverrais aussitôt. Mais (vous avez dû voir cela par les considérations sur la ressemblance de Gilberte Swann avec son père et avec sa mère dans les *Jeunes Filles en fleurs*) je suis toujours très intéressé par les réincarnations d'un type admiré, dans un autre sexe.[22]

Benoist-Méchin is flattered, but embarrassed. For the woman Proust had seen was not his mother, but his father's first wife. He sends the photograph, nevertheless, without clarification. Proust responds that the resemblance is astonishing. Benoist-Méchin is obliged to disabuse him. Proust counters:

... telles quelles, les choses sont infiniment plus intéressantes que vous ne pouvez l'imaginer, car votre photographie m'a confirmé le bien-fondé de mes conceptions de l'amour. Ne vous étonnez donc pas si je lui attache une grande importance. Je pense, en effet, que les hommes n'aiment pas telle ou telle femme isolée, mais un certain type de femme dont ils ne s'écartent jamais. Si, par suite d'un deuil ou d'une séparation, ils perdent la femme qu'ils aiment, ils courent après son type, qu'ils poursuivent obstinément, quoique souvent à leur insu. Si votre père a épousé en secondes noces Madame votre Mère, c'est qu'elle incarnait ce type spécial qu'il aimait plus que tout. Elle devait ressembler, par quelque côté, à sa première épouse. Il n'est donc pas étonnant que je retrouve sur votre image quelques traits d'une femme qui n'était pas votre mère et que vous n'avez jamais vue. A travers elle, un reflet du type de femme qu'aimait votre père est venu se poser sur votre visage, créant en quelque sorte une ressemblance au second degré. Cela confirme tout ce que je pense ...[23]

Benoist-Méchin can but submit to Proust's analysis: "Voilà ce qu'il en coûte de vouloir jouer au plus fin ... on ne trompe jamais les esprits supérieurs."[24]

If the light in the Wiesbaden Opera reproduced the *madeleine* episode, the struggle over maternal identification (which Benoist-Méchin loses), the decisive imposition of a mother on this son, repeats another nodal episode of Proust's novel: the celebrated good night kiss scene of *Combray*. Marcel's father fails to separate mother and son; she is dispatched to spend the night with him; his will undergoes a decisive decline ("Ainsi, pour la première fois, ma tristesse n'était plus considérée comme une faute punissable mais comme un mal involontaire qu'on venait de reconnaître officiellement; comme un état nerveux dont je n'étais pas responsable ...")[25] Now as Marcel's father climbs the stairs, we see the reflection of his lamp flickering on the wall. In his white nightgown, he is compared to Biblical Abraham in an Italian etching by Benozzo Gozzoli telling Sarah to get away from their son Isaac in anticipation of his sacrifice on Mount Moriah. But

Marcel's father fails to, the symbolic sacrifice is avoided, and ... the Jewish mother (Madame Weil?) swallows him whole. One result of that sequence, I have attempted to show elsewhere, is the obsessive assimilation throughout the novel of Jews and homosexuals as the two accursed races: the son, that is, *as* Jewish mother.[26] "Homosexuality is the truth of love" in Proust, writes Deleuze.[27] And our consideration of Proust's *S/Z* invites us to add – with reference to the other devouring passion in the novel, snobbery – that Jewishness is at some level the truth of snobbery. Together they form for Proust the disaster of life, which art – and the *madeleine* – alone can redeem.

With this linkage between Jewishness and homosexuality in Proust, our inquiry (into the literary fantasia of Benoist-Méchin) converges curiously with that of Hannah Arendt in her volume on *Anti-Semitism* in *The Origins of Totalitarianism*.[28] For in her effort to understand the roots of Nazism, the author on whom she draws most extensively is Proust, the "exemplary witness of dejudaized Judaism."[29] And the Proust she gives us is the virtuoso delineator of all the paradoxes informing the pariah status of Jews and "inverts." Arendt, of course, is a political theorist. Her strong suit, that is, is neither textual nor psychological analysis. (To reflect on the specific textuality of her *Anti-Semitism* would entail focusing on her rewriting of Marx's "farce" of Bonapartism as the "comedy" of the Dreyfus Affair, using Proust, for example, to bring *The Eighteenth Brumaire of Louis Bonaparte* an – anti-Semitic – step closer to the Hitler experience, with the "mob" – "the residue of all classes" – replacing Marx's *bohême*, and the anti-Dreyfusard Jules Guérin – "in whom high society found its first criminal hero" – replacing the Nephew.)[30] And yet Arendt's "political" analysis harmonizes eerily with our own comments on the structure of Proust's fable. For her subject is ultimately the degeneration of "Judaism," an ethical reality for both Jews and Christians, into the psychological essence – virtue or vice – of "Jewishness": "Jewish origin, without religious and political connotation, became everywhere a psychological quality, was changed into 'Jewishness,' and from then on could be considered only in the categories of virtue or vice ..."[31] And further on: "As far as the Jews were concerned, the transformation of the 'crime' of Judaism into the fashionable 'vice' of Jewishness was dangerous in the extreme. Jews had been able to escape from Judaism into conversion; from Jewishness there was no escape. A crime, moreover, is met with punishment; a vice can only be exterminated ..."[32] It will be perceived to what an extent this analysis prepares a comprehension of totalitarianism. But the degeneration of the ethical into the psychological, of a "faute punissable" into a "mal involontaire," was the upshot of the good night kiss scene in *La Recherche*. It is as though Arendt were taking her macropolitical cue from Proust's microtextual maneuver. At the end of which she is left to develop the imaginary reverberations of Proust's maternal identification into a sociology of Jews and/as "inverts."

The essential tenet of Proust's esthetic philosophy, as we have seen, posits a radical discontinuity between art and life, the realms epitomized in the novel by the *madeleine*, on the one hand, and the good night kiss scene on the other. For should the two overlap, should the esthetic blessings of involuntary memory be contaminated by the ethical curse of willlessness, Proust's idealism would be decisively stalled. Art could no longer reverse or redeem what would no longer be entirely distinct from itself. The most programmatic statement of that essential difference appears in *Contre Sainte-Beuve*, with its distrust of any appeal to an author's life in order to understand his art: "un livre est le produit d'un autre moi que celui que nous manifestons dans nos habitudes, dans la société, dans nos vices ..."[33] In *La Recherche*, the prototypal exemplification of the thesis is the inconceivability of any link between the wretchedness of Vinteuil's existence and the splendors of his music.

Yet in reading Benoist-Méchin on Proust–*Avec Marcel Proust* against *Contre Sainte-Beuve* – it was precisely that connection which interested us. The night at the Wiesbaden Opera, in our extrapolation, mapped the cult of art ("music in Proust," Vinteuil) onto the episode relating the horrors of degradation Vinteuil underwent at the instigation of his daughter. In that reading, Proust as guide in art is indistinguishable from Proust as victim in life. The project of *Contre Sainte-Beuve* would end in collapse.

In *A Structural Study of Autobiography*, in terms deriving from Lacan, I attempted to show that such a collapse was always already in effect in *La Recherche* itself, indeed in *Jean Santeuil*.[34] In the context of Benoist-Méchin's implicit apologia, and against the horizon of the political episode he has come to represent, I would like to expand that analysis – of the collapse of the thesis of *Contre Sainte-Beuve:* the radical autonomy of art – in the direction of the historical reality informing it. Against Sainte-Beuve? In the central chapter from which we have quoted, "La Méthode de Sainte-Beuve," Proust suggests that the future of Sainte-Beuve's thesis lay in its extrapolation to considerations of race by Taine ("Il considérait Sainte-Beuve comme un initiateur, comme remarquable 'pour son temps,' comme ayant presque trouvé sa méthode à lui, Taine").[35] The radicalization of Proust's argument, then, would read *Contre Taine*, or, in abbreviated form, art as opposed no longer to "life" so much as to "race." But that chapter is curiously framed by an anecdote imbued with a specific racial reference. Marcel reveals the idea of writing *Contre Sainte-Beuve* to his mother from a sickbed. Because of his extremes of mood, she hesitates to impinge on his privacy. In his affectionate largesse he finds himself reciting lines of Racine's Assuérus to his mother's Esther: the Gentile king and his Jewish bride ... On the one hand, then, in the frame we find an intrusive Jewish mother ("les belles lignes de son visage juif ..."), and, on the other, in the chapter, an implicit desire to defend art from incursions of "race."[36] But the Jews of Racine's *Esther* will surface in *Sodome et Gomorrhe* as ironic metaphorical equivalents of the "inverts" who have secretly invested all the strategic positions of mainstream society. Again we find the link between the two "accursed races," but in this context as the figural train of Esther-as-Jewish-mother.

From *Contre Sainte-Beuve* (or the thesis of art opposed to life) to *Contre Taine* (or that of art opposed to – the Jewish – race) ... That second formulation in fact brings us to the very end of the volume published posthumously as *Contre Sainte-Beuve suivi de nouveaux mélanges* and the specific light it casts on Proust's essential distinction – even as it totters on the brink of collapse. The final entry in the book is entitled "Léon Daudet," and deals with the famous polemicist, aide to Drumont before becoming a leader of Action

Française.[37] Daudet, arguably the most influential French literary critic of the century, launched the careers of Bernanos and Céline, and was responsible for the Goncourt Prize that marked Proust's consecration as a major figure in 1919. *Le Côté de Guermantes* was dedicated to him, presumably out of gratitude, but the ethical stake in Proust's homage to Daudet becomes clear only at the end of *Nouveaux mélanges*. From which:

Ne pouvant plus lire qu'un journal, je lis, au lieu de ceux d'autrefois, *l'Action française*. Je peux dire qu'en cela je ne suis pas sans mérite. La pensée de ce qu'un homme pouvait souffrir m'ayant jadis rendu dreyfusard, on peut imaginer que la lecture d'une "feuille" infiniment plus cruelle que le *Figaro* et les *Débats*, desquels je me contentais jadis, me donne souvent comme les premières atteintes d'une maladie de coeur. Mais dans quel autre journal le portique est-il décoré par Saint-Simon lui-même, j'entends par Léon Daudet ... [38]

Life and art are rigorously separated here, but life, in this case, is Jewish suffering (Dreyfus), and art, in a word, is French style. Might the latter redeem the former? In his next gust of praise for Daudet, Proust almost stumbles over his own distinction:

Cet homme si simple, si ami des "petits," du peuple, le moins snob en vérité des hommes, et qui a écrit, contre la richesse et le monde, les pages les plus délicieuses, cet homme qui semble s'être donné par patriotisme la tâche "héroïque" de détester, dans le sens où il dit le "faux héroïque" du colonel Henry (que je ne trouve pas héroïque du tout, si revenu que je sois depuis longtemps de tous les dreyfusards nantis qui essayent de se faire une position dans le faubourg Saint-Germain) ... [39]

Here we find Proust backing into a realization that the prose he admires is inseparable from the injustice (Henry's forgeries) it espouses and then latching onto the fact of the subsequent corruption of the cause of justice as a pretext for half-heartedly disavowing his discovery.[40] Finally, the distinction between art and life, the cult of French style and the torments of Jewish suffering, evaporates. Of Daudet's prose, he asks: "Qu'est-ce que cela doit être pour les victimes?"[41] And he answers: "Eux-mêmes, lisant le livre, doivent croire que les articles sont un affreux cauchemar, ou en lisant les articles que le livre est un rêve béni auquel on ne peut ajouter foi."[42] Art and life, the devotion to French style and the rigors of Jewish exclusion are, then, the *same* script, with a change of sign. But at this point, reverie takes over ("un rêve béni auquel on ne peut ajouter foi"), as though any fantasy would do to defend against the collapse of the assimilationist wish – French style as a balm for Jewish suffering – which the essay portends.

Toward the middle of *Le Côté de Guermantes*, the narrator offers a fable of redemption so complete as to resemble, in genre, a fairy tale.[43] The scene is a Paris restaurant divided into two rooms by the slimmest of partitions. On one side, the Hebrews; on the other, "les jeunes nobles." Marcel enters unaccompanied and is subjected to a rude surprise: "Pour comble de malchance j'allai m'asseoir dans la salle réservée à l'aristocratie d'où il [le patron] vint rudement me tirer en m'indiquant, avec une grossièreté à laquelle se conformèrent immédiatement tous les garçons, une place dans l'autre salle. Elle me plut d'autant moins que la banquette où elle se trouvait etait dejà pleine de monde et que j'avais en face de moi la porte réservée aux Hébreux qui (. . .), s'ouvrant et se fermant à chaque instant, m'envoyait un froid horrible . . ."[44] His humiliation seems total when Saint-Loup enters and he – and Marcel – are immediately accorded entry to the aristocratic room. Saint-Loup even commandeers the cloak *(manteau)* of the Prince de Foix to assure his comfort.[45] Marcel's triumph is complete. In the reading of Proust sketched in these pages, the autonomy of art, the new-critical prize presumably won *contre Sainte-Beuve*, is a transformation of the room in the restaurant reserved for aristocrats. The ultimate argument against the redemptive interpretation of *La Recherche*, that is, is its incoherence. "Art" cannot redeem the torments of "life" because it is their cause. French (literature) will not absolve from (Jewish) suffering because it is its enabling condition . . .

Perhaps we should imagine the encounter (in the Ritz) between Proust and Benoist-Méchin as an audition: the author secretly tries out his future critic for a role in the drama of his redemption from "Jewishness." The future collaborator with the Nazis waits thirty years to accept the role, but interprets it as his own absolution from collaboration . . . The "unconscious" of their transaction is perhaps the muteness of that unformulated pact. It is a silence in whose margins Hannah Arendt was able to read Proust as the exemplary sociologist of the world that would culminate in Nazism.

This analysis, it may be perceived, is a transformation of an effort to read Proust with Lacan undertaken ten years ago. To immerse an interpretation born of Lacan in the medium of European Jewish pariahdom at the beginning of the century is arguably to expose that discourse to its own most radical roots in Freud.[46] If this reading, that is, has allowed us to move further into Proust's narrative, it is my suspicion that in the proper light it might well take us further into Lacan as well.[47] In the interim, it is hoped that the substitution of a fantasy of "French exclusion" for "esthetic autonomy" at the manic pole of imaginary speculation in Proust will not be perceived as lacking in implication for an understanding of the vicissitudes of French thought in the United States in general.

CHAPTER 5

"Pierre Menard, author of Don Quixote*" again*

In an influential essay on Borges and his lessons for literary criticism, Gérard Genette, in his first volume of *Figures*, pays particular attention to the Argentine's celebrated parable of Pierre Menard, "Symbolist from Nîmes," and his quixotic decision not to copy, but to rewrite – "word for word and line for line" – Cervantes' masterwork.[1] The specific techniques brought to the art of reading by Menard's exploit, writes the narrator, are those of "deliberate anachronism" and "erroneous attribution." Genette warms to Borges' suggestion, but ultimately veers toward a more "structuralist" intuition that, in the last analysis, authorial attribution itself – be it true or false – is our critical error or self-imposed impoverishment. The true Borgesian payoff, Genette suggests, comes with the awareness that literature itself may be read as a vast anonymous text, reversible in time, homogeneous in space: "l'utopie littéraire," as he entitles his piece. As though the critic, in Paris, were inclined to read Menard's Nîmes the way Jarry reads Ubu's Poland – as nowhere.

No, it will be responded, not Jarry's Poland, but Valéry's Montpellier, barely an hour's drive from Nîmes. Menard, after all, is cousin to Monsieur Teste, and Genette has but reclaimed for French letters one of the extreme possibilities dreamed by France's premier poetician. Perhaps. Yet consider that with the displacement of Menard, the westering of Nîmes, the piquancy of Borges' text has been obliterated. If the "rhetorical eulogy of history" Borges quotes from Cervantes is not imagined as written by "a contemporary of William James," Anachronism loses its hold on the text. If its author is no one in particular, Erroneous Attribution drops out of the equation. There is perhaps, then, reason to resist Genette in his rushing of Menard toward Paris, his enlistment of Borges in the ranks of French criticism. Genette is perhaps right in implying that the critical task of the day is, at some level, to rewrite (not *Don Quixote*, but) "Pierre Menard, Author of *Don Quixote*," but it is a rewriting different from his own that I shall here undertake.

In the annals of French Symbolism, there was, it happens, but one poet who hailed from Nîmes, and who, moreover, was obsessed with a question of erroneous attribution. His name was Bernard Lazare.[2] And although there are few today who could name any of his works, he survives in the memoirs of Péguy – *Notre jeunesse* – as one of the few great Frenchmen of his generation because of his essential relation to what was perhaps the most carefully studied text of the entire nineteenth century, the *bordereau* or letter on arms erroneously attributed in 1894 to Captain Alfred Dreyfus.[3] Borges' narrator confesses that he has come to think of *Don Quixote* "as a palimpsest in which should appear traces – tenuous but not undecipherable – of the 'previous' handwriting" of Menard. In our reading of "Pierre Menard," we would be all the more inclined to detect the tenuous but not undecipherable trace of Bernard Lazare in Borges' fable of the Symbolist from Nîmes were it not, as we shall see, for Lazare's own problematical relation to the very topos of the identification of handwriting.

Let us begin by examining – for its emblematic qualities – an exemplary short story by Lazare, "Le sacrifice."[4] Corésos, a priest of the Bacchic cult, falls so deeply in love with a virgin, Kallirhoé, that he abandons the cult. She, however, resists his advances. Whereupon he concludes that the "virginal cruelty" of his beloved is guilty, and recalls "qu'il était prêtre d'un Dieu puissant qui jamais n'avait failli aux siens" (p. 159). He returns to the cult and indeed so moves the god whom he embraces anew that that god, to avenge him, strikes the city with madness. An oracle determines that only the sacrifice of the guilty party – or a willing surrogate – will end the public insanity. Kallirhoé, about to be executed, is saved *in extremis* by Corésos, who commits suicide in her place.

Now if the inaccessible virgin, marked by the seal of death, is to all appearances Lazare's version of Mallarmé's Hérodiade, his investment in Symbolist poetry itself, the return to an abandoned cult takes on proleptically a specific emblematic value.[5] For the turning point in Lazare's brief career, which ended with his death at the age of thirty-eight in 1903, was his realization, during the Dreyfus Affair, of the bankruptcy of the dream of Jewish assimilation in France, the return to an abandoned sense of Jewish national identity. The religious identity vs. the poetic mystique: it would appear that in sacrificing Symbolism's archetypal symbol, Lazare was moving – toward Judaism – away from Symbolism itself. And yet the tale ends with the substitution of the priest for the victim, the affirmation of a profound complicity – or identification – between adversaries which invites interpretation.

Note first of all that an identification with positions opposite those he was busy espousing was one of the hallmarks of Borges' Menard. The Symbolist from Nîmes had the "ironic habit of propounding ideas which were the strict obverse of those he preferred" (Borges, p. 52). Thus opines the narrator, intent on restoring the memory of his much maligned friend.[6]

Now consider that in Péguy's memoir – of his much maligned friend – Lazare, the forgotten hero of the Dreyfus Affair, author of a *J'accuse* far more daring than Zola's own, is said to have survived in his true dimension only in the obituary prepared by his enemy, Edouard Drumont, author of *La France juive*.[7] This circumstance, aside from evoking the idiosyncrasy of Menard, brings us deeper into the thought of Lazare. For it was his mixed blessing to have written a book on – and essentially against – anti-Semitism, just prior to the Dreyfus Affair, which won the praise of Drumont.[8] From *La Libre parole* of 10 January 1895: "C'est un livre remarquable, ai-je dit, que cet essai d'histoire de l'*Antisémitisme*, c'est un livre fort nourri de faits et dominé d'un bout à l'autre par un bel effort d'impartialité, par la consigne donnée au cerveau de ne pas céder aux impulsions de la race." Lazare, in his pamphlet "Contre l'antisémitisme (Histoire d'une polémique),'' gives every impression of being fixated to that remark, less interested in arguing his notion of anti-Semitism as a form of Catholic capitalist protectionism than in winning the approval – but on his own terms – of an increasingly indifferent Drumont. That will to identification with Drumont reached its uncanny peak in Lazare's "investigatory" service as sole Jewish member of Drumont's prize jury to determine the best solution to the urgent problem of destroying the nefarious influence of the Jews. Here is Lazare's successful letter of application to the jury:

Paris, 23 octobre 1895.

Monsieur le Directeur,

Jusqu'à présent, j'avais toujours reproché à l'antisémitisme de ne donner aucune solution à la question qu'il avait soulevée. A plusieurs reprises même, j'ai demandé, soit à vous, soit aux vôtres, quelles mesures vous préconisez pour échapper à ce que vous nommez la domination juive, à ce que j'appelle la tyrannie du capital qui n'est pas spécialement juif, mais universel. Je n'ai jamais obtenu de réponse.

Le concours que vous ouvrez satisfera, je l'espère, ma curiosité, et me fixera sans doute sur la doctrine antisémite. Voulez-vous me permettre de faire partie du jury? Vous pouvez être assuré de mon absolue impartialité, quoique d'avance, je trouve que la seule mesure logique serait le massacre, une nouvelle Saint-Barthélémy.

Si vous acceptez mon offre, je vous serai obligé de vouloir bien insérer cette lettre, qui l'explique.

Veuillez agréer, monsieur le Directeur, l'assurance de ma haute considération.

Bernard Lazare[9]

Just before making the crucial link between Dreyfus' inculpation and anti-Semitism, just prior to inventing, then, the Dreyfus Affair, the hero of the Dreyfusard effort wins exceptional membership in the prize jury of the nineteenth century's most adventurous anti-Semite by speculating on the necessity of a massacre of the sort executed by his leading twentieth-century heir. Identification with an adversary has rarely been pressed as far.

Now Lazare's letter to Drumont, immediately preceding his philo-Semitic engagement as Péguy's prophetic genius, as Hannah Arendt's exemplary Jewish intellectual, in fact marks the close of a period in his life – dominated by the identification with Symbolism – which was in a profound sense anti-Semitic.[10] But here a selection of quotations will be more eloquent than paraphrase or commentary. Lazare's anti-Judaism is grounded in a distinction between assimilated (French) Israelites and abject (foreign) Jews. The Jews: "Le juif ... c'est celui qui est dominé par l'unique préoccupation de faire une fortune rapide, qu'il obtiendra plus facilement par le dol, le mensonge et la ruse. Il méprise les vertus, la pauvreté, le désintéressement. La bête qu'érigèrent jadis dans le désert les tribus infidèles est restée son unique adoration …"[11] It should not be forgotten, however, that these "Jews" have little to do with French "Israelites": "Et tous ces Israélites sont las de se voir confondre avec une tourbe de rastaquouères et de tarés …" ("Juifs et Israélites," p. 179). The duty of the Israelite is to be unrelenting in his refusal of solidarity with "ce judaïsme misérable":

Je reviendrai une autre fois sur cette solidarité qui est une solidarité juive et non une solidarité israélite. Toutes ces fautes que commirent les Israélites de France, il faut les leur montrer, il faut leur crier bien fort, car un peu dorment-ils, de rejeter loin d'eux les lépreux qui les corrompent: qu'ils vomissent la pourriture qui les veut pénétrer. Mais l'erreur est vénielle, et il siérait que les anti-sémites, justes enfin, deviennent plutôt anti-juifs, ils seraient certains, ce jour-là, d'avoir avec eux beaucoup d'Israélites. ("Juifs et Israélites," p. 179)

In an article entitled "La Solidarité juive," the future hero of the Dreyfus Affair sounds the precise note on which a later generation, upon discovering it in *Pleins pouvoirs* (1939), has based its assessment of Giraudoux as an anti-Semite:

Que m'importent à moi … des usuriers russes, des cabaretiers galiciens prêteurs sur gages, des marchands de chevaux polonais, des revendeurs de Prague et des changeurs de Francfort? … A quoi voit-on du reste aboutir une semblable association [L'Alliance israélite universelle]? A accueillir chez nous des gens méprisables, à les aider, à les favoriser, à les implanter sur un sol qui n'est pas le leur et qui ne les doit pas nourrir, à leur en faciliter la conquête. A qui est-elle utile? Au Juif cosmopolite qui n'a d'attaches avec aucune nation, d'affection pour aucune, qui est le Bédouin transportant sa tente avec une indifférence complète.[12]

It will thus be perceived that an intolerance of "Jews" was the dominant note of Lazare's anarchist politics but a few years before he launched the campaign against anti-Semitism known as the Dreyfus Affair. The transition, moreover, finds its textual exemplification in the letter to Drumont in which he speculates on the only final solution adequate to his – strangely admiring – adversary's cause.

Lazare's early intolerance – for Jews – was in fact part of an esthetic. In 1892, he published "De la nécessité de l'intolérance."
His argument in that piece is that intolerance is the esthetic virtue
par excellence: "L'Intolérance est le levain des idées grandes, elle
est la vertu des âmes vigoureuses et hautes. Rien ne vaut que ce
que l'on pense, sinon on ne pense rien, on ne croit à rien."[13] The
necessity of such illiberalism seemed so evident to Lazare as to
find exemplary formulation in a rhetorical question: "Deman-
derait-on au corps humain d'accepter en lui des matières hostiles,
des toxiques mortels, des microbes dangereux? non. Pourquoi
donc demander à l'esprit d'accueillir des principes désorganisa-
teurs: d'élire des idées vénéneuses, de consentir à des théories en-
nemies de sa substance?" (p. 210). The biological metaphor seems
an anticipation of the rhetoric of twentieth-century racism. But in
this instance, it is linked to a will to esthetic radicalism: one that
has Lazare, for instance, unwilling to forgive Anatole France, in
an open letter, for his hesitation in applauding the Symbolists;
one that sees him positing as the critical virtue *par excellence*: "la
haine."[14] So that the intolerance of "Jews," in this case, seems integrally linked to an eccentric esthetic of Symbolism. The general
configuration might seem to partake of parody, our Symbolist of
Nîmes as quirky and contentious an esthete as Borges' exemplar,
Pierre Menard. Yet this appearance of parody emerges into a
new strangeness when we recall that within four years of
authoring the passage quoted Lazare had become the secret
champion of a struggle which quickly became modernity's
emblem of the imperative of tolerance itself.

There would appear, then, to be a Dreyfus Affair quite different,
as Péguy suggested, from Clemenceau's Manichaean version, centered on Zola.[15] Our Nîmes Symbolist confronts us with a chias-
matic crossing over from anti-Judaism to philo-Semitism, from
"intolerance" to tolerance. In that chiasmus, the moment of
crossing, I have suggested, finds its emblem in the letter applying
for membership in Drumont's prize jury: the effort to discredit
anti-Semitism from within. "Pierre Menard" again: his invective
being the "exact reverse of his true opinion" (Borges, p. 47).

The emergence of Lazare's "Jewish nationalism," however, is
fundamentally linked to an odd identification with another ideo-

logue of anti-Semitism. Here is the historian M. Marrus on that subject:

C'est peut-être bien à Barrès que pensait Bernard Lazare quand il écrivit, probablement en 1892, un essai intitulé *Le passé dans le présent*. Lazare évoquait "l'âme d'autrefois qui gît toujours dans notre âme présente"; il y décrivait une promenade qu'il avait faite dans le ghetto d'Amsterdam, faubourg "à l'aspect exotique et oriental," mais qui lui avait permis à lui, juif, d'entendre "des voix mortes depuis longtemps et dont l'écho se [répercutait] dans l'esprit qui [était] préparé à les recevoir ..."[16]

Whereby we find a Jewish nationalism modeled on that Barrèsian sense of roots which nourished France's fiercest tradition of anti-Semitism at the beginning of the century.

But if "anti-Jewish" sentiment and "intolerance," two causes championed by the early Lazare, cross over with the Dreyfus Affair to the category of realities he most opposes, what of the final cause he early made his own: "l'art d'enclore des symboles en des phrases précises," French Symbolism itself?[17] It is at this juncture that we should recall that Lazare's *Une erreur judiciaire: L'Affaire Dreyfus* turns on an "expertise d'écriture," that its principal villain is a theorist of "writing," Alphonse Bertillon. For to work through the theory of writing opposed by Lazare (in the name of common sense) is to encounter in surprising detail, we shall see, the textuality informing the history of the criticism of France's premier Symbolist, Mallarmé himself.[18] As though "Symbolism" – along with anti-Jewish sentiment and "intolerance" – would reveal itself subject to the chiasmus informing Lazare's destiny.

A science of writing? In 1897, the year of Lazare's explosive second edition of his pamphlet against the condemnation of Dreyfus, Alphonse Bertillon, principal witness for the prosecution, published two serene articles, without reference to Dreyfus, on "la comparaison des écritures et l'identification graphique" in *La Revue scientifique*.[19] In them, Bertillon, "chef du service de l'identité judiciaire," presents himself as a structuralist consolidating an epistemological break with the thematic interpretation of the institution of writing that preceded him. Structure: "C'est l'étude approfondie de la corrélation des caractères entre eux qui

fournit la clef des déguisements ou altérations graphiques ..."
(*Revue scientifique* 8: 25, p. 774). That fundamentally relational
reality attributed to writing might, for instance, take the form of
a delineation of "l'écriture sinistrogyre": "[qui] dans son mouvement général est ... entraînée vers la droite, cela va de soi, mais
elle ne chemine qu'en évoluant continuellement sur elle-même
vers la gauche ..." (*ibid.*, p. 774). The investment in an unstable
relation beyond a received binary opposition, its independence
of all semantic value, is opposed to the thematic reading to
which the study of writing had hitherto been restricted: "Toutes
les questions qui se rattachent à l'écriture ont été, dans les vingt
dernières années, l'objet, de la part des graphologues, de remar-
ques aussi ingénieuses qu'aventureuses, en vue d'établir des relations entre le caractère du scripteur et son écriture" (*ibid.*, p.
774). That notion of writing as an expression of identity is a
remnant of the prehistory of Bertillon's science, which posits, on
the contrary, that human identity is best definable *as* the plurilinear specificity of varieties of script. Bertillon's brave science
works at the epistemic rift – "pour tracer sur ces questions la
ligne de démarcation entre la fantaisie et la vérité" – fully cogni-
zant that it is in the nature of a mystical system such as gra-
phology to give way to an authentic science – writing
identification (*ibid.*, p. 774).

There is as well what might be called a post-structuralist
horizon of Bertillon's science, in which questions of form are sub-
verted by matters of force.[20] This pertains to the tricky business of
forgery: "Dans cet ordre de recherche, ce n'est plus à la forme
géométrique des lettres qu'il faut s'attacher, mais au mouvement
qui a présidé à leur confection" (*ibid.*, p. 782). It is, that is, the
palpable trace of an imitative script, the rhythm of inhibition – or
hesitation – in inscription which gives the forger away. Bertillon
touches here on one of the paradoxical limits of his enterprise, for
whereas writing identification is based on resemblance of script,
beyond a certain limit, degree of resemblance becomes a basis for
discounting any possibility of identification.

There are other perturbations of Bertillon's "structuralism" as
well. One concerns a kind of unconscious contagion of script,
Bertillon's version of Freud's counter-transference:

Une observation curieuse dans cet ordre de faits est la facilité inconsciente avec laquelle un scripteur reproduit les formes graphiques sur lesquelles son attention a été attirée vivement, d'une façon ou d'une autre. Ainsi toutes les personnes qui ont fait des expertises en écritures ont pu remarquer que, durant cette période d'observations réitérées, il leur arrivait fréquemment de reproduire elles-mêmes involontairement, au courant de la plume, telle forme graphique qu'elles avaient la veille déclarée absolument caractéristique chez le sujet dont ils venaient de s'occuper. (*ibid.*, p. 776)

Bertillon's new science is perpetually threatened by a collapse of its status as metalanguage – i.e., of its claims to scientificity itself.

Finally, there is the contamination of writing identification by the claims of a rival science – fingerprint analysis. For the status of the plurilinear pattern called "handwriting," in Bertillon's perspective, is ultimately no different from that of the intricate "arabesque" of a fingerprint: "tracé des mille petites stries capillaires formées par les hasards de l'agglomération des glandes sudoripares qui tapissent la pulpe des doigts d'un chacun" (*Revue scientifique* 9: 1, pp. 5, 7). Ultimately, for the contingent reason of its greater availability to classification, Bertillon, in his paper, opts for identification through handwriting. But in principle at least, his enterprise seems marked by a fundamental indecision as to whether man is the text his fingers write or the text written on them. The identificatory "chip" inscribed on – or just beyond – an individual's digital extremities takes on the qualities of a "partial object," a perpetually oscillating index of identity whose very vibrations play havoc with the possibility of identity itself.

Now all the threats to Bertillon's "structuralism" – through forgery, contagion, and the rival analysis of fingerprints – are ultimately short-circuited by an affirmation that in the last analysis handwriting analysis should be submitted to criteria having little to do with the discipline itself: "*Les affaires civiles obligent souvent à une interprétation plus étendue des conclusions de l'expertise*" (*ibid.*, p. 4). It is that italicized maxim which will stabilize conjecture into conclusion, and ultimately surrender the entirety of Bertillon's elaborate technique to the dictates of social dogma. We approach at this point Bertillon's participation in the Dreyfus Affair, his role as *bête noire* of Lazare's tract.

But a reference to Bertillon's technique brings us as well in remarkable proximity to an important chapter in the history of contemporary literary criticism. For Bertillon's method was quite simply – or complexly – the superimposition of texts. One begins, in his summary, with two series of texts, one "authentic," the other the "anonymous" subject of attribution. These two series are then photographed and enlarged to double their size. The photographic proofs are cut up into their individual words, and each piece of paper is glued to an easily manipulable "fiche mobile," tinged differently – e.g., blue or red – according to the series in which the word originated. The two sets of cards are then combined into a single series: "les fiches de ce répertoire bicolore sont brouillées et battues comme un gigantesque jeu de cartes" (*Revue scientifique* 8: 25, p. 778). That enlarged deck is then available for redistribution according to various criteria: alphabetical order, inverse alphabetical order (or rhyme), alphabetical order of second syllables, etc. In each case adjacent blues and reds are superimposed: the greater the degree of coincidence, the more sure the attribution, with the exception of total coincidence, which is always an index of forgery (i.e., tracing).

As we observe Bertillon proceed – through a technique of "dissociation graphique" – to the discovery of what he calls "syllabes-matrices" (e.g., *méri* from the superimposition of *numérique* and *immérité*), we are reminded of Saussure's search a few years later for the anagrammatic subtext of Latin poetry. (Saussure: "Avant tout, se pénétrer des syllabes, et combinaisons phoniques de toute espèce, qui se trouvaient constituer son THEME."[21]) But the "photographic" superimposition of texts, more precisely still, is the metaphoric scheme informing the critical *oeuvre* – born of a passion for Mallarmé – of Charles Mauron.[22] In his effort to extrapolate the lessons of his seminal reading of Mallarmé to literature itself, to elaborate a style of interpretation sensitive to what might be construed as the Mallarméan stratum of every text, Mauron formulated the initial stage of his "method" as follows: "En superposant des textes d'un même auteur comme des photographies de Galton, on fait apparaître des réseaux d'associations ou des groupements d'images obsédants et probablement involontaires" (Mauron, *Des métaphores obsédantes*, p. 32).

Mauron's metaphor, that is, entailed transferring a method derived from facial photography to that of script. But that metaphor is precisely what is realized in the case of Bertillon's "science."[23] Bertillon: "Pour tous, les faits parlent d'eux-mêmes sans choix pour ou contre l'hypothèse initiale" (*Revue scientifique* 8: 25, p. 778). Mauron: "pareille découverte [de la superposition des textes] est objective et ne saurait être confondue avec un commentaire" (*Des métaphores obsédantes*, p. 335). A common will to empiricism seems to weld the efforts of the principal witness against Dreyfus and the seminal reader of Mallarmé into a common tradition.

Turn then to Bertillon's "expertise" against Dreyfus, the sole juridical basis, according to Lazare, for the captain's inculpation and the principal target of his polemic. For the general configuration of events appears to have been such that the Dreyfus case, in the importance of its stakes, imposed a special strain on Bertillon's theory of the text, pressed it to its limits. Dreyfus himself, in the course of his refutation of the case against him, seems to be invoking a thinker far more interesting than himself, when he professes in exasperation:

Il a fallu une ingéniosité aussi extraordinaire que celle de Bertillon pour découvrir l'emploi prétendu d'un système comportant clef, gabarit, réticulage, mesurage, calquage, décalquage, avancements, reculements, abaissements, repérage tantôt sur le bord supérieur, tantôt sur le bord inférieur, tantôt sur l'encoche latérale du Bordereau, pour produire finalement comme résultat une écriture d'apparence évidemment rapide et courante.[24]

At a certain level, the debate over Dreyfus boiled down to the question: can the *bordereau* be read as a non-problematic transcription of thought or is that appearance an illusion – what Mallarmé would have called "une apparence fausse de présent" – generated by an elaborate textual labyrinth? Or, to formulate matters differently: our best means of understanding the howl of laughter which, according to Poincaré, greeted Bertillon's testimony at the first Dreyfus trial might be in terms of imagining a jury's reaction to an awkward deposition by a not very adept practitioner of deconstruction on the subject: What is a text?

The special twist brought by Bertillon to his attribution of the *bordereau* to Dreyfus lay in claiming that Dreyfus had deliberately forged his own handwriting in order to be able to disassociate himself from the document – which he could claim to be a manifest forgery planted on him – should it ever be discovered in his possession. The large number of precise coincidences with "authentic" documents of Dreyfus, combined with the fact that the *bordereau* was written on paper – *papier pelure* – of a transparency no "genuine forger (*vrai faussaire*)" would have used, lead Bertillon to the conclusion that Dreyfus is a "false" forger.[25] Dreyfus wanted to be able to say, according to Bertillon, "Voyez comme c'est tremblé! donc c'est calqué." The next step lay in reconstructing the precise modality of the self-forgery. For the key to a successful forgery consists in reproducing the precise "pulsation" or "espacement" of a script.[26] It is here that Bertillon introduces his curious hypothesis of a doubly inscribed template (or "gabarit") orienting the forgery. Paul Painlevé, in his refutation of Bertillon's "system," evokes it economically as follows:

Le scripteur du bordereau s'est servi, pour guider son écriture, d'une sorte de transparent que M. Bertillon appelle un gabarit, glissé à chaque ligne sous le papier-calque du bordereau. Ce gabarit se compose d'une double chaîne: la première chaîne est constituée par le mot intérêt, calqué bout à bout indéfiniment et imbriqué (*sic*), c'est-à-dire écrit de façon que l'*i* initial se confonde avec le *t* final qui le précède: la seconde chaîne est identique à la première, mais reculée de 1 millimètre 25.[27]

There is, then, an always already deferred proto-writing, deprived of reference, which generates the identity of a "natural writer" (Dreyfus), subverts that identification as forged, and subverts that subversion, since the forgery itself is "forged."

But at this point one feels an obligation to quote the hapless Dreyfus, fending off what one is hard put to think of in terms other than those of a ludicrously inept – though historically determinant – effort at deconstruction:

Bertillon a cru enfin prouver, de manière décisive, l'emploi d'un gabarit avec le mot "intérêt" pour clef, au moyen de la photographie dite "composite" de tous les mots du Bordereau passant successivement devant l'objectif d'un appareil photographique. Le résultat de cette épreuve a été une image d'une telle confusion qu'il a été impossible d'y rien distinguer. Mais il a alors imaginé de ne faire passer devant l'objectif qu'une partie des mots du Bordereau, choisis arbitrairement, et il a obtenu ainsi une ligne de brouillards coupée de raies noires inclinées au milieu de laquelle, dit-il, "semble apparaître" (à l'agrandissement) la silhouette du mot "intérêt." ("Mémoire du Capitaine Dreyfus," p. 132).

If we bracket the question of the accuracy of Dreyfus' attack against the "superimposition" of texts, we recognize the rhetoric of an incredulous positivism resisting the first incursions of "structuralist" criticism in the University: "Picard," if one likes, vs. "Mauron." But, then, the positivist University was in many ways consolidated around the struggle for Dreyfus . . .

Our Dreyfus Affair in these pages, like Péguy's, is, however, less that of Dreyfus than of Bernard Lazare. Here then is the Symbolist from Nîmes in *Une erreur judiciaire*, evoking the performance of the prosecution's star witness:

M. Bertillon fit circuler aussi deux petites cartes superposées dont la supérieure, jouant dans une sorte de coulisse, pouvait recouvrir l'inférieure. Sur l'une d'elles était écrit le mot "adresse," sur l'autre le nom "A. Dreyfus." M. Bertillon voulait, à l'aide de ce petit appareil, démontrer la culpabilité du capitaine Dreyfus. Pour arriver à ses fins, il faisait jouer rapidement les deux cartes l'une sur l'autre et convainquait ses auditeurs qu'au bout d'un temps fort court il leur était impossible de distinguer les deux mots qu'elles portaient. Il est indifférent, disait-il, que la superposition de leurs lettres soit impossible au repos, il suffit de retenir la confusion qui s'établit entre les deux mots lorsqu'on les fait glisser l'un sur l'autre.[28]

The example is nicely emblematic. For if the expert's task were to assign the purloined letter or *bordereau* to Dreyfus, there could be no more appropriate superimposition than one between "adresse" and "A. Dreyfus." But the example offers us as well a historical prototype that was to come to maturity – or intellectual rigor – in (or as) Mauron's seminal reading of Mallarmé.

Bertillon proceeds a step further in his demonstration as evoked by Lazare: "Craignant de n'être pas compris, il ajoutait qu'euphoniquement la constatation était la même et qu'en prononçant alternativement et avec volubilité le mot 'adresse' et le nom 'A. Dreyfus' on arrivait à les confondre et à dire l'un pour l'autre, ce qui, d'après cet étonnant expert, prouvait leur identité" (*Une erreur judiciaire*, p. 49). After the superimposition of texts, we find a vibration of inscriptions pressed to the point of hallucinating a voice. From Mauron's "Mallarmé" to the "centre de suspens vibratoire" of Derrida's, it is as though the Symbolist of Nîmes were charting proleptically a history of Mallarmé criticism.[29] To denounce it as Bertillon's "hallucination."[30]

In the course of these pages, we have seen Lazare cross over in chiasmus from advocate to adversary of "anti-Jewish" sentiment and "intolerance." At the instant of crossing, we have seen him enroll – against Drumont – in Drumont's prize jury, take up – against Barrès – a Barrèsian nationalism. In retrospect it would appear that the early championing of *symbolisme* was subject to a similar chiasmus, that Lazare's Dreyfus Affair, a protracted denunciation of the "charlatan" Bertillon, was a prescient and proleptic break with the future of – the reading of – Mallarmé himself. Let the precision of Lazare's anticipation serve to exemplify the enigmatic moment of crossing.

Much of contemporary literary criticism, in France and elsewhere, finds its metaphorical anticipation in the "techniques" of Bertillon. In reading Lazare with Menard, how far, it may be wondered, have we departed from Bertillon's gesture of sliding "A. Dreyfus" over "adresse," of "clinching" the case against the Jewish captain? Thus our own frame-up: a Symbolist of Nîmes, obsessed with questions of erroneous attribution, surviving in the defensive memoir of a friend, and endowed with the ironic habit of propounding ideas which were the strict obverse of those he preferred … Imagine, then, to clinch our case, the moment of crossing over for Lazare (or ourselves), the moment of identification with Bertillon. Part of the lore surrounding Bertillon's eccentric performance at the Dreyfus trial, the presumed confirmation of his attribution, was the uncanny exploit of systematically reproducing – without copying – the detailed text of the *bordereau*. As though he had mastered the inner logic of its confection. Painlevé, in his classic refutation of Bertillon's expertise, develops an ingenious comparison of a savant intent on reproducing from memory a map of the French coast of the English Channel. With some skill, a variety of mnemonic notations in relation to lines of latitude and longitude will allow him to arrive eventually at a fairly close likeness:

Si c'est un homme raisonnable, il en conclura simplement que sa patience lui a fourni un bon procédé mnémotechnique. Si c'est un fou, ou si son effort d'attention a dégénéré en idée fixe, il déclarera que la côte française de la Manche "est une véritable épure géométrique dont les lignes suivent une loi déterminée," que les coïncidences qu'il a relevées sont trop singulières et trop nombreuses pour être fortuites, que la côte de la Manche est truquée, tracée artificiellement sur un rythme géométrique, dont la clef est dans son tiroir. Pour le prouver, il s'offrira à dessiner la côte de mémoire, d'après son procédé géométrique, *et il y réussira* . . .[31]

Alphonse Bertillon ou le fou de la Manche. (Borges: "He did not propose to copy it. His admirable ambition was to produce pages which would coincide – word for word and line for line – with those of Miguel de Cervantes," p. 49.) Symbolist from Nîmes for Symbolist from Nîmes, and madman of La Mancha for madman of La Manche . . . As we conclude our superimposition (of two fables of superimposition), uncertain whether Lazare's "Bertillon" is best regarded as a metaphorical anticipation of our own effort, or our own effort as an unwitting repetition of his, we can but hope that the Borgesian frame, with its insistence on the radical difference with which time divides identity, will impart to these pages the measure of heterogeneity best defined as *new*.

CHAPTER 6

Iphigenia 38: deconstruction, history, and the case of
L'Arrêt de mort

In the already considerable annals of the naturalization of recent
French thought in this country, one of the most rewarding documents is a collective volume of 1979 entitled *Deconstruction and Criticism.*[1] Its publisher, Seabury Press, billed the book as a
"manifesto" of what has elsewhere been called the "Yale
School": Messrs. Bloom, de Man, Derrida, Hartman, and Miller
telling it as it presumably never quite manages to *be*. The anthology, moreover, was originally conceived as a series of readings
of Shelley's dense and elusive final fragment, "The Triumph of
Life." There was, I suspect, a measure of perfidy in that choice:
the English poet falls into a "trance of wondrous thought" and
enters into dialogue with his great French precursor, Rousseau.[2]
For Bloom, Rousseau plays Virgil to Shelley's Dante.[3] And
therein lay the trap; for Shelley ultimately supersedes Rousseau.[4]
Consider that scenario as the intertext of the anthology-manifesto:
the "working through" of Derrida, exemplary reader of Rousseau, in English would take the form of allowing him to take his
stand amid the enigmatic rhymes of Shelley's most problematic
poem – smack in the land of Bloom. If there were ever terms on
which the Frenchman (like Rousseau) might be superseded in and
by English, these were they. The binding of the book, as if in anticipation, identifies the author as "Bloom *et al.*"

Derrida, in his shrewdness, was not about to fall into that trap,
and his tack in retreating from – treating – Shelley's text lay in au-
daciously assuming as his own Rousseau's presumably imperfect
English: "The Triumph of Life"? What if one were to hear
"triumph" as the French verbal form: *(ce qui) triomphe de la vie?* As
though the triumph of life might be appropriately (mis)read in

82

French as a triumph *over* life. It is sufficient to assimilate that triumph over life to a death sentence – an *arrêt de mort*, as Blanchot entitled his short novel of 1948 – for Derrida to land in familiarly uncanny territory. For it is indeed a reading of Blanchot's *L'Arrêt de mort* which is the core of Derrida's contribution to the "manifesto," the substance of what is in many respects a protracted epistle to the Americans.[5] It is that impressive reading which I propose to examine in these pages, with particular attention to its failure to deal with what I hope to show to be one of the novel's more disturbing intricacies: its way of negotiating its own perverse embeddedness in literary history and, ultimately, in European history *tout court*.

Let me begin by summarizing, however inadequately, the elusive events of *L'Arrêt de mort*. The book, something of a metaphysical ghost story, is divided into two sections. In the first, a narrator recalls a shattering experience he underwent in October 1938, during the most sombre days of the Munich crisis. Writing for him has since then been no more than the register of his retreat from its truth. An initial effort to give literary form to the events, in 1940, ended in the narrator's destruction of the manuscript. Indeed the work begins with a request never to disclose the "proof" of the events, to destroy without reading whatever pertinent documents the narrator may leave behind after his death.

Whereupon we are told of his ordeal, in those October days, when he is told by their common doctor that his friend J., an ailing young woman, has but three weeks to live. It is as though the death of the *other* brings home to the narrator the alterity of what, in Blanchot's terms, can never be one's "own" death.[6] Part I then recounts the specific rhythm of his participation – or implication – in her agony – or "death sentence." He has a cast taken of J.'s hands; a palm reader consults the imprint of her "ligne de chance" and concludes: "elle ne mourra pas." Particularly disabling pain-killers are administered. She asks to die: "Si vous ne me tuez pas, vous êtes un meurtrier." There hovers an almost Heideggerian wish to force death into a situation of "greater loyalty." Before she dies, he visits and has the impression of calling her back from death; she has an interlude of gaiety.

Toward the very end, she pronounces the words "une rose par excellence." He believes she is referring to the flowers he has brought, and which, because of their strong fragrance, are kept outside the room. He is told that on the contrary, those were the "last words" she pronounced the previous night upon momentarily emerging from a coma. "Ce récit me glaça. Je me dis que la nuit dernière recommençait, d'où j'étais exclu, et qu'attiré par quelque chose de terrible, mais peut-être aussi de séduisant, de tentant, J. était en train de retourner d'elle-même dans ces dernières minutes où elle avait succombé à m'attendre." (p. 44).[7] This "end" which "rebegins" in a moment of "return" provokes the precipitous end of Part I. J. wakes to point to the narrator and to say to the nurse: "Maintenant voyez donc la mort" (p. 48). He eventually seizes a large syringe and injects into her a quadruple dose of pain-killer. She dies.

The second part of the book relates more tentatively the narrator's subsequent liaison with a second woman, Nathalie. She is a translator of Russian and English, and the narrator knows the exhilarating irresponsibility of speaking to her in a foreign language. Indeed, gratuitously, he twice proposes marriage to her in her tongue. Now as the narrative develops, the reader and the narrator are overwhelmed by an odd aura of resonance between Nathalie and J. Could they, at some level, be the same woman? Is the narrator an unwitting Orpheus bringing back Eurydice from the dead? The climax comes when he discovers that Nathalie has taken his key and the address of the sculptor who had set the cast of J.'s hands. He insists that she renounce her "project." As if to remind us that whatever relation to Heidegger is being entertained in the text, it is not Sartre's, she responds: "Ce n'est plus un projet" (p. 123). Then: "Vous l'avez toujours su?" Response: "Oui, je le savais." Exaltation, triumph, jubilation at seeing "face à face ce qui est vivant pour l'éternité" (p. 125). By this time, moreover, the temporal – or historical – reference has become unhinged. The first pages of the book situate events on specific days in October 1938, against the backdrop of the Munich accords. By the end of the book we are told that the dates may not be trustworthy, "car tout a pu remonter à un moment bien plus ancien." An eternal return irrupts in 1938.

Let us turn now to Derrida's lengthy discussion of *L'Arrêt de mort*. It might well be extrapolated from his consideration of Blanchot's title; for the death sentence – an *arrêt de mort* – may also be read as a suspension or stopping *(arrêt)* of death.[8] Here then is a superb instance of a would-be "event" precipitated by its own deferment, and it may be imagined how that intuition might be developed into a reading of Blanchot's text as an exercise in deconstruction: an inconceivable *arrêt* which arrests itself, finding its locus in the interruption – or fold – dividing two apparently heterogeneous *récits*.

What is initially most surprising in Derrida's essay is the conclusion: the "mad hypothesis" that "the two women should love one another, should meet, should be united in accordance with the *hymen*."[9] *Hymen*, the archaic French term for "marriage," is thus displaced from its initial mention in Derrida's text, where it refers to the narrator's gratuitous proposal of marriage to Nathalie, and becomes an imagined marriage, excluding the male narrator, between the two women who, in Blanchot's book, have no contact with each other, emerge from apparently separate narratives. But readers of Derrida will recognize the term *hymen* as an importation from his extended analysis of Mallarmé, "La Double Séance."[10] In that text, *hymen* – like *arrêt* in the essay we are examining – is the pivotally perverse instance: at once consummation (marriage) and barrier preventing consummation (membrane). Let us precipitate matters and posit what is never explicit in the essay on Blanchot: Derrida's speculative conclusion, the presumably unspeakable revelation from which *L'Arrêt de mort* seems in retreat, would appear to assign as paradigm of Blanchot's text Mallarmé's masterpiece, "L'Après-midi d'un faune." The male, in search of "trop d'hymen," dreams at high noon of interrupting the Lesbian embrace of two nymphs whose very dissolution into wakefulness is his own discomfiture.[11] The "mad hypothesis" consecrates a lineage that moves decorously from Mallarmé to Blanchot to Derrida.

There is an interesting political point registered by that virtuality. In an excursus on J.'s vision (or mention) of "la rose par excellence," Derrida quotes Bataille's fragments on the death of his wife Laure, which transpired at exactly the time of J.'s death,

October 1938. Her last words: "La rose."[12] We have, by implication, a gruesome version of Freud's paradigmatic *Witz*: two male friends (Blanchot, Bataille) share the pleasure of observing a woman compelled to leave the premises. Derrida's implicit critique is to imagine a man excluded, condemned, by the liaison of two women. For those who remember the day when the last word in avant-garde feminism consisted in quoting Derrida's line on wanting to write like a woman, the next (masochistic) step is indicated: I would like to write like, say, Charles Swann . . .[13]

Let us remain with the rose. Late in his volume of criticism, *L'Entretien infini*, Blanchot incorporated a short text, entitled in English, "A rose is a rose." It begins with an exorbitant formulation of the notion that the very will to develop one's thought is politically nefarious: "Une pensée développée, c'est une pensée raisonnable, j'ajouterai que c'est une pensée politique, car la généralité à laquelle elle tend, est celle de l'Etat universel . . ."[14] Better, he suggests, the refusal to advance, the repetitive skid exemplified by Gertrude Stein's famous tag: "A rose is a rose . . ." Whereupon the author forgets Gertrude Stein and takes up the putative pretext of his essay: the "enigma of repetition" in a novel by Nathalie Sarraute.[15] Consider then that, whereas *L'Arrêt de mort* gave us a political danger averted (Munich), a woman (J.) disappearing in the enigmatic repetition of the word "rose" only to be superseded by a second woman named Nathalie, the essay from *L'Entretien infini* repeats in the void that configuration, offers us its very ghost. As for the political peril, the "universal State," turn to the next essay after "A rose is a rose." It is called "Ars nova" and would also exonerate modernist art from a burden of political guilt. Its subject is Mann's *Doktor Faustus*, which, we read, erroneously metaphorizes twelve-tone music in its daring as an image of German history in this century: a pact with the Hitlerian demon.[16] Blanchot would free contemporary art from any contamination by that pact. From "A rose is a rose" to "Ars nova": "a rose is a *rosa*." But the pact with Hitler brings us back to Munich, the political catastrophe simultaneous with the first section of *L'Arrêt de mort*.

Might there then be a political legacy of Blanchot's rose? Consider the articulation of the pivotal episode in *L'Arrêt de mort*. It is while saying *rose* that "the last night" "begins anew," that J. enters her slide out of history into a death-like repetition. The narrator's initial thought is that she is referring to the flowers he has brought, and which she has given signs of wanting out of the room. But no, that reference – or situation – proves irrelevant, since the utterance "une rose par excellence" repeats her words of the "last night." Consider now that Blanchot's first separately bound publication on literature, "Comment la littérature est-elle possible?," is a commentary of 1942 on *Les Fleurs de Tarbes ou la terreur dans les lettres*.[17] The central conceit of Paulhan's essay is that poetry has traditionally – and unduly – exercised a reign of terror against *flowers* of rhetoric insofar as they are imagined as debased manifestations of linguistic repetition. In this, poetry has resembled that sign in the public park of Tarbes denying access to its garden to anyone who would enter its precincts with flowers in hand.[18] The room in which J. dies, that is, resembles Paulhan's garden in Tarbes: flowers had best be left outside. Blanchot, in his early essay on Paulhan, attempts to demonstrate, however, that iterability does not threaten poetic language from without, but is, on the contrary, a structure which contaminates poetry in its core: repetition is indeed the enabling condition of poetry. The Terror castigated by Paulhan – the search for the discursive equivalent of "virginal contact" with reality, what deconstruction would later thematize as "logocentrism" – is thus vitiated in its inception: "Il s'agit de révéler à l'écrivain qu'il ne donne naissance à l'art que par une lutte vaine et aveugle contre lui, que l'oeuvre qu'il croit avoir arrachée au langage commun et vulgaire existe grâce à la vulgarisation du langage vierge, par une surcharge d'impureté et d'avilissement ... il n'écrit que par le secours de ce qu'il déteste."[19] But in precisely that manner was the narrator at J.'s deathbed chilled ("glacé") to realize that the repetition of a rose transpires outside and against the scenario of "Terror," without *reference* to those flowers he was advised to deposit outside J.'s room.

J.'s death in October 1938 or the untenability of (logocentric) terror, of Terror as logocentrism ... In *Legacies: Of Anti-Semitism in France,* I have attempted to establish a connection between Blanchot's forgotten political writings of the 1930s, activist, fascist, a

protracted apology for terrorism, on the one hand, and the metaphor of terror as an untenable discursive posture in "Comment la
littérature est-elle possible?," on the other.[20] "Le terrorisme,
méthode de salut publique" is a call for acts of terrorist violence
against "the conglomerate of Soviet, Jewish and capitalist interests" governing France in 1936.[21] After the German reoccupation
of the Rhineland in 1936, Blanchot's ire was above all directed at
the "unfettered revolutionaries and Jews" who perfidiously "demanded against Hitler all possible sanctions immediately."[22] His
text on the subject was entitled "Après le coup de force germanique" and appeared in April 1936.[23] It is anti-German, but
above all French fascist. Two years later Munich would present a
new "coup de force germanique." But by that time, I would
submit, it was virtually impossible to maintain a line that was simultaneously "fascist" *and* "anti-German." For it should be underscored that those who did maintain a fascist line – Blanchot's
position of 1936 – in the wake of Munich tended massively to join
the Collaboration a year or two later. Rebatet's comments on the
situation in 1938, to cite the most notorious example, are virtually
identical to those of Blanchot in 1936: "Une des pires ignominies
de l'histoire de France aura été certainement l'abominable chan-
tage au patriotisme exercé par les désarmeurs, les juifs errants, les
socialistes internationaux, etc."[24] But it is precisely at this point,
October 1938, when one could no longer maintain a line that was
both anti-German and pro-fascist (terrorist) that the scenario of
the untenability of literary terror – or logocentrism – is (retrospec-
tively) activated as the scene of J.'s death in *L'Arrêt de mort*.

Through a strange act of piety none of this political reality has
entered the analysis of *L'Arrêt de mort*. That Blanchot's novel of
Munich might be related to his exorbitant text on Jewish guilt in
the wake of Hitler's "coup de force" barely two years before
Munich does not enter Derrida's purview, for instance, in his ingenious text on that novel. A discussion of the multiple valences
of Blanchot's "rose" is cut short by a self-addressed note in Derrida's running commentary: "Do not go on about the symbolism of
the flower (have done so elsewhere, at length, precisely about the
rose)."[25] *The* symbolism of the rose? The arresting of the play of
Blanchot's signifier is simultaneous with an eclipse of the political

reference. For "the rose," we are told, see *Glas* – rather than Blanchot on *Les Fleurs de Tarbes*. It is to that impoverishment of the intertextuality of Blanchot's *récit*, concomitant with an elision of all political reference, that I shall now turn.

There are several passing references in *L'Arrêt de mort* to J.'s mother, called ironically the "queen mother." Derrida is taken with the *insignificance* of the maternal point of origin, the mother as origin, in Blanchot's narrative, and rhapsodizes to that effect: "The figure of the mother, the 'queen mother,' a mere walk-on, almost a supernumerary, a figurant, a figureless figure, the vanishing origin of every figure, the bottomless, groundless background against which J.'s life fights, and from which it is snatched away, at every moment."[26] Now J.'s mother is indeed a walk-on, but it is important to realize from where she has arrived. There is an ironically conceived "queen mother" in Blanchot's *other* novel of 1948, *Le Très-Haut*.[27] She is the mother of the narrator and of his sister Louise. But Louise is as well the name of J.'s sister in *L'Arrêt de mort*. Derrida's "walk-on" mother has arrived, then, from *Le Très-Haut*. *Le Très-Haut?* The theological ramifications of Blanchot's novel have received their most extensive commentary in a Heideggerian context from Pierre Klossowski.[28] The Heideggerian reference, moreover, is all but dictated by the name of Blanchot's protagonist, *Sorge*, the key term for "solicitude" or "care" which irrupts midst a consideration of the *unheimlich* in the last chapter of the first part of *Being and Time*.[29] What I find most striking in Klossowski's reading is his failure to perceive that Blanchot's novel developed as a patent adaptation of the scenario of the Greek Orestes plays to a contemporary frame. It is sufficient to recount the plot to perceive this. Thus the anonymous author of the entry on *Le Très-Haut*, whom I have ascertained to be Michel Foucault, in Laffont-Bompiani's *Dictionnaire des oeuvres:* "Sous un masque transposé de la tragédie grecque – avec une mère menaçante et pitoyable comme Clytemnestre, un père disparu, une soeur acharnée à son deuil, un beau-père tout-puissant et insidieux –, Sorge est un Oreste soumis, un Oreste soucieux d'échapper à la loi pour mieux se soumettre à elle."[30] Blanchot's oft quoted line at the end of "La Folie du jour" – "Un récit? Non, pas de récit, plus jamais" – has led us not to expect the coherence of classical plot from his fiction.[31] In Derrida's terms, writing of *L'Arrêt de mort:* "In this sense, all organized narration is 'a matter for the police...'"[32] And yet the Electra-Orestes scenario, unnoticed by Klossowski, runs manifestly through *Le Très-Haut.*[33]

At this juncture, the question may be raised: if Louise "is" at some level Electra, who is her sister J. in *L'Arrêt de mort?* Classical tragedy provides but a single candidate, Iphigenia, condemned to death, and it is to a demonstration of Iphigenia's insistence as subtext of *L'Arrêt de mort* that I shall turn at present.

Note first that Euripides, our source here, composed, in accordance with the myth, two Iphigenia plays. In the first (in terms of plot sequence), *Iphigenia at Aulis,* the basis of Racine's play, Iphigenia is condemned to death so that Agamemnon's fleet might begin an unworthy war. In the second, *Iphigenia among the Taurians* (Goethe's source), after the war, after committing his fatal deed of revenge against Clytemnestra, Orestes encounters in the land of the Taurians, modern Crimea, a foreign woman. She turns out to be Iphigenia herself, who, unbeknown to him, had been miraculously saved from sacrifice by the goddess Diana. In *L'Arrêt de mort,* then, as in the Iphigenia cycle, we find a bipartite structure, two separate units across which a woman, assumed to be dead, undergoes a miraculous and threatening return. Foucault, who perceptively detected Orestes in *Le Très-Haut,* sees no further than Orpheus, the organizing myth of *L'Espace littérataire,* in *L'Arrêt de mort:* Eurydice returning from the dead.[34] Let us see what he has missed in the process.

The setting of *Iphigenia at Aulis* is the Greek army mobilized but stalled in its wish to begin what is by common agreement a bad war. Helen of Troy is described as a "wicked wife," a "harlot."[35] Menelaus is told it is a blessing to be rid of her. The setting of the first part of *L'Arrêt de mort* is Munich: the French army is mobilized, but stalled, in what appears to have been a "dress rehearsal" for the beginning of World War II.[36] From the point of view of French fascism, it was a bad war, bound to end in disaster, and all for the sake of maintaining the "honor" of a despised regime, the Third Republic, disdainfully dubbed *la Gueuse,* the slut.[37]

At the beginning of the play, we find Agamemnon jealously guarding a secret – his intention to sacrifice his daughter, whom he has summoned on a false pretext of marriage – or rather trying to undo that secret, writing a letter to her attempting to defer "indefinitely" her arrival.[38] He is described by his puzzled servant as follows: "You have written upon this tablet which you carry about in your hands, then you scrape off your own writing. You seal your letter, then open it again, you throw it upon the ground ..."[39] At the beginning of *L'Arrêt de mort*, we find the narrator jealously guarding a secret; instructions are given "surtout de ne pas ouvrir ce qui est fermé: que [ceux qui m'aiment] détruisent tout, sans savoir ce qu'ils détruisent, dans l'ignorance et la spontanéité d'une affection vraie" (p. 10).

Efforts to give form to the narrator's unrevealed obsession have led to an "unwriting" of his text which may be superimposed on Agamemnon's gesture: "Dans le désoeuvrement que m'imposait la stupeur, j'écrivis cette histoire. Mais, quand elle fut écrite, je la relus. Aussitôt je détruisis le manuscrit ..." In our two texts, then: secret, inscription, effacement.

Whereupon *l'arrêt de mort*, a death sentence undone, arrested, in its own execution. Euripides: "He [Agamemnon] will slash the poor girl's white neck with a sword."[40] Blanchot: "Je pris une grosse seringue, j'y réunis deux doses de morphine et deux doses de pantopon, ce qui faisait quatre doses de stupéfiants. Le liquide fut assez lent à pénétrer ..." (p. 52). The injection precipitates J.'s death. For an uncanny responsibility is attributed to the narrator. J., just before the end, points to him and says to her nurse: "Maintenant voyez donc la mort" (p. 48). It is a revelation of the sort Euripides' Agamemnon manages to forestall until he is confronted with Clytemnestra's question: "Are you going to kill her?"[41] And then the infinitely imperfect "death" or "survival" of the victim. Blanchot's palm reader, consulting the cast of J.'s hands, had said: "Elle ne mourra pas." In act III of Racine's adaptation of Euripides, Achilles says presciently: "Votre fille vivra ..."[42] Both are in their way correct. Significantly, in *Iphigenia at Aulis*, Euripides' final play, the confusion as to whether or not Iphigenia has died (or been replaced by a sacrificial deer) is simultaneous with a degenera-

tion of the Greek text. The Hadas edition inserts the words:
"From this point on, the Greek becomes more and more
suspect."[43] The ending of the play as we have it is regarded as
"spurious."[44] The play, that is, like Iphigenia, fails to *end*. And
it is precisely that failure which Blanchot has given us as the
death of J. in *L'Arrêt de mort.*

An interpretation? Earlier, in a discussion of the "rose" sequence of the novel, we superimposed the narrator's flowers, left
outside J.'s room, on the *fleurs de Tarbes* which Paulhan's poet-ter-
rorist would be forbidden to bring into the arena of poetry. J.'s repetition of "une rose par excellence" was taken to signify the
ultimate untenability of (poetic) Terror, the irrelevance of the scenario of terrorism. But since Blanchot had been an ideologue or
propagandist of terrorism a few years earlier, the dismantling of
the terroristic – or logocentric – imperative was read as an
encoded farewell to his investment in French fascism itself. The
crux, it will be recalled, lay in the virtual impossibility in 1938 of
retaining a line that would be simultaneously fascist and intent on
resisting the peril for France represented by Germany. The
painful solution: a farewell to the cherished eventuality of a fascist
insurrection against the Republic, the dissipation of the hopes of
6 February 1934; the agonizing death sentence of J ...[45]
Iphigénie 38 or *La Guerre de Troie aura lieu.*[46]

Years pass. The war subsides. Orestes wanders in exile, bearing
the burden of "the disasters of royalty."[47] He alights in the land
of the Taurians, modern Crimea, charged with the mission of retrieving a sacred "image" of the goddess Diana. He encounters a
redoubtable "stranger woman," whom he will recognize in a climactic scene as none other than his own sister Iphigenia, long believed to be dead.[48] Under Diana's protection, they flee the land
of the Taurians together, intent on bringing the salvatory image
back to Argos.

Now the second part of *L'Arrêt de mort.* The narrator, heir to
the narrator of the first section, has slipped out of the historical
past (Munich, 1938), and writes from a tentative present which
has yet to transpire.[49] We are in the temporal medium initiated
by the "rose par excellence," a last night about to begin anew.
Within the ghostly exile of "literary space," the narrator

wanders and encounters Nathalie. "Longtemps après, elle me dit –, et elle resta persuadée que je n'avais su à aucun moment qui elle était et que cependant je la traitais, non pas en inconnue, mais en personne trop connue" (p. 70). She is a foreigner, translating Russian and English, of manifestly "Slavic" appearance, perhaps from the region known as Crimea, the land of the ancient Taurians. Their exchanges find the narrator speaking her (foreign) tongue. There occurs, nevertheless, on the path to recognition, a crucial irruption of French: "Il me semble que quelque chose de furieux me poussait, une vérité si violente que, rompant tout à coup les faibles appuis de cette langue, je me mis à parler en français, à l'aide de mots insensés que je n'avais jamais effleurés et qui tombèrent sur elle avec toute la puissance de leur folie. A peine l'eurent-ils touchée, j'en eus le sentiment physique, quelque chose se brisa. Au même instant, elle fut enlevée de moi, ravie par la foule, et l'esprit déchaînée de cette foule, me jetant au loin, me frappa, m'écrasa moi-même, comme si mon crime, devenu foule, se fût acharné à nous séparer à jamais" (p. 103). The brute intensity of that contact in French, the narrator's mother tongue, is cut short. The recognition will be consummated, however, around the motif of a cast of her hands and head that Nathalie orders from the same artisan used by the narrator of the first part to retain an "impression" of J: "N'est-ce pas: vous l'avez toujours su? – Oui, dis-je, je le savais" (p. 124). In Goethe's *Iphigenia (auf Taurus)*, a confusion is maintained between the sacred statue of Apollo's sister, Diana, on the one hand, and Orestes' sister, Iphigenia, on the other. In Blanchot's, no sooner is a statue invoked than the rhetoric of the book takes an unexpected turn toward the sacred: "Et que maintenant cette chose est là-bas, que vous l'avez dévoilée et, l'ayant vue, vous avez vu face à face ce qui est vivant pour l'éternité, pour la vôtre et pour la mienne!" (p. 125). With this conjunction of the statue and the sacred, however enigmatic their relation, it is as though the repertory of motifs from the second *Iphigenia* were complete: exile (or foreign tongue), recognition of the woman, statue, divinity, and triumph ("une gloire qui ... me touchait, moi aussi, du même orgueil grandiose, de la même folie de victoire," p. 125).

But what are we to make of Blanchot's second installment? If *Iphigenia at Aulis* had been an encoded farewell to a no longer tenable fantasy of *action française*, indeed of fascism in France, what could be the parallel import of *Iphigenia among the Taurians?* In 1948, the year of *L'Arrêt de mort*, Blanchot published as well "La Folie du jour." Concerning that text, Emmanuel Levinas, Blanchot's privileged reader, has suggested enigmatically that it was to find its proper application twenty years later in 1968.[50] During the failed political upheaval of that year, many were surprised to find Blanchot, participating in the *comité d'action écrivains-étudiants*, among the most politically active of French intellectuals.[51] Here, for example, is the text of a tract he composed in May of that year:

En Mai, il n'y a pas de livre sur Mai: non par manque de temps ou par nécessité "d'agir", mais par un empêchement plus décisif: cela s'écrit ailleurs, dans un monde privé d'édition, cela se diffuse face à la police et d'une certaine manière avec son aide, violence contre violence. Cet arrêt du livre qui est aussi arrêt de l'histoire et qui loin de nous reconduire avant la culture désigne un point bien au-delà de la culture, voilà ce qui provoque le plus l'autorité, le pouvoir, la loi. Que ce bulletin prolonge cet arrêt, tout en l'empêchant de s'arrêter. Plus de livre, plus jamais de livre, aussi longtemps que nous serons en rapport avec l'ébranlement de la rupture.[52]

The final lines ("plus jamais de livre") echo the end of "La Folie du jour" ("pas de récit. Plus jamais . . ."). But the play on *arrêt* and *s'arrêter* recalls specifically the verbal knot around which Derrida, for example, has built his reading of *L'Arrêt de mort*.[53] In 1936, Blanchot was calling for a renewal of the fascist insurrection against the Republic of February 1934. The ultimate failure of its eventuality, indeed of any authentic *action française*, I have suggested, was encoded in *L'Arrêt de mort* as the sacrifice of Iphigenia. In that context, I would suggest that the abortive events of May 1968 – *arrêt qui s'arrête* – find their prescient anticipation in the recognition of Iphigenia in the land of the Taurians: the moment in which the narrator draws on unimagined resources in French only to find Nathalie swept away by the crowd.[54]

That construct – Blanchot's politics of 1968 scripted by his rewriting of Euripides in 1948 – finds unexpected confirmation in the writings of one of France's premier historians. In his 1980 memoir, Philippe Ariès, whose youth was passed in the ranks of *Action française*, recalls his astonishment at listening to the radio in May 1968: "Quelle fut notre surprise! Sous le déluge de discours, de graffiti, nous retrouvions des thèmes familiers de notre enfance, de notre jeunesse réactionnaire, la méfiance de l'Etat centralisateur, l'attachement aux libertés réelles et aux petites communautés intermédiaires, à la région et à sa langue ... Alors quoi? Ce que nous aimions jadis, nous, et nos parents et nos grands-parents, avait disparu de notre milieu social, de notre famille politique, comme feuilles mortes, et voilà que nous le voyions reparaître aux antipodes, chez des jeunes qui pourraient être nos enfants, à la gauche d'un communisme conservateur? ... Il y avait de quoi s'étonner. Le choc fut grand ..."[55] Blanchot's affiliation before the war, *Combat*, was not classically reactionary, but represented something of a fascist (or national-socialist) dissidence within the Maurrassian context.[56] With that single modification, however, the reading of *L'Arrêt de mort* proposed in these pages would offer nothing so much as the scenario of the chiasmus informing Ariès' shock. Blanchot, propagandist in 1936 for a renewal of the rightist insurrection of February 1934, emerges from his literary labors, his explication of literature as the realm of "a passivity beyond all passivity," in order to join the leftist insurrection of May 1968. Midway between the two, he rewrites the Iphigenia cycle as part history, part anticipation of the entire sequence. In the first section, he dreams his implication in 1938 in the shattering (or apparent) death of Iphigenia or J. (I. or J.), figure of his generation's aspiration toward a no longer tenable fascism in France. In the second section – whose anticipatory status is uncannily conveyed in an opening paragraph: "tout ne s'est pas encore passé" – Blanchot dreams a shocking recognition of the allegedly dead Iphigenia in the figure of the Slavic Nathalie. The political dream of insurrection is re-emergent, but at the other end of the political spectrum: Iphigenia – or February 1934 – will return as – the ultimate impossibility of – May 1968. After years in the desert of *l'espace littéraire*, the former partisan of *Action française* knows in his narrator a gust of French that transfixes him until Nathalie is swept away by the crowd. There will remain with him but the "truth" ("Vous l'avez toujours su") or "imprint" ("moulage") of that chiasmus.

In 1974, in an analysis of Blanchot's writings on Rilke, I attempted to show that Blanchot's investment in the myth of Orpheus constituted a last metaphysical attachment to notions of archetype and originary voice which the very Rilkean corpus he was examining could be mobilized to dismantle.[57] Within Rilke's Orphic voice, I suggested, could be found a bizarre writing machine utterly disruptive of every mythic – and vocal – plenitude: Derrida, in brief, as the horizon of Blanchot's text.[58] In the years since then, Derrida has written his way into Blanchot's *oeuvre*, in a perspective ultimately compatible with that of my essay on Blanchot, Rilke, Derrida.[59] This was perhaps clear from my references to his analysis of *L'Arrêt de mort:* "L'Après-midi d'un faune" as implied subtext of Blanchot's *récit;* Mallarmé, Blanchot, Derrida as the pertinent line in French thought.

In these pages, I have departed from my program of 1974. Beyond the myth of Orpheus, quite properly detected by Foucault in *L'Arrêt de mort,* I have insisted not on a "writing machine" (Rilke's "phonograph" or Derrida's problematic), but on a second myth, Iphigenia, and the historical burden that it bears. If that reading has been able to convince, to impart something of the shock experienced by Ariès in the fragment of his memoir quoted above, I confess that I will shoulder any accusation of residual logocentrism or metaphysical deviation with relative calm.

CHAPTER 7

Writing and deference: the politics of literary adulation

There is an error – or infelicity – of translation in the English version of *Grammatology* which is so deeply anticipatory (if not performative) of the future of deconstruction in the United States as to deserve exemplary status. It concerns nothing less than the origin of language. Rousseau, it will be recalled, imagines passion's first utterance as a woman tracing with a stick (or "baguette") the outline of her beloved's shadow on the ground.[1] What sounds, he suggests, could ever match that inscription? Derrida, as well he might, reinscribes that "mouvement de baguette" as a chapter heading in his book.[2] Here, now, is the English rendering of Rousseau: "How she could say things to her beloved, who traced his shadow with such pleasure! What sounds might she use to render this movement of the magic wand?"[3] In the translation, it is the beloved who appears to be tracing his – own – shadow. The origin of language, that is, appears to have been lost in the translation. But the translation seems to convey its own myth: in between languages, the woman appears to have deferred to her beloved, to have handed him the stick or wand and invited him to speak (or trace) her love for him to himself. Communication has been lost, the inscription of difference (i.e., Derrida's argument) has been botched as the beloved is made to speak the other's admiration of himself ...

It is tempting to view this sequence as a kind of primal scene of literary adulation – an obliteration of difference by deference (to refer to my own attempt at a mistranslation in the title of these remarks, although it is not nearly as eloquent as the case just quoted). For anyone in American academia who came to deconstruction at a time when it had to be engaged against the expectations (and wishes) of one's teachers – and it is from that perspective that I speak – the myth conveyed by the mistranslation of the Rousseau passage has an uncannily accurate ring to it.

Let me illustrate that point by referring to three texts by Derrida. In their crescendo, they appear to be a virtual acting out of the mistranslation:

1. In "Living On," Derrida's contribution to the 1979 volume *Deconstruction and Criticism*, the author, discussing Blanchot's *L'Arrêt de mort*, discreetly but provocatively dangles the "Yale key" lost by the narrator before his New Haven audience.[4]

2. In "The University in the Eyes of its Pupils," the text of a lecture published in 1983, the model of reason perched precariously above its abyss is the Cornell campus atop its suicidal gorges.[5] There is much attention, moreover, to the epistemological importance of that abrupt interruption of vision which the French renders *clin d'oeil*, which the translators render most often *blink*, but which is also, beyond doubt, the lecturer's ironic *wink* at his Ithaca audience being told less where he than they, as the locution goes, are at.

3. Finally, *Otobiographies*, a volume reproducing a lecture at Charlottesville and most interestingly about Nietzsche and the sorry political legacy Derrida would no longer *entirely* absolve him of ("il ne suffit pas de dire que 'Nietzsche n'a pas pensé ça,'" 'pas voulu ça,'" p. 82), begins, nevertheless, with twenty pages on the plight of Thomas Jefferson, author of the Declaration of Independence and as such representative of those Representatives of a people that would paradoxically have no existence as such prior to the complex interplay of signatory representations that would – after the fact – endow it with existence.[6] Substitute *signifiant* for *représentant* and the Declaration of Independence emerges as the charter of deconstruction. All this at the University of Virginia.

It will be intuited just how pregnant the error in translation was. In each of these lecture texts, we find Derrida – with consummate *politesse* and customary ingenuity – reflecting the American academy's adulation of him back toward its source in a gratifying ritual of mutual deference. The situation, I submit,

is inherently worrisome, and the worry it elicits might be formulated as a question: How much deference can the discourse
of difference tolerate before its claims to heterogeneity begin to
ring hollow?

Perhaps I can convey my concern over deconstruction in the
era of its academic respectability (despite such lines as "la plus
grande indécence est au contraire de rigueur en ce lieu" in the
Charlottesville lecture) by another fable, everyone's favorite fable
of literary adulation, "Le corbeau et le renard."[7] In La Fontaine,
it will be recalled, the fox, coveting the cheese in the crow's beak,
flatters the bird into singing a song:

> Sans mentir, si votre ramage
> Se rapporte à votre plumage,
> Vous êtes le Phénix des hôtes de ces bois!

Whereupon the crow sings, the cheese drops out of his beak and
the falsely adulatory fox makes off with the cheese ... Let us
now adjust the fox's words to the present context: If your voice
is as good as your plumage – your penwork, your texts – then
you are really something ... Or: we loved your texts, can you
give us a lecture? Note how fine La Fontaine is here in capturing
the precise nuance of flattery: the word for voice is *ramage*, a
metonym for branchwork, the voice as that which emerges from
the plurilinear network of branches... Or: we have read you
and will not mar your visit with any untoward gusts of logocentrism (we know, that is, what a "voice" is) ... Whereupon the
lecture begins and the cheese drops out of the crow's beak. Shall
we read the cheese as the problematic of difference at its most
radical? There is a text by Michel Serres on cheese – and
Nietzsche (cheese as a culinary move "beyond good and evil") –
which might authorize as much ...[8] It was inspired, he writes,
by a New York customs official who seemed particularly concerned lest Serres attempt to bring cheese into the United
States.[9] New York: one thinks of Freud arriving in New York
harbor and telling Jung (upon seeing the enthusiastic welcome
party ashore): "The poor fools! They don't realize we're
bringing them the plague ..." One thinks as well of how little
time it took for America to prove him wrong. And then one

thinks of the apocalyptic beauty of the opening pages of *Grammatology* ...[10] And passes the cheese ...

Let me return for a moment to the texts by Derrida just mentioned. Jefferson and a Nietzsche no longer entirely absolved of the use the *Führer* was to make of him ("mais il serait aussi court de dénier que quelque chose passe et se passe ici qui appartient à *du même* [un même quoi, l'énigme reste], depuis le *Führer* nietzschéen qui n'est pas seulement un maître de doctrine et d'école jusqu'au *Führer* hitlérien ...").[11] Thus the two poles of *Otobiographies*. It may be recalled that Ezra Pound, one of the tutelary figures of *Grammatology* ("la première rupture de la plus profonde tradition occidentale"), wrote a maddeningly wrongheaded *Jefferson and/or Mussolini*, an attempt to neutralize – if not deconstruct – the opposition between the father of democracy and the fascist leader ("The heritage of Jefferson ... is HERE, NOW in the Italian peninsula at the beginning of second fascist decennio, not in Massachusetts or Delaware.")[12] Wrong, risky, and juridically soon to be judged crazy. Very far, however, from the decorative use made of Jefferson in *Otobiographies*, a text that seems less risky than an invitation for others to take risks.

"Living On" is a reading of *L'Arrêt de mort*, a novel crucially set during those days in October 1938 known as the "Munich crisis." As such, Blanchot's text, I have attempted to show elsewhere, demands reading in terms of French reactions to the threat posed by Nazism, a subject not unrelated to that of *Otobiographies*.[13] But the cult of Blanchot, the failure to take any of Blanchot's own political writings of the 1930s into account, has obliterated any sense of this from Derrida's reading of *L'Arrêt de mort* We approach our subject...

But first: is not writing and deference, far from being a description of the fate of deconstruction in the age of its academic respectability, the very – logocentric – subject *of* deconstruction? Consider that in the middle of *Grammatology*, we find Lévi-Strauss bemoaning the corrupt deference which a Nambikwara chieftain manages to exact from his tribesmen by his fraudulent association with the Frenchman's knowledge of *écriture*.[14] He pretends to know how to write and hoodwinks the natives into deferring to him on that account. The political evil of writing, the politics of literary adulation, are thus fundamental topoi of lococentrism. There is soon a resistance movement against writing-and-deference, which Derrida is quick to dismantle.[15] For – in both senses of the question – how can one resist writing? We are always already in the toils of the written, always already collaborators *dans le texte.*

And so we are left with the question: Is the scene of writing and deference the very one that deconstruction was invented to dismantle, a matrix prior to the advent of grammatology? Or is it, on the contrary, the destiny into which deconstruction has lapsed in the course of time, the state of deconstruction in what I have called the age of its academic respectability? And are affirmative answers to those two questions of necessity mutually exclusive?

Let us return to *Grammatology.* It begins by invoking the general problematic of "language" as the one against and out of which the new understanding of *écriture* was in the process of emerging. An "inflation" of the sign "langage," ultimately indistinguishable from the inflation (or pneumatics) of the sign itself, was seen to have reached a point of explosion.

Of those in France most deeply involved at the time in the consideration of the "problem" of "language" was Jean Paulhan, who in fact died in 1968, the year following the publication of Derrida's opus. Paulhan's role as grey eminence of French letters between the wars has often been noted, but there has perhaps not been an adequate appreciation of the extent to which his "grammarian"'s obsession with the conundra of language was pregnant with future developments. His importance for Blanchot, of course, has been acknowledged.[16] Indeed in 1942, for Blanchot, to ask the most fundamental of questions: How is literature possible?, meant to delve deeper into Paulhan's *Les Fleurs de Tarbes* for an answer.[17] But it is a different (although related) legacy, the convergence of Paulhan's thought with concerns that Derrida would take up after Paulhan's death that interests me here.

Consider the 1953 text *La Preuve par l'étymologie.*[18] It is an empirical critique of that desire to uncover etymologies or "original meanings" of words, what deconstruction would later thematize as "transcendental signifieds."[19] The etymological passion, according to Paulhan, is haunted by the Cratylist dream. His effort in the book consists of demonstrating that the etymologist's activity in plumbing the primal depths of language at key junctures is indistinguishable from the infinitely superficial exploits of the punster. First, two words or series of words are confronted for reason of their similar sound. A story is invented to integrate their diverse meanings. Louis XIII, it is said, prized the grammarian who demonstrated to him that *jeunesse* (youth) is the age when games begin (*les jeux naissent*) and that *pantalon* is a garment that hangs to the heel (*pend jusqu'aux talons*).[20] At this stage, it is indeed difficult to distinguish an etymology from a pun. The etymology emerges when a recessed meaning in the sequence is arbitrarily isolated and projected as having been at the origin of the entire chain. An etymology, that is, is a joke passing itself off as wisdom. The book concludes: "C'est qu'il n'existe guère de l'étymologie au calembour – par ailleurs si proches et le plus souvent indiscernables – qu'une différence morale: le même écart qui sépare le licite de l'illicite, le permis du défendu. Comme si l'étymologie exigeait, pour donner son plein, de nous laisser le change sur sa nature et que la rhétorique en général ne jouât pleinement qu'à la condition de ne point nous apparaître comme telle."[21]

That is: the signified (of signifieds), the etymon (and Heidegger's metaphysics, Paulhan reminds us, is fundamentally etymological in orientation) is but the precipitate of a play or interference between signifiers.[22] It is the illicit play of signifiers which grounds the deluded moral and moralizing quest for primal meanings. If philosophers, in Valéry's phrase, were unwitting practitioners of a literary genre (philosophy), etymologists were unwitting punsters – with Heidegger, no doubt, somewhere between the two. Paulhan gave us, in brief, a local instance of what might be called, before the letter, applied grammatology. That in 1953.

Toward the end of his life, Paulhan's fascination with puns brought him to the bizarre project of wanting to rehabilitate Karl Abel's pamphlet of 1884, "On the Antithetical Sense of Primal Words."[23] What interested him was the central role of what Etiemble has dubbed "homophonic antonyms," and he was of the opinion that Abel's work, which had been written off by all of modern linguistics, was the key to their understanding: "C'est un livre que *tous* les linguistes ont traité avec mépris, comme l'exemple à ne pas suivre en linguistique. Tous, même Bloomfield, même Hjelmslev, même Benveniste. Freud seul, mais qui n'est pas linguiste, l'a traité avec égards. C'est Abel que je voudrais réhabiliter. Il a pu dire des sottises en étymologie, mais il a eu une intuition du sens qui passe de loin tous les linguistes."[24] In the last letter he was to write (3 March 1968), Paulhan recalled that Abel's work was one of the ten books that Nietzsche kept at his side – in the thought that they merited endless rereading.[25] One perceives the configuration, then, of our grammarian ultimately feeling closer to Freud and Nietzsche on the question of language – and specifically on that of homophonic antonyms – than to the linguists.

Etiemble has criticized Paulhan's interest in Abel because the cases examined by the latter can in no way be construed as "primal."[26] But etymology, we have seen, was not at all a quest indulged by Paulhan. So that we are left with a Paulhan – whom Blanchot described as a "mystic" of language – fascinated by the possibility of a decisive discordance affecting certain linguistic terms.[27] Decisive? Their homophonic character would, on the contrary, render discursive thought undecidable (as Etiemble objected) except in a written language following the model of Chinese ideograms.[28] Homophonic antonyms would authorize what Paulhan would eventually call a principle of "counteridentity" ("A = non-A").[29] In Pierre Oster's terms, Paulhan was in search of a polysemy *other* than the superficial variety acknowledged by linguists: "une polysémie radicale."[30] I propose that that other more radical polysemy is what Derrida was soon to dub "dissemination." To take but a single case: "hymen," in Derrida's essay on Mallarmé – with its twin valences of consummation (of marriage) and membrane (impeding consummation) is made to function as a homophonic antonym, a term whose lack of identity with itself is seen to structure the entirety of Mallarmés *oeuvre.*[31]

From illicit puns grounding consecrated primal meanings (etymons) in 1953 to the constitutive homophony of founding antonyms ... Let us recede to the period before that progress and consider a 1947 text by Paulhan, *De la paille et du grain.* It begins

with a series of reflections on language whose horizon my previous remarks will have prepared. The metaphor for language
itself is a masked ball. "Ce bal a ses règles, comme tous les bals
... Or la première des règles veut qu'on déguise les mots étrangers avant de les admettre dans la salle. Cela va parfois jusqu'à
la grosse farce: dans *choucroute* c'est *chou* qui veut dire (à peu près)
croûte, et *croute* qui veut dire chou ..."[32] That is: although
"choucroute" sounds roughly like a French transcription – or
mispronunciation – of *Sauerkraut*, in fact it is its reversal. Phoni-
cally, the *croute* seems to be dictated by the *Kraut* and the *chou* by
the *Sauer*, but lexically the situation is reversed. In German, the
predicate (*sauer*) precedes the subject (*kraut*); in French, the
subject (*chou*, meaning *Kraut*) precedes the predicate (*croute*).
There has been, in sum, within the rough interlingual pun, a reversal of sense or direction. Whereby we find ourselves again
confronting something of a homophonic antonym – a common
sound reversing its sense ...

Now Paulhan's subject – in 1947 – is already (as it would be in
1953) the shortsightedness of any moralistic attitude within the
constitutive arena of language's masked ball. This time, however,
the moralist is not the etymologist, but a specific group of writers
– the Comité National des Ecrivains – presiding over the purge
(or *épuration*) of French letters after the German occupation of
France.

Let me summarize Paulhan's argument: The moralism of the
CNE is based on a willful blindness to a kind of constitutive
chiasmus at the heart of French political life. The great paradox
of World War II was that the national Resistance to foreign occupation was the achievement of an ideological group which had
long been denigrating all national values with a view toward a
future Collaboration – with the Russians. In addition, the Collaborators with the Germans were a group that had long been
training as future Resistance fighters – against the Russians.
"Quelle étrange aventure: la France a failli être ruinée par des
hommes qui priaient chaque matin la déesse France; elle a été
sauvée (entre autres) par ceux qui jetaient chaque jour l'armée
française au panier."[33] The parenthetical "entre autres" leaves
room, of course, for the likes of Resistance leaders like Paulhan

himself, but it seems almost a regretted concession to empirical reality. As though the analysis, for its full eloquence, depended on the reversal allowing of no exceptions. In the beginning, then, "tout se passe à l'envers"[34]: aspiring collaborators lead a resistance struggle and are opposed by would-be resistance fighters committed to collaboration. By the end of Paulhan's analysis, *résistant* and *collaborateur* each appear to be all but "homonymic antonyms" – primal words apt to lapse into their opposite. (But: "chacun sait que les mots ont tendance à glisser d'un sens au sens opposé."[35]). Like *choucroute-Sauerkraut?* It is enough to expand the temporal frame of analysis to be authorized – by Paulhan's text – to conclude in the affirmative: in the thirty years' war that went from 1914 to 1944, writes Paulhan, the (leftist) pacifists of 1914 have no moral superiority over the (rightist) pacifists of 1940: "c'est bonnet blanc ou blanc bonnet."[36] It is, that is, *choucroute* or *Sauerkraut.* Which is why, I take it, Paulhan makes the case that there is perhaps a mystery of patriotism which is both metaphor and metonym of the mystery of language, the mystery of Letters. Metaphor: "C'est donc qu'il existe un mystère de la patrie, comme il en est un des langues, et des Lettres."[37] Metonym: "Qui sait, un mystère voisin sans doute."[38] There is a kind of essential hitch – reversal and/or displacement – in French national awareness which makes for a situation in which the grave question of French patriotism can only be broached with the kind of obliqueness ("de biais et par raccroc") appropriate to "languages, games, and literature."[39]

The degeneration of the Resistance and Liberation into the *Epuration* or post-War purges is, of course, one of the great unresolved dramas of recent French history. For Paulhan, the national tragedy reproduced the sequence denounced by Péguy, in the wake of the Dreyfus Affair, as the decline of *mystique* into *politique.*[40] Perhaps it would help to imagine it in other terms as the loss of what Benjamin called "aura" (a reasonable translation of Péguy's *mystique*) into the organized juridical violence of the purges ...[41] Paulhan's notorious "Lettre aux directeurs de la Résistance" of 1951 elaborates the political analysis just presented to considerable polemical effect: "Etonnez-vous que ... Eh bien, par exemple, que nos collaborateurs n'aient pas rencontré d'ennemis plus acharnés – plus courageux aussi (dans les temps où il s'agissait encore de courage) – que d'*autres* collaborateurs. Qui refusaient de collaborer avec l'Allemagne; mais c'était – ils nous l'ont très bien dit, ils n'ont cessé de le répéter sur tous les tons – parce qu'ils avaient fait choix d'une autre collaboration. Ils ne voulaient pas du tout s'entendre avec l'Allemagne: non, ils voulaient s'entendre avec la Russie ..."[42] In moving back from the "Lettre" of 1951 to *De la paille et du grain*, the somewhat indistinguishable wheat and chaff of 1947, we have situated Paulhan's political point – the Resistance as always already a dream of Collaboration – as solidary with a view of language and letters: Language as a masked ball rudely intolerant of any moralizing stance. The rough interlingual pun joining *Sauerkraut* and *choucroute* provided the context – literally the frame – for exonerating those French authors who had collaborated with the Germans.

By 1953, however, in the sequence of texts we are examining, the political moralism of the CNE was replaced by the highmindedness of etymologists whose claims to primordial or originary sense were seen to be the precipitate of the slightly illicit form of signifying contamination known as punning (*calembours*). With the transcendental signified (or etymon) generated after the fact by a tension between signifiers, the problematic later to emerge as deconstruction was already broached. A few years later the grounding nature of puns would take a turn toward the almost "mystical" effort to rehabilitate Abel on homonymic antonyms. With the principle of "counteridentity" based on the irreducible (silent) difference affecting certain signifiers, a "more radical polysemy" emerged that would later be dubbed "dissemination." But that irreducible difference, I am arguing, harked back to the grounding discrepancy or paradox of French history at the time of the War: a certain *logical* undecidability affecting the categories of resistance and collaboration. Paulhan's dream was that the dilemma might some day be resolved by the only category of Frenchman authorized to do so: "Ah! je voudrais être juif, pour dire – avec plus d'autorité que je n'en puis avoir [and yet Paulhan was a leader of the Resistance] – que j'ai pardonné à la France, une fois pour toutes, son impuissance à me défendre."[43]

Amnesty – a radical forgetting – was the legacy of Paulhan's thought, an amnesty of the type arranged by the French government after the Dreyfus Affair, but which was not yet possible after the War ... Let the problematic survive, but let its painful political crux be voided.

Enter the age of Grammatology ... At whose center, a last trace of that political dilemma: the analytical defeat of the Nambikwara "resistance" to writing at the hands of Derrida's analysis. The resistance, as we suggested, always already in the toils of collaboration ... *dans le texte*.

With the passage of time, Grammatology was to know its own bizarre destiny and emerge as the object of the literary adulation of a foreign intellectual community – our own – marginal to but very much part of the most powerful country in the world, perhaps, the most powerful foreign presence in France, to be sure. Derrida's discourse ironically appears to have found its privileged audience in the American academy. (A brief note of comparative sociology: Derrida was cited some years ago as the name most often referred to in PMLA. In 1981, however, the French journal *Lire* conducted a poll of 600 French intellectuals asked to identify the three living French-writing intellectuals whose writings exercised the deepest influence on the evolution of thought, letters, the arts and sciences, etc.[44] Thirty-six names were listed according to the number of times they were mentioned. At the top of the list – which P. Bourdieu, with appropriate scorn, calls "le hit-parade des intellectuels français" – was Lévi-Strauss. Derrida's name does not appear...) And yet the address to the somewhat marginalized academics of the United States seems curiously haunted by a different hegemony in France. The lecture to Yale on Blanchot's *L'Arrêt de mort* dangles a Yale key before its audience, but shuns consideration of the timing of the novel's action – or passion – in October 1938: the period of the Munich crisis. The lecture at Charlottesville would invite consideration of the precise conditions allowing for the Nazis' misappropriation of Nietzsche, examination of the extent to which they may have been "right" to be wrong ... As though deconstruction were haunted anew, in the presence of its foreign audience, by the dilemma for which, in our speculative construct, we have viewed it as constituting something of a protracted amnesty. As though no sooner did the problematic take on the appearance of a foreign franchise in French thought than the old dilemma – resistance, collaboration, a certain undecidability between the two – revived. With deconstruction become the object of the American academy's adulation, moreover, there appeared in France, after the fact, in 1981, a bizarrely revealing text on literary adulation dating from the earlier era. As though alive to the very parallel we are drawing, it was entitled: *Un Allemand à Paris, 1940–1944*.[45] It is to that earlier instance of literary adulation, and the light it may cast on our current situation that I now shall turn.

Un Allemand à Paris is the memoir of a middle-level cultural bureaucrat named Gerhard Heller. An essentially apolitical student of Romance languages in the 1930s, he was talented enough to win a year's grant to the Scuola Normale in Pisa and the opportunity to visit Paris as well. But his gifts were not of an order allowing him, in those difficult times, to look forward to writing a dissertation and enjoying an academic career. His career took a remarkable turn in 1940 when the German Propaganda Service found itself in need of a bureaucrat to take charge of the seemingly minor business of organizing the censorship of books in France. The Francophilic Heller was chosen, named Sonderführer of the Propaganda-Staffel, and was delighted to arrive in Paris on his 31st birthday. That initial delight was cut short by the uncanny experience of witnessing the (occasionally abject) deference with which he was treated by writers before whom he had stood in admiration – as a bedazzled student of French culture – only a few years earlier. That somewhat servile posture, moreover, would persist despite the political power at his disposal: Heller's chapter on Drieu, for instance, finds the occupying German addressing the author of *Gilles* as "Monsieur Drieu" and being addressed by him as "Heller."[46]

Now Heller quickly conceived of his role – within the new German order – as that of a protector of French culture. Giraudoux was to regard this as a particularly Machiavellian touch on the part of the Nazis: to assign a genuine enthusiast for French letters to woo the French intelligentsia to the German cause.[47] If that was in fact the case, there can be little doubt that Heller himself – if we can believe his apparently candid memoir – was among the first to be deceived by the stratagem. Perhaps the best symbol of the self-contradictory character of his pathetic struggle to further the cause of French letters from within the Nazi apparatus was the fake wooden revolver he apparently had made so that he could simultaneously appear to satisfy his military obligations as Sonderführer and know himself incapable of harming any of the French writers with whom he came in daily contact. The fake revolver figures as something of a fetish object in what might be called his political unconscious – the materialization of a deluded private belief that irreducible differences might be papered over. And yet Heller was also capable of actions of real decency and even minor heroism: tipping off the *bouquinistes* that a raid was imminent; saving lives of various threatened personalities (including Paulhan's); rescuing a number of condemned books from destruction; authorizing a remarkable quantity of quality publications. (In 1943, there were apparently more titles published in France [9,348] than in any other country in the world. The figures for the United States and Great Britain are, respectively, 8,320 and 6,705.)[48]

From Heller's point of view, his crowning official achievement was the organization of two major colloquia on French culture held – with all expenses paid – in Weimar in 1941 and again in 1942. Representing what he and Jünger had come to regard as a "demonic" power, but perhaps for that reason capable of acts of heroism that cultural bureaucrats in more placid times would never have the option of executing, Heller spent much of his time engaged in the business of organizing French cultural occasions for the benefit of his homeland, wooing French intellectuals to perform as nothing more than French intellectuals under German auspices. His work, that is, as cultural impresario on behalf of a dominant power offers an odd prototype for the activities of many a French Department chairman in the United States. That suggestion may seem scandalous, but consider that at the end of the War, Heller, who had already fallen out with the Nazis by 1944, re-emerged in Germany as a publisher and translator of French texts and interpreted his activities as follows: "We thus pursued what the War had given me the opportunity of beginning: a rapprochement among European cultures, and particularly between those of France and Germany."[49] From his point of view, the War was the beginning of a life of Franco-German cultural collaboration, conducted with diligence and a certain mediocrity after 1945, and with remarkable freedom and intensity during the four years of the War. From Heller's point of view? Not only, since in 1980 the Académie Française awarded the former Sonderführer of the Propaganda-Staffel its Grand Prix du Rayonnement Français. Thus ends the memoir of this cultural bureaucrat, in the tawdry fulfillment of a dream worthy of any French professor anywhere.

Now my reason for invoking the case of Heller is that the principal figure of his memoir of the Collaboration is Jean Paulhan. The central chapter of the book is entitled "Mon Maître Paulhan" and offers us the bizarre spectacle of a leading official of the Nazi occupying apparatus describing himself as a disciple of one of the leaders of the intellectual Resistance. For Paulhan, of course, was one of the founders of the Comité National des Ecrivains and – along with Jacques Decour – of *Les Lettres françaises*. And yet we find Heller, who appears to have spent much time with Paulhan during the War, writing: "I learned everything from him; he was my master..."[50] In the beginning – of the genealogy we are constructing – as at the end, then, a paroxysm of literary adulation.

Is there a link between the political dilemma with which Paulhan emerged at the end of the War – a resistance movement which had historically been a school of collaboration (i.e., the left), a collaborationist movement all of whose traditions had been oriented toward resistance (i.e., the right) – and this odd configuration of the Nazi official become disciple of the Resistance leader (his "spiritual father")? Perhaps ... After the War, Paulhan was to write: "Après tout, Pétain faisait sans doute ce qu'il pouvait. Je suppose que sans lui nous aurions eu cent fois plus de martyrs et de morts. Et c'est la chance de la France qu'elle ait eu à la fois de Gaulle et Pétain. A la fois des résistants et des obéissants: les uns pour sauver les principes, et les autres pour sauver – dans la mesure du possible – les hommes et la terre de ce pays."[51] For Heller that attitude was already Paulhan's during the War and would explain the fact that whereas he was capable of denouncing Drieu's *NRF* in an unsigned text in the journal *Résistance*, he also assumed the full burden of bringing out issues of the *NRF* when Drieu proved unequal to the task.[52] Here then was a "double jeu" which preceded the paradoxes of *De la paille et du grain* and which – mediated by Heller's adulatory discipleship – may have conditioned their emergence in Paulhan's thought.

There is a remarkable case in which mentor Paulhan's influence aided Heller in living his own contradictions as anti-Nazi Nazi occupant. The Frenchman one day brought Heller to visit Picasso's apartment. The German was overwhelmed: "Throughout all the works [I saw], in the cruel decomposition of forms, the tragic violence of colors, the horror of the War (which was nevertheless never directly expressed) was present in an almost unbearable way."[53] Heller quotes Jean Cayrol, for whom Picasso "was the painter par excellence who could easily have set up his easel on the Appel-Platz of Mauthausen or Buchenwald ..." [54] A page later, Jünger advises Heller: "One has to learn how to domesticate the mysterious energies of these paintings." Heller: "It was to that that I was initiated by Paulhan." Without Paulhan's aid, they would have remained "demonic," "unbearable." Paulhan's remedy was the course on Braque which was initially delivered to Heller and subsequently published under the title: "Braque le patron." Heller: "Whereas the War was exploding through the screaming work of the Picasso of that period, Braque, in order to flee it, appears to have muted his tones and mellowed his lines even more ..."[55] Paulhan's esthetic, that is, allowed the Sonderführer to "domesticate" the demonic reality of the situation, of the Nazi cause ...

Let me cut short these comments here and summarize what I have – and haven't – said. At both extremes of the fable (or speculative genealogy) I have sketched, we find very similar, very different cases of literary adulation: the Americans for Derrida; Heller for Paulhan. The differences are too great to need rehearsing. The similarity lies in the hegemony – be it financial, political, or military – enjoyed by the national community of the adulators in relation to the France of the adulated – and the inevitability of that superiority's figuring in the relation. In the middle of the construct, I attempted to stitch a suture between the obsessions of the later Paulhan (homophonic antonyms, the critique of etymologism, etc.) and the newly emergent problematic of Grammatology. The fact that those obsessions were integrally linked to Paulhan's perception of the political dilemma of the degeneration of the Resistance and Liberation in France in turn allowed me to imagine Derrida's opus as the textual instantiation of the amnesty or radical forgetting that seemed to constitute the horizon of Paulhans writings on post-War politics in France. Should additional authority be needed, I would not be averse to citing Derrida himself on the "rejected sources" (Freud, Nietzsche) of Valéry.[56]

Why attempt such a construct? Ithaca, I have been told, was the original home of the American motion picture industry, before it moved to Hollywood. The classic *Perils of Pauline* was filmed in its gorges. When I read Derrida's text on reason-above-its-abyss-like-the-Cornell-campus-above-its-gorges, I thought of that fact as well as of the Hollywoodization of Franco-American academic relations in recent years. There was something distressing about the spectacle of Deconstruction sharing the set of the *Perils of Pauline* and it was with that thought in mind that I have attempted to situate its concerns in a context radically different. That my scenario – of Deconstruction as a forgetting of the perils engaged by Paulhan – requires a few particularly vigorous intertextual leaps to achieve its coherence has seemed to me more to recommend than to invalidate the effort. My sense is that the discourse of difference will be able to make good its claims to heterogeneity only on the condition of running just such interpretative risks.

CHAPTER 8

Perspectives: on Paul de Man and Le Soir

Some years ago, in a text of homage to Derrida, Emmanuel Levinas, without malice but with a touch of the unwitting resentment that only the deconstructed perhaps harbor, proposed the oddest of analogies. The historical sequence he was invariably reminded of upon reading Derrida, he wrote, was the "exodus" of 1940: "L'unité militaire en retraite arrive dans une localité qui ne se doute encore de rien, où les cafés sont ouverts, où les dames sont aux 'Nouveautés pour dames,' où les coiffeurs coiffent, les boulangers boulangent, les vicomtes rencontrent d'autres vicomtes et se racontent des histoires de vicomtes, et où tout est déconstruit et désolé une heure après."[1] Such would be the *frisson nouveau* introduced by Derrida: a traumatic rendering of the traditional sites of thought so "uninhabitable" that the principal shock it evokes out of Levinas' memory is the evacuation of town after town in anticipation of Hitler's surge westward. Ortwin de Graef's discovery of the numerous articles published by Paul de Man in *Le Soir* during the first half of World War II is perhaps first of all an invitation to imagine Levinas' improbable metaphor as metonymy, his analogy as sequence. For de Man, it now appears, served, in the course of his life, as champion of two radical cultural movements from abroad: as partisan of the Nazi "revolution" among the Walloons in the 1940s and as advocate of "deconstruction" among the Americans in the 1970s. Hitler's jolt to European sensibilities – too devastatingly rapid, as de Man repeatedly suggests in *Le Soir*, to have registered in psychological terms – and Derrida's, that is, are less the stuff of grotesque analogy (Levinas) than nodes of a complex continuum one name of which may be the "life of Paul de Man."[2]

Metonymy is the trope of contamination, which is one source of its appeal to deconstruction in its efforts to dismantle what de Man, on Proust, has called "the totalizing stability of metaphorical processes."[3] But the intertextual contamination deconstruction all but *demands* between de Man's two "revolutions" (of the 1940s and the 1970s) is open to a restricted – or remetaphorized – reading we should do well to confront at the outset. For those who have always warmed to the liberatory aspect of deconstruction's destabilizing tendencies, the revelation of de Man's enthusiastic endorsement of a Nazi Europe might be contained by claiming that deconstruction was plainly the remedy – acknowledged or not – for the ill of collaboration. *Ecclesia super cloacam*: the church remains no less splendid for being built over the sewer of European history. That such a proposition repeats in its structure the triumphalist interpretation of Proust that de Man rejected should give us pause: to "save" deconstruction by subsuming the relation between de Man's "deconstruction" and his "collaboration" with the Nazis to that between "art" and the "life" it would redeem is to affirm a dialectical configuration pre-emininently vulnerable to deconstruction. Nevertheless, Geoffrey Hartman, in a piece in *The New Republic*, concludes on precisely that note: "In the light of what we now know, however, his work appears more and more as a deepening reflection on the rhetoric of totalitarianism ... De Man's critique of every tendency to totalize literature or language ... looks like a belated, but still powerful, act of conscience."[4] Might it be that in order to "save" deconstruction one is reduced to resorting to language that ought to make any deconstructor blush?

How serious a collaborator with the Nazi regime was Paul de Man? A reading of the sum total of de Man's articles in *Le Soir* reveals that political issues were far from a daily obsession for the young journalist. Still there can be no doubt of de Man's avid support for the New Order. On 25 March 1941, five months after the *Militärbefehlshaber* of Belgium issued the first anti-Jewish decrees, de Man could speak shamelessly of "the impeccable behavior of a highly civilized invader."[5] On 14 November of that year, in an article on Daniel Halévy's *Trois épreuves*, de Gaulle's resistance movement in London was dismissed as a "parody"; moreover, immediate collaboration with the occupier was said to be an "imperative obvious to any objective observer." Lest de Man's reading of the situation be interpreted as a response to geo-political (rather than ideological) realities, note should be taken that two weeks later (28 October), in an article on Jacques Chardonne, one of the stars of the Collaboration in Paris, de Man rejected as inadequate any effort to distinguish between Nazism and Germany; on the contrary, "the war will have but united more intimately the two quite kindred realities which the Hitlerian soul and the German soul were from the beginning, fusing them into a single unique force. This is a significant phenomenon, since it means that the Hitlerian dimension cannot be judged without simultaneously judging the German dimension and that Europe's future can be anticipated only within the framework of the possibilities and exigencies of German genius." The time had come for Germany's "definitive emancipation," but such emancipation, for de Man, meant German "hegemony" within Europe, and within such a context no distinction was to be made between Germany itself and Hitler.

On 20 January 1942, in a review of French apologists of the Collaboration (Brasillach, Drieu la Rochelle, Chardonne, Montherlant, Fabre-Luce), Belgium is referred to as "a country which has not yet made its revolution and for which these war years are like a meditative pause in the face of future tasks." The prospect is of the "intoxication" of great collective efforts in the New Europe; in the interim, Belgians, we read, will have "rarely felt closer to the French" than in the "anguished and quivering (*frémissant*)" reflections of the *gratin* of the Collaboration whose reading de Man recommends. By 31 March 1942, the future revolution has already become "the current revolution," and a significant contribution to it is said to be made by Alfred Fabre-Luce's *Anthologie de la nouvelle Europe*, admired for its attempt to "defend Western values against increasingly threatening intrusions." With the final solution (unmentioned) well under way, the article offers a rare display of indignation by the (already) aloof de Man – against "the criminal errors of the past." (Such language should be read, I believe, as implicitly endorsing the prosecution of Léon

Blum and other pre-War anti-Nazi leaders in show trials.[6]) On 20 April 1942, de Man weighed in with a strong endorsement of Paul Alverdes' journal *Das innere Reich*, which was created in order to counter the impression of a massive flight of the German intelligentsia from Hitler's Germany.[7] De Man was just then translating Alverdes' novel *Das Zweigesicht*, a book here described as participatory in the "virile" outlook of the journal. It is in fact Alverdes' success in evoking "virile, patriotic, and exalting" materials in a work of art of "quasi-feminine finesse" that de Man most admires in the author. Wherein he appears to be toying with Nazi ideology in its more jaded manifestations.

Of all the articles cited as evidence of de Man's sympathy with the New Order, his contribution on 4 March 1941 to a special section on "cultural aspects" of the Jewish question has been most frequently referred to. "Les Juifs dans la littérature actuelle" is a very curious piece. For it grafts the question of the Jews onto a second issue, which is in fact a far more insistent concern in his articles for *Le Soir*: the subject of literature's ultimate autonomy in relation to the impure world of politics, history, etc. Against the "vulgar" anti-Semites de Man would take his distance from, the author maintains that modern literature – *unlike the modern world* – has not been contaminated (or "polluted") by Jewish influence. On the one hand, "the Jews have in fact played an important role in the factitious and chaotic existence of Europe," so much so that a novel emergent from such a world might indeed be qualified as *enjuivé*. On the other hand, however, it is the specificity of literature to maintain its own autonomy relative to the world: "It seems that esthetic developments (*les évolutions esthétiques*) obey quite powerful laws whose action persists even while humanity is racked by formidable events." In all its crudity, the analogy informing the article is between literature and history (or "reality"), on the one hand, and Europe and the Jews on the other. The argument, moreover, is clinched by a demonstration. In the case of France, "Jewish writers have always been of the second rank"; figures such as "André Maurois, Francis de Croisset, Henri Duvernois, Henri Bernstein, Tristan Bernard, Julien Benda, etc. are not among the most important, and certainly not among those who have oriented in any way the genres of literature." On these grounds, de Man congratulates the West on its ability to fend off "Jewish influence" (or "Semitic infiltration") and signs on to an embryonic form of the "final solution," mass deportation: "In addition, it will be seen that a solution to the Jewish problem intent on the creation of a Jewish colony isolated from Europe would not entail any deplorable consequences for the literary life of the West."

De Man's analogy – whereby art, in its purity, need be protected from a reality whose degradation is tantamount to a Judaization – is bizarre, but not unique. Surprisingly enough, the only figure of stature to have embraced such an ideology, at times unwittingly, was Marcel Proust. The most succinct expression of the reverie – or fairy tale – on which Proust's position was based is a sequence in *Le Côté de Guermantes.*[8] The scene is a Paris restaurant divided by the slimmest of partitions. On the one side, the "Hebrews"; on the other, "young aristocrats." Marcel enters, makes for the side of the restaurant reserved for nobility, but is ignominiously shunted into the other room; his humiliation (and physical discomfort) are all but total until Saint-Loup enters and offers to sweep Marcel into the blissful warmth of the aristocratic section. That division between (Jewish) suffering and (French) salvation, I have demonstrated elsewhere, is a motif that is affirmed throughout Proust's writings.[9] It is cognate both with the opposition between life and art in *Contre Sainte-Beuve* and with the scenario of salvation-through-art in *La Recherche.*[10] It begins, in the novel, when all of life's ills are placed, in the good night kiss scene, under the sign of Abraham, Isaac and Sarah, continues in the protracted metaphor assimilating Jews and homosexuals as the world's "accursed races," and is perhaps most revealing in a later text in praise of Léon Daudet, in which Proust ponders the cruel imperative that has a Dreyfusard such as himself choosing *Action française* as his sole newspaper, despite the injustices it espouses, out of sheer love of Daudet's vintage prose: "dans quel autre journal le portique est-il décoré à fresque par Saint-Simon, lui-même, j'entends par Léon Daudet?"[11] "Art", in brief, in its opposition to "life," is as (French) style in its opposition to (Jewish) suffering, and the triumph of the former lay in its utter imperviousness to the latter.

But is not Proust's position, thus construed, almost identical to de Man's in the article under consideration? Between the future novelist Marcel's possibility of rescue from the "Hebrews" of Paris and de Man's affirmation of literature's salutary autonomy in relation to a desperately Judaized (*enjuivé*) world the similarity is patent. Indeed one might almost imagine de Man quoting Proust in support of his position. But, of course, he didn't. Not only is Proust not quoted, but in the list of exemplary French Jewish authors he is not even mentioned. For the mere mention of his name would have shattered de Man's argument that such writers were invariably second-rate. This bit of dishonesty, I believe, is the most egregious moment in the article. For de Man was not unaware of Proust's stature; he is referred to as a major figure in several other pieces.[12] Yet in order to make his anti-Jewish point stick, he suppressed the principal item of evidence on the subject.

De Man's fling with anti-Semitism, that is, was not a good-faith error, but an indulgence in deception. His subsequent reputation for probity – exercised over the years in the discrimination between the first- and second-rate in American academia – no doubt deserves to suffer as a consequence. The relation to deconstruction, however, is another matter. Consider that the one figure of stature, Proust, who might have been quoted to bolster de Man's argument about literature's autonomy from a Judaized world was the one figure the mere mention of whose name would have destroyed de Man's argument. And that irreconcilable tension between the constative worth of Proust's testimony and the performative vice of its provenance is, I take it, as convincing a demonstration of a certain validity of deconstruction as one might hope to encounter. Deconstruction, that is – but the term is beginning to fray – provides as illuminating a reading of the shoddiness of de Man's text as one might want, and I see no reason to be anything other than grateful for it.

Might it be, however, that de Man's indifference to the Jews during the War was actually a function of his indifference to the "Jewish question" itself? The presupposition of "Les Juifs dans la littérature actuelle," the autonomy of literature in relation to political reality, paradoxically resurfaces in other articles in *Le Soir* in the form of admonitions to literary collaborators with the

Nazis to return to their literature. Thus, an article (12 August 1941) on Brasillach's *Notre avant-guerre* begins, like the essay on the Jews, by establishing a water-tight distinction between (flourishing) art and (decadent) politics in French life, and warns that the eminently "sympathique" Brasillach, a leader of the Collaboration in Paris, was plainly out of his element when treating such matters as the triumph of national-socialism in Germany, the failure of the Popular Front in France, and the Spanish Civil War. Similarly, on 11 November 1941, we find de Man upbraiding Montherlant for *Solstice de juin*, the book that earned him an accusation as a collaborator after the war, with the following generalization: "there is no reason to grant men of letters such authority in an area of human behavior which manifestly escapes their competence. One is astonished by the naïveté and insignificance of certain of their judgments once they are stripped of the brilliant veneer they derive from their carefully elaborated form." Better, de Man suggests, leave such matters as the "spiritual" grounds of European unity to "specialists." Taken together, the three articles on Brasillach, Montherlant, and the Jews lead one to suspect that de Man's commitment was to the proposition that art was autonomous in relation to political life, and not to any view on the Jewish question. Of course, the fact that de Man was sufficiently opportunistic to tack his specious argument about the Jews onto the more fundamental proposition is not precisely a recommendation . . .

There is an odd sense in which the more insistent target of de Man's collaborationist articles is not at all the Jews, but the French. For what gives so many of the pieces for *Le Soir* a recognizably de Manian tone is a certain disabused skepticism as to the abilities of the majority of his audience to rise to the occasion they celebrate. On 12 August 1941, writing of Brasillach, de Man characteristically ponders whether the "French elite will be able to perform the about-face demanded by circumstances and adapt to disciplines entirely opposed to their traditional virtues." A month later (30 September), the new French literary generation is said to be "hopelessly mediocre." On 14 October, observing the "incoherent convulsions" rocking France since the armistice, a skeptical de Man "can but formulate pessimistic views as to future possibilities." Perhaps the most explicit article to this effect is a review of a re-edition of Sieberg's *Dieu est-il français?* on 28 April 1942. De Man manifests "very little optimism as to the future possibilities of French culture." Given the "mystical age" Europe was about to enter, an era of "suffering, exaltation, and intoxication," France would plainly have to modify its secular cult of reason to survive. Worse yet, France in its chauvinism suffered from what de Man, following Sieberg, calls "un nationalisme religieux," a spirit the new Europe would not tolerate. The reference to "religious nationalism," the vice (of intolerance) anti-Semitism has traditionally found intolerable in the Jews, all but clinches the shift: de Man's obsession during the War was less the evil of the Jews than the inadequacies of the French: not Zionism, but what he calls "Gionism," the cult of the writings of the regionalist novelist Giono, is characterized as "detestable" (22 April, 30 September 1941).

The fact that the articles seem on the whole more consistently anti-French than anti-Jewish (the day after the piece on the irrelevance of the Jews de Man was capable of invoking Yehudi Mehuhin as exemplary violinist) is worth recording not simply to set the record right. Rather it establishes an odd continuity between the earlier and the later writings. For in both his writings in French on behalf of the Nazi "revolution" among the Walloons in the 1940s and his writings in English on behalf of "deconstruction" among the Americans in the 1970s, the idiosyncratic discursive feature binding the two endeavors, each in furtherance of a radical cultural movement from abroad, is a pronounced pessimism regarding the abilities of his broader audience (the French in the 1940s, American academia in the 1970s) to muster the wherewithal needed to respond to the demands each movement was putting on them. Consider an admirable piece, such as "The Return to Philology" (1982), in this light. It concerns a deluded "resistance" to an invasion from abroad: "the final catastrophe of the post-structural era, the invasion of departments of English by French influences that advocate 'a nihilistic view of literature, of human communication, and of life itself.' "[13] This invasion is, in fact, part of a movement that is "revolutionary," for which reason local "resistance" to the occupation from abroad has been quick to organize. De Man asks: "Why, then, the cries of doom and the appeals to mobilization against a common enemy?"[14] And the first answer he comes up with is the havoc the "common enemy" is wreaking on a traditional investment in ethics: "the attribution of a reliable, or even exemplary cognitive, and by extension, ethical function to literature indeed becomes much more difficult." The new "return to philology," an apparently "revolutionary" restoration led from abroad, will, however, in all probability, know failure: "The institutional resistances to such a move, however, are probably insurmountable."[15] The new skepticism is so far-reaching as to spare not even itself: "One sees easily enough why such changes are not likely to occur." What remains is an unswerving commitment to an ideal whose glory, in defeat, will no longer be able to be denied even by its adversaries: "Yet, with the critical cat so far out of the bag that one can no longer ignore its existence, those who refuse the crime of theoretical ruthlessness can no longer hope to gain a good conscience."

Many who read "The Return to Philology" in the *Times Literary Supplement* in 1982 cannot but have been moved by its libertarian gesture of countering on their own traditional – philological, but also Harvardian – grounds those who would shut a younger generation of scholars out of tenure. Yet within the echo chamber excavated by Ortwin de Graef, the piece sounds almost like an unwitting parody of the position repeatedly voiced by de Man forty years earlier in *Le Soir*. Specifically:

1. The idiosyncratic phrase "crime of [theoretical] ruthlessness," used to characterize the "revolution" from abroad, however ironically pitched in 1982, takes on a sinister aptness in light of the *Le Soir* articles. It is one thing, that is, for Geoffrey Hartman, in *The New Republic*, to fault de Man for "underestimating the ruthlessness of the Nazi regime."[16] It is another, far stranger one for de Man himself to conjure up "ruthlessness" as the characteristic *par excellence* of the movement he was championing in 1982.

2. The skepticism as to the prospects of "deconstruction" in American academia is very much of a piece with the skepticism regarding the French – the broader audience a French-language

critic of literature could not but be addressing – in Hitler's new Europe. It will be perceived that what binds "The Return to Philology" and its attendant texts to the articles of the 1940s is a chiasmus. In 1941–42, we have seen, a deluded resistance to the salutary revolution from abroad was the vice of the French; in 1982, "resistance" (to theory) was an American shortcoming in the face of a "revolution" coming *from* France. In each case, moreover, there was an enlightened enclave among the benighted recipients of the good news in whom de Man placed exceptional faith. On 30 September 1941, the future of Francophone culture lay for de Man with the Walloons: "I do not believe it a lack of objectivity to claim that the young are closer to this goal in Belgium than in France ..." And again: "these books [by Belgians writing in French] are more attuned to the desired revolution than those presently being written by Frenchmen of the same age." At some level, one imagines, the Yale graduate students were cast in the role of the Walloons of the 1970s.

3. The traditional investment in literature's "ethical function," threatened by the new (theoretical) "ruthlessness" of the 1970s, serves as a reminder that de Man's articles for *Le Soir* were shot through with statements about ethics. Specifically, the repository of ethical wisdom in the West was the German novel: works of a Germany, it will be recalled, whose soul was essentially "Hitlerian." Whereas the French novel, we are told on 5 August 1941, is essentially "psychological," the Germans introduce us to a dimension that is ethical: "not a psychological drama, but a conflict between Good and Evil." By 2 March 1942, the Germans are said to be "un peuple moraliste par excellence," and their perennial investment in intervening in the "struggle between good and evil" has issued in the current "fine example of patriotic fidelity" on the part of German authors. No sooner, however, does de Man confront a German work of apparently anti-Hitlerian tenor, Jünger's *Auf den Marmorklippen* (31 March 1942), than he begins retreating from the centrality of the ethical dimension in German literature. True, the book is about the struggle between "Good and Evil," but it must not be confused with a "pale moralizing sermon." Moreover, "the conflict does not interest [Jünger] for its

ethical consequences,but as an inspiring pretext (*thème d'inspiration*), as a motif his imagination can translate into a sequence of images of sun, fire, and blood." Hitlerian Germany, that is, is essentially "ethical" until the issue of Hitler's evil is confronted, however indirectly, at which point the ethical is deflected into ultimate irrelevance. But that deflection of the ethical, at the hands of a new "ruthlessness," is precisely what is reaffirmed forty years later, in the face of a new resistance, in "The Return to Philology."

The superimposition of the 1982 text and the articles of the 1940s – however intriguing the chiasmus it enables (or is enabled by), however uncanny the return of the motifs of "ruthlessness," "skepticism" and "ethics" – remains, it will be objected, a mere formal exercise. Deconstruction, of course, is ill suited to object to considerations of "mere form" (in the name of "substance"?), and at its most forceful will in fact be inclined to think matters of difference (say between the writings of the young and the mature Paul de Man) in terms of repetition ... As a style of reading, that is, deconstruction is singularly ill equipped to contain contamination by the articles in *Le Soir*. A generation that has thrilled to the intertextual oscillation, in Derrida's *Glas*, between the philosophy of Hegel and the erotics of Jean Genet, cannot, I believe, in good faith, claim that between the writings of de Man's youth and those of his maturity there is, in Hillis Miller's words to *The Nation*, "no connection."[17]

Ultimately, the effort to spare "deconstruction" any contamination by de Man's collaborationist texts is dependent on reviving, on the whole without acknowledgment, the quaint notion of a *coupure épistémologique*. Thus Christopher Norris, in an attempt to demonstrate the "utter remoteness" of the early from the later de Man, falls back on the notion of the later work as an "ideological critique" of "organic" values and metaphors.[18] If dividing line there must be, of course, the critique of the organic is as good a theme as any around which to elaborate it. But not only is the notion of a *coupure épistémologique* – Althusser's dubious marriage, within the text of Marx, of a motif from Bachelard with Lacan's reading of Freud's "castration" – deconstructively problematic, it also fails to acknowledge the striking continuities: a scorn for the values of liberal – or individualist – humanism (see de Man's contempt, on 20 January 1942, for the French dream of "saving man"); the investment in dismantling binary oppositions (*Ni droite ni gauche*, it will be recalled, is the title of Sternhell's masterly study of Fascist ideology in France) ...[19]

The question of deconstruction-and-fascism, if there be one, however, is sufficiently idiosyncratic as not to be available to resolution in terms of thematic continuity or discontinuity. I refer to a phenomenon so glaring and so unacknowledged as to loom as something of a purloined letter over the entire debate: the fact that no fewer than three of the most sterling careers flanking deconstruction (that is, Derrida's own career) were profoundly compromised by an engagement with fascism. Indeed, my first fantasy upon hearing of de Man's writings during the War was of a caricature entitled the Passion of Deconstruction with Derrida on the cross flanked by Blanchot, crucified under the sign *Combat* on the one side, and de Man, suffering similarly beneath the rubric *Le Soir*, on the other. As for the Father-who-has-forsaken-him, the cruelest moment of the fantasy would have Heidegger, from whom Derrida received the word "deconstruction," flashing from above the Nazi membership card he did not relinquish until after the war ...[20] Blanchot (in France), de Man (in the United States), and Heidegger (in Germany) are arguably the three most important contemporaries to figure in the international enterprise we have come to recognize in Derrida's work, the subject, in fact, of three recent books he has authored: *Parages* (1986) on Blanchot; *Mémoires: for Paul de Man* (1986); and *De l'esprit: Heidegger et la question* (1987).[21] My point is that "deconstruction" is centrally the thought of Derrida, that de Man's "deconstruction" was in many ways born of his relation with Derrida, and that the question of deconstruction-and-fascism (in de Man or elsewhere) is perhaps best broached in the works of Derrida, specifically on those thinkers, central to his writing, who had at one time or another invested in the ideology of fascism.

Now almost more striking than the fascist careers of our trinity (Blanchot until 1938, de Man until at least 1942, Heidegger throughout the War) is the role that dimension plays in the books Derrida has devoted to them:

1. Maurice Blanchot's writings for *Combat*, apologies for acts of terrorism against the "degenerate" government of Léon Blum, receive no mention in *Parages*.[22] Surely, in a writer as intent on assessing the radical heterogeneity of writing, the omission of such texts (which were known to Derrida) from a discussion of his work is troubling. More specifically, I have shown elsewhere, Derrida's failure to bring Blanchot's *Combat* pieces into play in a long reading of *L'Arrêt de mort* (whose action transpires in October 1938) has led to a failure to perceive the structuring role of the myth of Iphigenia in that novel and, consequently, to a misreading of it ...[23] But for the moment, what is of interest is simply the omission of the fascist articles of the 1930s from the Blanchot texts discussed by Derrida in his book.

2. *Mémoires: for Paul de Man* is a moving work, written on the death of Derrida's friend, partially, perhaps, out of identification with Blanchot himself, whose *L'Amitié* was conceived in memory of Blanchot's departed friend, Georges Bataille. For its subject is, in part, "the unique, the incomparable friendship that ours was for me."[24] The book was written, of course, before the revelation of the articles for *Le Soir*, and thus makes no reference to them. Thus we are confronted with yet another book bypassing a politically nefarious past. And one wonders: was there no room in that "incomparable" friendship – or its record, *Mémoires* – for revealing writings of such importance? As if in unwitting mockery, Derrida's book (on the writings of a man who, one suspects, spent considerable energy forgetting his assent to a Nazi Europe) responds: "that he [de Man] existed himself in memory of an affirmation and of a vow: yes, yes."[25] Surely, to have gotten the configuration so *precisely* wrong is a feat worth pondering.

3. It is the third of Derrida's three recent books, however, *De l'esprit: Heidegger et la question*, which is most central to the question of deconstruction and fascism, since it confronts the issue of Heidegger's collaboration with the Nazis *dans le texte*. To what end? The book, it should be noted, is one of the most surprisingly and intricately conceived of all Derrida's works. For those who have lamented a certain predictability in the author's recent work, a reading of *De l'esprit* will serve as a reminder – indeed much more than a reminder – of the glory days of deconstruction.

Perhaps the book's import is best broached through a consideration of structure. We are presented with the discovery of a particularly liberating problematic, its subsequent repression, and a later (sublime) return of the repressed. The discovery – of an authentic interrogation of the being of *Dasein* – comes in 1927. Crucial to its consolidation is a relegation of mind (*Geist, esprit*) to the category of those (all too Cartesian) words that Heidegger would have one use only "in quotation marks." The repression comes in 1933 with the celebration of *Geist* or Mind – without quotation marks – as the motivating theme of the Freiburg Rector's Speech, traditionally regarded as the principal document of Heidegger's career as a Nazi. (What were "repressed," that is, were the quotation marks.) The sublime return of the repressed comes in 1953, in a discussion of Trakl's poetry, wherein *Geist* makes its reappearance no longer as a derivative of the Platonic *geistig*, but of the sacral, if un-Christian, adjective *geistlich*. *Geist*, in 1953, comes into its old-Germanic own as *fire*: *l'esprit*, in a phrase rife with Derridean indeterminacy, *en-flamme*.

Now concerning this scenario, the most surprising development is the reading of Heidegger's Nazism as a humanism. The appeal to Mind, the forgetting of Being, or rather: the repression of the quotation marks, of the question of *écriture*, is read as an effort to save Nazism from its own biologism, to "spiritualize Nazism." And between the collaboration with Nazism and the lapse into humanist metaphysics, Derrida seems hard pressed to decide which is worse: Heidegger "capitalise le pire, à savoir les deux mots à la fois: la caution au nazisme et le geste encore métaphysique."[26] Simultaneously, in two long footnotes, Derrida is particularly severe on the great humanists of pre-Nazi Europe, Valéry and Husserl. The latter, in particular, is taken to task for a "sinister" passage in which "Indians, Eskimos, and Gypsies" are excluded from the realm of European spirituality.[27] The implication is plain: if Heidegger, to the extent he was a Nazi, was a humanist, the humanists Husserl and Valéry, to the extent they were humanists, were racists. In strict logic, between Nazis and anti-Nazis, we are given little to choose. For which reason Derrida and his readers can only be relieved at the passing of the Nazi interlude – which is perhaps best characterized, within the logic of *De l'esprit,* as the Nazi-anti-Nazi interlude – and the re-emergence of the original problematic (of 1927), in even more extreme form: it is within the splendidly and eminently *written esprit-en-flamme* of the 1953 meditation on Trakl that Derrida's Heidegger, one feels, and Derrida himself, come into their deconstructive "own." The Nazi-anti-Nazi interlude, within the logic of the book, was a misreading of 1927, comically beside the point, a ludicrous performance: "Here comes the Rector!" one all but hears as Derrida hoists the curtain for his reading of Heidegger's *Rektoratsrede.*

Concerning *De l'esprit,* I should like to make two points, the first of which concerns an essay of my own. In 1985, in "Writing and Deference: The Politics of Literary Adulation," I speculated that one unacknowledged ancestor of deconstruction might be Jean Paulhan.[28] Paulhan, a particularly adroit delver into the conundra of language, a former leader of the Resistance, became after the war a champion of the cause of amnesty for collaboration with the Nazis. His position was based on a – questionable – chiasmus. The crux of recent French history, he maintained, was that the majority of the wartime Resisters in France had long been trumpeting, prior to the War, their eagerness to collaborate – with the Russians; and simultaneously the majority of the Collaborators had long been preparing a resistance, in the name of French national values, against the Russians. Given that configuration, Paulhan claimed there could be no basis for moral outrage after the War against either group. His only regret, wrote Paulhan, was not being a Jew so that he might forgive France for not having defended him better. In my essay, I suggested that the advent of deconstruction might be read speculatively as a fulfillment of Paulhan's dream of amnesty, retaining the irreducible form of the chiasmus, but voiding the political crux in which it was grounded. (That conclusion was somewhat misrepresented in a truncated quotation in the *Newsweek* article on Paul de Man.[29]) The reaction of deconstructors near and wide, I have been told, was less than enthusiastic.[30] In retrospect, however, *De l'esprit* strikes me as confirmation of my point. Between Paulhan, on the one hand, claiming his collaborators were originally resisters and his resisters collaborators, and Derrida, on the other, that Heidegger was a Nazi only to the extent he was a humanist and Husserl and Valéry humanists only to the extent they were (Eurocentric) racists, the continuity seems to be so substantial as to be conclusive.

My second point concerns the return of a radicalized *Geist* in 1953 as irreducibly metaphorical fire. For if the Nazi-anti-Nazi interlude was a misreading (of 1927), a deluded literalization of what is fundamentally figural or written (in quotation marks), then one is left with the sense that a literalization of the metaphorics of *das Flammende* (p. 132) would similarly be beside the point. But note that for Derrida, the interpretation of old-German *Geist* as more originary than Latin *spiritus* or Greek *pneuma*, is part of a "brutal foreclosure or exclusion" (p. 165): of the primordial Hebrew *ruach*. In addition, Derrida goes to pains to modify the received translation of *entsetzt* in the Trakl essay: mind aflame does not merely *displace*, it *deports* (*déporte*) (p. 158). Nazism, fire, exclusion of the Jews, deportation: does not the whole of Derrida's text, with its implied warning against any literalization of what is irreducibly figural (Heidegger's comic error in 1933), move toward a "deconstruction" of what has, after all, served as transcendental signified *par excellence* for two generations: the Holocaust? To read Derrida seriously is, I fear, to arrive at no other conclusion.[31]

To take Paul de Man seriously is to imagine him perennially vexed by his implication in the Nazi order, a wound, one hopes, that did not heal easily. What better balm for it than the philosophy that was to reach a brilliant culmination after his death in *De l'esprit*? For *that*, not *Mémoires*, is the volume, one suspects after the fact, which might best have been subtitled *For Paul de Man*. With its inability to find an anti-Nazi stance not always already contaminated by the rot of metaphysics (or racism: *la mythologie blanche*), its implied "deconstruction" of the Holocaust, *De l'esprit*, or the thought from which it emerged, was *the* solution to the ethical quandary one imagines de Man struggling with throughout his life.

One of the mythical moments of contemporary criticism, related by both de Man and Derrida, centers on their first enunter in Baltimore.[32] What brought them together was a shared interest in Rousseau's *Essai sur l'origine des langues*. But if ever there was a misencounter around a text it was this, for the two were manifestly working at cross purposes. This is clearest in de Man's misreading of both Derrida and Rousseau on the subject of music. For whereas the point of departure for Rousseau (and Derrida) is a denigration of harmony (resembling writing in its intervalic or differential essence) in relation to melody (as voice, plenitude, imitation), de Man gets things precisely backwards, maintaining that discontinuity – or writing – is on the side of melody ("a succession of discontinuous moments . . . chronology is the structural correlative of the necessarily figural nature of literary language".)[33] Once that position is consolidated, there is indeed little ground for any true dialogue on the text. All of which is to suggest that the mythical meeting of minds over Rousseau was perhaps steeped more deeply in myth than has been acknowledged. And that suggestion in turn, combined with our knowledge of the articles for *Le Soir*, leads one to speculate that the true meeting of minds, which of necessity never took place, was the one all but staged within the intricacies of Derrida's *De l'esprit*.

The popular press has seized on the similarities between the cases of de Man and Waldheim, and – from the failure to acknowledge past complicity with the Nazis to the exalted post-War eminence – such analogies are surely there to be drawn. Yet in retrospect the most instructive aspect of the link between the two cases is a fundamental disparity. For the election of Waldheim to the presidency of Austria, a country that provided three-fourths of extermination-camp commanders during World War II and committed forty percent of all war crimes, was in important ways enabled by that sorry history: in electing Waldheim, Austria was in effect normalizing (if not exalting) its own Nazi past.[34] For the relatively small group of American critics affected by the de Man revelations, the situation has led to anything but a normalization. To the contrary: a generation raised in the belief that Nazism was evil – or *otherness* – itself has suddenly been forced to negotiate the spectre of Nazism as it has surfaced, after the fact, from within their own identification with de Man. For many, it is not simply that the "great man" turned out to have collaborated with the Nazis, but that the individual they had, at some level, been bent on *being* (through an act of identification with either his person or the force of his signature on the letters of recommendation to which they owed their careers) turned out to have done so. And if he had, what of them? "Certain historic destinies place individuals before quite exceptional circumstances . . ." wrote de Man in an article of 17 June 1941. We now know that de Man himself had such a fate. But how many of his adepts now feel secure that under identical (exceptional) circumstances they would not have acted similarly? That such a question should now be consigned to the realm of the "undecidable" is perhaps the final lesson of Paul de Man.

Unless, of course, the current polarization around the de Man case is further exacerbated. For there is a sense in which the present configuration resembles nothing so much as the final chapters of *Madame Bovary*: after the death of his beloved, Charles indulges in an orgy of sentimental grief, only to stumble one day on Emma's cache of adulterous love letters. A spell of "howling" and "sobbing" subsides into "somber fury," and then, as Charles puts the whole episode behind him, into a particularly degraded mode of the "dismal lifelessness" which has characterized him from the beginning. "It is the fault of Fate," is his final abject comment (in de Man's revised translation of the book) on the whole abortive episode. One can already hear, after the sentimentalities of the *Yale French Studies* tribute, the posthumous discovery of the pro-Nazi articles, and the "howling" that ensued, the academic equivalent of Charles Bovary's *mot*: So he was a Nazi . . . That is: so what! That what has been called the "relativization" of Nazism, already well under way in academic Germany, might end up being an item on the agenda of American "deconstruction" is a particularly grim prospect.[35] The fact that the opposition, momentarily riding high, is for the most part peopled by the academic counterparts of Monsieur Homais should, needless to say, be of no consolation at all.

CHAPTER 9

Prosopopeia revisited

Prosopopeia, during the last years of Paul de Man's life, served as something of the abracadabra of his own brand of deconstructive criticism. In the strict sense, the term designates the figure through which an absent or deceased person is represented as speaking. De Man, however, through a series of ingenious but arbitrary analyses, sought to generalize it to the very bounds of literature: through epitaph, it became the "dominant figure" of autobiography; through apostrophe, the "master-trope" of poetry; through etymology ("to confer a mask or face"), something akin to personification; and finally, through its appeal to an absent other, the "very figure of the reader and of reading." Jacques Derrida's gesture of fidelity in *Mémoires: for Paul de Man*, the three baroque essays he devoted to his deceased friend, lay in returning to prosopopeia in the strict sense, giving voice to his friend in the form of a masterly rehearsal of de Man's thoughts on memory, but also in the concluding discursive gesture of reading an unpublished piece by de Man, as it were, from beyond the grave. A certain amount of fanfare prepares Derrida's revelation of that text, the first letter he received (in 1971) from de Man, in which the critic, in rather mannerly fashion, runs through his differences with Derrida on the subject of Rousseau and refers in passing to Rousseau's madness. Derrida puffs up his prose and wonders (in a decrescendo Proust might have savored) whether the mere act of quoting personal correspondance in a public forum is not "abusive, violent, indiscreet"? He makes bold to go on, invents a new transgression. The reference to Rousseau's madness arouses a will to consider de Man's thought "under the light of lunacy." For that reference has revealed to the commentator that de Man's entire career was pursued under the aegis of madness: Rousseau, Hölderlin, and Nietzsche, the "three madmen of Western modernity." Such would be the message reserved for Derrida from beyond the grave.

Unfortunately, the disparity between the professorial decorousness of de Man's early letter and the pathos of Derrida's commentary makes this particular prosopopeia ring singularly false. How false, however, did not become clear until several years later when Derrida found himself visited by a far more disturbing message from beyond the grave, the much touted discovery of a series of articles published by de Man between 1940 and 1942 in the Belgian collaborationist newspaper *Le Soir*. It was as though beyond the botched prosopopeia in *Mémoires* there were another more authentically transgressive one waiting to be voiced. Oddly enough, the entire – unintended – configuration rehearses something of a genealogy of the genre of the essay in France. For Montaigne too began his essays, invented the genre, in (and as) mourning over a deceased friend, La Boétie. And he too had planned to center his effort on a prosopopeia: a posthumous edition of La Boétie's youthful tract, *Discours de la servitude volontaire*. Montaigne, however, withdrew that publication when, in the context of the religious wars in France, he learned that the text was already being exploited by those "seeking to trouble and change the state of our governance." He replaced it with a rather conventional set of love sonnets by La Boétie – the pseudo-prosopopeia masking the real one. Derrida, to his credit, did all he could to facilitate the publication of de Man's (very different) discourse of "voluntary servitude" or collaboration. But he accompanied that gesture with a text, published in France as the fourth essay of *Mémoires* (and in the United States [initially] in the journal *Critical Inquiry*), whose contradictions are so reminiscent of Montaigne's own in exonerating La Boétie that one suspects that the most interesting prosopopeia in *Mémoires* is, in fact, a third – unwitting – one: Derrida giving voice to neither the critic of the 1971 letter nor the journalist of the 1940s articles, but, in his own prose, to Montaigne inventing the genre of the essay in the first volume of his masterwork.[1]

What then of de Man's 170 articles published in *Le Soir* during the War? They are, on the whole, articles of a young intellectual more interested in literature than politics, indeed concerned with protecting a certain autonomy of literature from extra-esthetic impingements, but nonetheless unstinting in his support for Hitler's new Europe. In this regard, the most extreme of the articles, a 4 March 1941 contribution to a page on cultural aspects of the "Jewish question" is characteristic. Against the "vulgar" anti-Semites de Man would take his distance from, the author maintains that modern literature – *unlike the modern world* – has not been contaminated (or "polluted") by Jewish influence. Since I have analyzed that article (and the bad faith behind its omission of any reference to Proust) in the preceding chapter, I shall turn now to Derrida's treatment of de Man's writings in *Le Soir,* the prosopopeia behind the prosopopeia in *Mémoires.* At its center it too confronts the "unbearable" article on the Jews in contemporary literature and expresses the shock it caused him. But only to do an about-face. De Man's reference to "vulgar anti-Semitism" may indeed be pitted against a more genteel variety. "But the phrase can also mean something else, and this reading can always contaminate the other in a clandestine fashion: to condemn 'vulgar anti-Semitism,' *especially if one makes no mention of the other kind,* is to condemn anti-Semitism itself *inasmuch as* it is vulgar, always and essentially vulgar." A speculative paragraph more, and that second reading wins out over the first. But this is mere wishful thinking – and poor reading – on Derrida's part. The genteel anti-Semitism, far from being unmentioned, is the very stuff of de Man's article, the attitude that has him finding no problem with the mass deportation of the Jews. Moreover, if de Man were in fact offering a subtle denunciation of anti-Semitism itself, why should Derrida react – and continue to react – to his article as though it were an "indelible wound"? Undecidability, the master stance of deconstruction, when confronted with a political crisis, here reveals itself to be no more than the desire to have things both ways. Derrida's concluding reverie on de Man in the essay is of a piece with the analysis of the article on Jews in contemporary literature. "He must have lived [his internal conflicts concerning his past] according to two temporalities." One would see that past as a "prehistoric prelude," the other as the center of his existence, turning all the rest into a kind of "posthistory." Temporality for him would be the reiterated disjunction between that prehistory and that posthistory. The formulation is esthetically intriguing, but ethically amounts to allowing Derrida to exonerate de Man (since it was all prehistory) even as he pretends to condemn him (since everything else was posthistory).

Montaigne on La Boétie's *Servitude volontaire* sounds an almost identical note: "Je ne fay nul doubte qu'il ne creust ce qu'il escrivoit ...": I have no doubt that he believed what he was writing, but this after all was a mere rhetorical exercise, a youthful game ... And like Montaigne, Derrida appears to want to mute or distort his friend's writing lest it be unduly exploited in a religious war. The word *war*, in the subtitle of the essay ("Paul de Man's War"), is a carry-over from the text of *Mémoires*, where it designates the "war" over deconstruction. *Mémoires* presents the image of the leader of a persecuted sect naming and reviling its "enemies" (Searle, Danto, Wellek, Bate, etc.), surveying its triumphs ("l'Amérique, mais *c'est* la déconstruction"). The religious character of that war, moreover, is underscored by the almost liturgical aspect of Derrida's prose. *Mémoires* may stand for that period of his work which increasingly finds expression in books originally delivered as lectures to the faithful. Familiar motifs are less analyzed than embroidered upon; footnotes seem less to fellow scholars than to distinguished members of the congregation ... And this sense of de Man's wartime writing as a potential weapon in a religious – or critical – war seems central to the 1988 article in *Critical Inquiry*. Derrida's tactic is again infuriatingly two-faced: on the one hand, all must enjoy complete freedom to react to de Man's writings as they wish; on the other, he, personally, plans to "denounce" any "trial of Paul de Man" in "the most uncompromising manner." The word "trial" here is a rhetorical ploy invoked by Derrida to discredit in advance any effort to take the implications of de Man's wartime writings seriously, and the threat to use his considerable institutional muscle to "denounce" any who would is hardly compatible with the liberal gesture of making the texts available for public consideration in the first place. In an additional effort to discredit de Man's would-be critics, Derrida hints at a parody of any future effort to align the motifs of de Man's critical writing with those of his wartime journalism. Let any "symptomatologists in training" write him, he says; he "will point out a few tricks." So much for the invitation to undertake serious consideration of the wartime journalism!

Note should be taken of the curious title of Derrida's article. "Like the Sound of the Sea Deep within a Shell" is a quotation of de Man quoting Montherlant's *Solstice de juin* approvingly in 1941. Montherlant, in the book which earned him an accusation as a collaborator after the war, claims he can already hear the indifference of the future rolling over the newspapers of the day, "comme on entend le bruit de la mer quand on porte à l'oreille certains coquillages."[2] The same will to affirm literature's autonomy which had found expression in the anti-Semitic piece already discussed, that is, could similarly serve de Man in urging writers to steer clear of collaboration. And Derrida no doubt entitled his essay as he did in an effort to underscore that aspect of de Man's thought. What he may not have realized was that the very same words he chose for his title had already appeared as the last lines of Maurice Blanchot's wartime volume of criticism, *Faux pas*, and as such constituted a coded farewell to Blanchot's own career as a fascist journalist during the years prior to World War II. The motif of the coded farewell to a fascist past not quite acknowledged, that is, seems to threaten deconstruction from more than one quarter. And Derrida's own failure to deal with (or even mention) that past of Blanchot's in a book on the author (*Parages*) is of a piece with his muting of the import of de Man's wartime writing.

All of this, of course, seems somewhat removed from the "theoretical" concerns discussed in *The Resistance to Theory*.[3] Perhaps the "theory" of literature espoused in de Man's title essay is best apprehended in psychoanalytic terms. Freud's split between ego and unconscious becomes for de Man a rift in the medieval *trivium* between grammar and logic, on the one hand, and rhetoric on the other. Figurality (rhetoric) is endlessly productive of blindness concerning the scope of its own perverse agency, and "theory" itself – like the unconscious – is never so confirmed as in the "resistance" it generates. "Theory," that is, is the theory of the resistance to theory, even as psychoanalysis is an ongoing meditation on the repression of its own most virulent discovery: repression itself. For the French Freudians, the intra-psychoanalytic repression of the theory of repression is classically that of American ego psychology. For de Man the analogous instance is the "regrammatization" of the rhetorical; his "ego psychologists" – intra-theoretical exemplars of the resistance to (the primacy of rhetorical indeterminacy in) theory – in this book are Michael Riffaterre and Hans Robert Jauss. A third long essay, on Benjamin's "The Task of the Translator," offers an exemplification of "theory" as de Man espouses it. On the whole these essays offer a particularly eloquent statement of a problematic that has been convincingly demonstrated, at considerable length, in the realm of psychoanalysis, particularly in the reading of Freud, but which seems to me so rapidly and arbitrarily illustrated by de Man in *The Resistance to Theory* as not to carry conviction.

I shall take two cases, each of which turn out to have a surprising relation to the wartime journalism. The essay (originally a lecture) on Benjamin pulls the theological anti-humanism of Benjamin's thought in the direction of Nietzsche and deconstruction and ends by rejecting that theological – or messianic – dimension entirely. It does so, moreover, through the conceit of discussing the errors Benjamin's French and English translators have made. At times the results are convincing, at others less so: *das Wehen des eigenen*, de Man claims, must be rendered as the "suffering ... of the original language," a prefiguration of the deconstruction of origins. But Harry Zohn's English rendering of "birth-pangs" is entirely appropriate since Benjamin is referring to the "mother-tongue" of the translator (not the original). Elsewhere de Man claims to improve on the rendering of Benjamin's Kabbalistically inspired image of translation as a reassembling of fragments of a vessel, and ends up with the arbitrary image of translation as a fragment of a fragment. The most surprising statement in the discussion of Benjamin, however, comes during the question period (at Cornell University) following de Man's lecture: "Benjamin would be closer to certain elements in

Nietzsche than he is to a messianic tradition which he spent his entire life holding at bay. The man who bears a strong responsibility in this unhappy misinterpretation is Scholem, who deliberately tried to make Benjamin say the opposite of what he said for ends of his own." This statement, and the truncated reading of "The Theologico-Political Fragment" on which it is based, is, in a different political context, every bit as outrageous as the omission of Proust's name from the essay on Jews and literature in 1941. Indeed, Harry Zohn's one undeniable error as a translator of the Benjamin essay is the omission of the word "messianic": the growth of languages *bis ans messianistische Ende ihrer Geschichte* is inexplicably rendered by Zohn "until the end of their time." Surely here was a slip-up worth de Man's attention. And yet he did not signal it to his readers because it confirmed his own misreading of the text. Much has been made of the fact that de Man's final lecture was a tribute to Benjamin, a Jew who died while fleeing the Nazis. Such would be a measure of the distance he had traveled since the sorry days of 1941. But the decision to strip a Nietzscheized (and de-Judaized) Benjamin of both his friendship for Scholem and his overwhelming investment in the messianic is very much of a piece with the earlier move to cleanse French literature of the "Jewish influence" of, say, Proust.

The most sustained reading of a literary text in the volume is de Man's treatment of Michael Riffaterre's analysis of the Victor Hugo poem (from *Les Rayons et les ombres*) "Ecrit sur la vitre d'une fenêtre flamande." The poem begins with an apostrophe to Flanders "où le Nord se réchauffe engourdi / Au soleil de Castille et s'accouple au Midi." The chimes or carillon of Flanders are evoked as a Spanish "danseuse" descending on the "toits léthargiques" of Flanders, symbolizing Time (*l'Heure*), pitilessly awakening the somnolent. By the poem's end, Mind (*Esprit*), all eyes and ears, is evoked following the dancer as she rises and descends on a stairway of invisible crystal. Now de Man's analysis insists on the apostrophe at the beginning of the poem ("J'aime le carillon ... O vieux pays"), but pressures the reader into accepting it as a prosopopeia, in the vague etymological sense of "giving face to two entities," Time and Mind. "By the end of the poem, it is possible to identify without fail the *je* and *tu* of line 1 as being time and mind." The bullying "without fail" is our clue that something is amiss, for the I and thou of the poem's beginning are the poet and Flanders and the slippage to mind and time is far from a given. To the extent that de Man assumes it, in fact, he trips over another line: the singularity of the poem, we read, lies in the fact that its "descriptions" can occur only because a "consciousness or a mind is figurally said to relate to another abstraction (time) as male relates to female in a copulating couple (line 5)." Line 5, however, turns out not to have anything to do with coupling. The verb *s'accoupler* appears in line 4, where it describes the relation not between mind and time, but between North (Flanders) and South (Castille). The "seduction scene" de Man reads into Hugo's lyric, before being between time and mind, is between Castille (the Spanish dancer) and Flanders. Now de Man's insistence on seduction is all the more striking in that Riffaterre's reading of the poem embeds the text in a thematic matrix concerning the hostile relation between time and mind: the relation of Time to men is thematically "one of executioner to victim." The reader of Hugo detects the tocsin or death-knell behind the carillon. But even the carillon, according to Riffaterre, evoked for the readers of the day such commonplaces as the "resistance of the Low-Countries to Spanish oppression." In brief, Riffaterre has implicitly written a scene of the harsh military occupation of Flanders, the cruellest of whose episodes was what one historian, A. de Meeus, has called the "blitzkrieg" of the Duke of Alba. De Man, on the other hand, dropping the Flemish and Spanish references entirely, has misread the apostrophe and the line on "coupling" and recast the poem as a "seduction scene" of his own invention (under the auspices of Prosopopeia) between female Time and male Mind. But to the extent that Hugo's Time and Mind are, as Riffaterre points out in passing, figures of Spanish occupant and Flemish victim, de Man has implicitly rewritten the poem as a scenario of Flemish collaboration with a foreign occupant, a rehearsal, as it were, forty years after the fact, of one of those Germano-Flemish cultural events celebrated by de Man in the pages of *Le Soir*.[4]

CHAPTER 10

The paranoid style in French prose
Lacan with Léon Bloy

For some time now I have had on my desk three brief passages which might serve as epigraphs for these pages, but which I am inclined to think of as pieces in an elaborate jigsaw puzzle or mosaic that remains to be assembled. The first is Drieu la Rochelle's epitomization of Céline: "Céline, c'est Léon Bloy moins Dieu."[1] The second is a rather pregnant allusion to Léon Bloy's *Le salut par les Juifs* in Lacan's *Seminar*: Freud as the prototypal Jew in Bloy's sense of the term.[2] The third is from the first volume of Foucault's history of sexuality. It concerns what he calls the "political honor of psychoanalysis," its "theoretical and practical opposition to fascism," which lay in reintroducing an archaic political dimension – of the law, of sovereignty, and of the symbolic order – into the newly emergent and tendentially totalitarian realm (or "analytic") of sexuality.[3] It is, then, the politics of a certain archaic strand in Lacan's prose and its affinities with the figure of the Sovereign – be he God or Father – in Bloy which form the horizon against which these remarks are offered. That the absence – or elimination – of such a strand in the case of psychoanalysis would modulate toward fascism (according to Foucault) and in that of Bloy toward Céline (according to Drieu) provides both an implicit confirmation of the homology herein constructed and an indication of the political perils it skirts.[4]

Let me begin with one of Bloy's *Histoires désobligeantes*. It is called "Propos digestifs," "Table Talk," and is at once a superb introduction to Bloy and to his affinities with Lacan.[5] The scene is a salon of the intellectual bourgeoisie, whose leading denizen is called the Psychologist, and whose habitués, after dinner, are debating just how to do away, once and for all, with the poor – *"la classe guenilleuse.''* Massacres, penal colonies, mass deportations are among the options bandied about as the group drives itself to a pitch of grotesque enthusiasm. The improvisatory theme, in brief, is Baudelairean: "Assommons les pauvres." Whereupon a bizarre and "precariously decked out" individual makes his appearance. He is called Apemantus the Cynic – after the "churlish philosopher" of *Timon of Athens* – and is plainly a surrogate for Bloy himself. "De quoi vivez-vous?" he is rather nastily asked by the bitchiest – *la plus acariâtre* – of the poetesses in the group. "D'aumônes, madame," – alms – he answers with the *sang-froid*, we are told, of a dead fish. The circumflex over the *o* in *aumônes* pierces his interlocutor like an arrow, and allows us already to grasp the complication Bloy brings to the scenario of *Le Spleen de Paris*. For if Baudelaire regularly pitted the dandy against the beggar, Bloy here gives us the beggar *as* dandy. Apemantus is regularly tolerated by the group, partly out of fear, partly out of respect for a kind of "barbarous eloquence" he would on occasion "unsheathe" and which succeeded in imposing its will on "the most retractile of the inattentive," the most "tautly strung of the sensitive." Unsheathed ... retractile ... the eloquence is essentially phallic, fundamentally removed from the grotesque "digestive" drivel of the Psychologist and his crowd. It allows him to speak his mind on all issues. He is requested to speak to the question at hand, and agrees, if he must, to tell a story, "une histoire aussi désobligeante que possible," but insists on prefacing his fable with a series of didactic observations: "mais auparavant, vous subirez, – sans y rien comprendre, j'aime à le croire –, quelques réflexions ou préliminaires conjectures dont j'ai besoin pour stimuler en moi le narrateur." I find it hard to read the contempt for the audience in those lines without simultaneously being reminded of a tone occasionally struck by Lacan in his seminars. Which is why I would suggest that the remainder of the tale, which consists of the didactic session held by Apemantus, be read as Bloy's fictive seminar.

Apemantus, after subscribing to the proposed massacre of the poor, moves gingerly toward the apparently unrelated theme that most interests him, the difficulty of vouching for one's own identity: "Pour parler d'une autre manière, où trouver un homme, non encore vérifié et catalogué comme idiot de naissance ou comme gâteux, qui osera dire qu'il n'a pas l'ombre d'un doute sur sa propre *identité?*" That reflection is, in fact, inspired by the parable of the Gerasene demoniac in Mark (5: 1–20), whose demons were cast out into a nearby herd of pigs. Here is Bloy's version: "Très ingénument, je déclare que, songeant parfois au récit de l'Evangile et à l'étonnante multitude de pourceaux qui fut nécessaire pour loger convenablement les impurs démons sortis d'un seul homme, il m'arrive de regarder autour de moi avec épouvante . . ." The discourse thus modulates toward rather spectacular insult (You are perhaps not merely pigs, but demons to boot), and Apemantus will be duly interrupted by an attendant paleographer: "Pardon, monsieur, il me semble que vous allez un peu loin." The imperturbable response: "Je suis donc dans mon chemin . . . car c'est justement très loin que je veux aller." But more interesting than the implied equivalence pig = demon is the threat posed to identity by the multiplicity of pigs, the notion that one may not simply be other, but many (component others).

At this point the seminar drifts toward literature, reduced for the needs of the demonstration, to its supreme gimmick (*son truc suprême*). Which is what?: "Quelle est, si j'ose m'exprimer ainsi, la ficelle qui casse tout, l'arcane certain, le *Sésame* de Polichinelle qui ouvre les cavernes de l'émotion pathétique et qui fait infailliblement et divinement palpiter les foules?" Answer: "Mon Dieu! c'est très bête ce que je vais vous dire. Ce fameux secret, c'est tout bonnement l'*incertitude sur l'identité des personnes.*" Such is the gimmick which has had them crying ever since Sophocles: someone turns out to be not at all the person one supposed, but a lost mother, son, or – why not? – uncle. Now Apemantus claims that the trick works because it is in intuitive contact with a far more fundamental mystery, which is the essential relation between poverty and mistaken identity: "Cette mécanique émotionnelle est inconcevable sans le Pauvre." The Pauper – poverty's essential relation to displaced identity – as the hidden enabling condition of Literature itself. As opposed to the Pauper, the Bourgeois (*le riche*) is a virtual ideologue of identity: at home everywhere, he knocks your eyes out: "il crève l'oeil, il sue son identité par tous ses pores, du moins en littérature." Literature is where the bourgeois exudes his identity through every pore.

Whereupon Apemantus circles back to the original project of massacring the poor. For in order to implement such a project, one would first have to determine who exactly *is* a Pauper. And once one views things – as Bloy and his narrator do – from the perspective of the poor, poverty itself wreaks such havoc on any criterion of verification or identification that the proposed extermination turns into a practical impossibility. For "nul ne sait son propre *nom*, nul ne connaît sa propre face, parce que nul ne sait de quel personnage mystérieux – et peut-être mangé des vers, – il tient *essentiellement* la place."

That last bit of sophistry provokes the impatience of Apemantus' audience as much, perhaps, as it does the reader's. The hostess calls him back to order: "Vous vous fichez de nous, Apemantus, intervint alors Mme du Fondement. Vous nous aviez promis une histoire." Agreed, comes the response. Here it is: A rich man had two sons, of whom the younger asked for all that was coming to him. The father obliged him, the son took off, and squandered all his wealth in a life of dissipation . . . This time the affront proves too much. "Ça!" shoots back one of the assembled women, her rage rising: "mais c'est la parabole de l'Enfant prodigue qu'il nous débite, ce monsieur. Il va nous apprendre que son héros fut réduit à garder les porcs, en mourant de faim et qu'un beau jour, las du métier, il revint à la maison de son père, qui se sentit tout ému, le voyant arriver de loin." "Hélàs, non, madame," Apemantus corrects her in a solemn voice, "ce furent les cochons qui arrivèrent." At which point "Quelqu'un" – with a capital Q – who doesn't smell good enters the room and Bloy's story comes to an end.

The pigs who improbably force their way back in at the end of the story may be read as a return of those who came to lodge the multiple demons rushing out of the demoniac toward the beginning. That multiplicity, it will be recalled, was already thematized as subversive of human identity: so many out of one . . . But more fundamentally still this crossing – or condensation – of one parable with another plays havoc with the identity of the animals themselves. For one cannot tell whether these pigs are rushing their way *out* (of the demoniac down to the lake) or *in* (to the paternal home). They are inherently at odds with themselves. The three words used for pig in Bloy's tale are *pourceaux, cochons,* and *porcs.* But that last signifier is already sounded elsewhere in the story, when Literature is characterized as the locus in which the bourgeois – *le riche* – exudes identity through his every pore (*par tous ses pores*). The attack is thus lodged at some metaphorical bodily surface whose function is to exude (or contain) bourgeois identity. Let us say: the ego. And its tactic is to invest that surface with a particularly slippery – or slimy – signifier: PORC, specifically those furious *porcs* of which it cannot be determined whether they are on their way out or on their way back in, that is: whether they are inside or out. Let us say: "alien internal entities," which was Freud's characterization of the unconscious drive. Finally, should one want to derive a literary lesson from Apemantus' seminar it would evolve from the opposition between Literature (with its affinity for bourgeois identity) and that crossing of parables, which renders the *porcs* internally discordant and suspends the possibility of interpreting the parables in which they appear.[6] On the one hand, an integral form whole unto itself (Literature); on the other, a crossing – or condensation – of parables which is a crossing out of their meaning . . .

Thus, then, Léon Bloy, reserving for the end of his tale, the end of Apemantus' seminar, a "shock" of decidedly Baudelairean tenor: the dandy strikes his degraded interlocutor with a devastating blow – virtuoso in its wrongness – from which he (or she) will be hard put to recover.[7] But it is the afterlife of Bloy's writing that interests me. Consider that the blow we find Bloy in the seminar inflicting on his audience – the crossing or condensation of signifiers – is what Freud would call a primary process. To situate that impoverishment of discourse at the limit (or skin, the pores) defining human identity, and to castigate that identity as essentially bourgeois (a property of the rich) strikes me as a significant anticipation of much that was to be developed in Lacan's seminars. For the ego, illusory guarantor of human identity, is a metaphor of the organism, a fantasied "sack of skin," in Freud's terms. And within the *Ecrits,* its reprehensible defence is regularly associated with the increasingly Americanized middle-class establishment of psychoanalysis, and more specifically with the will to annex psychoanalysis to the field of general psychology. The Psychologist, we recall, was the prime ideologue of the gathering addressed by Apemantus in Bloy's tale. "Nul ne sait de quel personnage mystérieux – et peut-être mangé des vers, – il tient *essentiellement* la place." So ran Bloy's version of the communion of Saints. And what if it were Bloy, in the economy of French intellectual history, whose place Lacan, who spoke of the psychoanalyst as saint, was essentially fulfilling?[8]

By condensing two parables, that of the demoniac and that of the prodigal son, Bloy ultimately forestalls the possibility of assigning a meaning to either. That suspension of interpretation of the text of the New Testament, the postponing of its fulfillment, is, in fact, the focus of the work that Bloy regarded as his most significant achievement, *Le Salut par les Juifs*. For the fascination exercised by the Jew there is a function of his status as an obstacle to the advent of the figural fulfillment of the Old Testament in the meaning of the New. It is the Jew who impedes the delivery of the letter of the *préfigurant* to its destination in the *préfiguré*. Bloy's theology, that is, like Lacan's psychoanalysis, is one of letters *en souffrance*, and it is for that reason, I have argued elsewhere, that Bloy's Jew, in his unassimilable abjection, comes close to figuring something in the order of what Lacan would later call the "unconscious."[9] Against the illusions of Progress, and in thwarted anticipation of Apocalyptic fulfillment, time for Bloy becomes that of what he calls "le renouveau sempiternel des itératives préfigurations de la Catastrophe" – the eternal return, that is, of the signifier of a Reality that fails to take place.[10] Indeed, between the total Failure figurable as Apocalypse and the repetitive failure of that Failure to materialize, a contamination is effected. Once again, the convergence can be sensed: a theology of tragically irreducible prefiguration might easily draw on rhetorical resources related to those exploited by a psychoanalysis of the irreducible priority of the signifier. As we shall see ...

That theology, in "Propos digestifs," was contemptuously conveyed, it will be recalled, to a group of diners gathered about someone called the Psychologist. Now the Psychologist was the abusive term used by Bloy for the most frequent target of his polemic, the edifying novelist, Paul Bourget. His polemical violence is worth savoring: "Ses *analyses* boréales amalgamées de Renan, de Stendhal et de quelques pions germaniques, où l'absence infinie de style et de caractère est symétrique au double néant du sentiment et de la pensée, furent sucées avec dévotion par tout un public de mondaines, ravies qu'un auteur qui leur ressemblait condescendît, en leur présence, de ses pâles doigts en glucose, à traire les vaches arides qu'elles gardent avec tant de soin dans les ravissantes prairies de leurs coeurs."[11] Those lines are from an article which relates how Bourget became "le Psychologue," but which bears as its title a somewhat different archetype of abuse. It is called "L'Eunuque." The theology of irreducible prefiguration is polemically directed against the eunuchs of psychology, that propensity to spiritual emasculation which the very virile Bloy would rail against to no end. Add to the combination the fact that such emasculation was linked to a pronounced Anglomania – for resistance to the English was a constant in Bloy: "un excrément anglais à toutes les intersections de l'infini" – and we have in encapsulated form the principal addressee and target of Bloy's polemic: an Anglicized, psychologized, emasculated Christendom.[12] From Lacan's point of view, of course, those three epithets might well be used to characterize the psychoanalytic community – Anglo-Americanized, psychologized, emasculated – on which he of necessity first unloaded his theory of the unconscious. It was an unconscious whose discourse was theorized as fundamentally determined by the person or persons to whom it was being addressed.

And yet the term "eunuch," the ultimate abuse, is subject to odd pressures in Bloy's writing. For the theologian of irreducible prefiguration, for all the virility of his stance, nonetheless was giving prophetic voice to a divine discourse strangely powerless to achieve fulfillment. In the absence of Apocalypse, Bloy's surrogate, the hero of the autobiographical novel, *Le Désespéré*, convinced himself: "qu'on avait affaire à un Seigneur Dieu volontairement eunuque, infécond par décret ..." (p. 58).[13] He has the intuition of a kind of divine impotence, "*provisoirement* concertée entre la Miséricorde et la Justice ..." (p. 59). Not the styleless Bourget, but Christ here is the "eunuch," unable to right the balance between the prefigurative and the prefigured, and the first consequence is stylistic: "Situation inouïe, invocatrice d'un patois abject. La *Raison* Ternaire suspend ses paiements depuis un tas de siècles et c'est à la Patience humaine qu'il convient de l'assister de son propre fonds" (p. 59). Human patience – or patient-hood – consists in taking on the burden of a transcendental eunuchdom, suffering with the letter *en souffrance* of a *préfigurant* cut off from its *préfiguré*. It is for that reason, I would suggest, that the most striking evocation of the Church, to whom Bloy's hero Caïn willfully submits, is as "the Eunuchs of the Harem of the Word (*les Eunuques du Sérail de la Parole*)" (p. 61). Here again we find a link between eunuchdom and language. But language here – specifically the Logos – is in the position of the Sultan. What the Eunuchs of the Church would presumably do is allow for Christians to be sexually traversed by the Logos, to know passively that quintessentially impotent language of the *préfigurant* doomed to repetition. Modulate to Lacan and we find a precise homology between the eunuchdom within which Bloy would have humanity assume its place and the "castration" Lacan would have his patients "assume." It may be noted that the phrase "Eunuques du Sérail de la Parole" was not untinged by a sense of the Church's mediocrity. For which reason, the phrase, I believe, finds its perfect rendering in the polemical idiom of the 1970s: "les Eunuques du Sérail de la Parole" or "les docteurs de la Castration."[14]

Let us summarize our results thus far: on the one hand, a theology of the unredeemed and "iterative" *préfigurant*, centred on the metaphor of eunuchdom, and flamboyantly directed at a Christendom deemed to be psychologized, Anglicized, and emasculated into utter opprobrium; on the other, a psychoanalysis of the unredeemed and repetitive *signifiant*, centered on the metaphor of castration, and flamboyantly directed at an analytical community deemed to be psychologized, Anglo-Americanized, and emasculated into utter triviality. (As for the apocalypse that fails to materialize, I would propose the mythical role attributed by Lacan to Freud's quip, upon entering New York harbor, that the poor enthusiasts in his greeting party didn't realize he was bringing them the plague.)[15] We are still a considerable distance from the paranoid tradition of my title. But of course, in psychoanalysis, as Freud and Lacan both said, one is never very far from paranoia. Let us consider the great novel, *Le Désespéré*, in that light. It is the story of the elaborator of the theology I have just sketched out. Here, in summary, is the not very complicated plot. Caïn, the starving protagonist, upon his father's death, accuses himself of having contributed to it through his unrelenting refusal to compromise, and writes a humiliating letter to none other than the Psychologist (a surrogate for Bourget) to request a loan that might allow him to bury his father. Bourget shunts Bloy off to another associate and is happy to be rid of his former and extremely importunate friend. Psychology, shall we say, in a more recent idiom, will never help you negotiate La-Mort-du-Père ... Whereupon Caïn (Bloy) goes off to a monastery and works on his theology of history, a "new science," which "genius alone could save from ridicule" (p. 131).[16] He realizes that the monastic vocation is not his, however, since he continues to long for the prostitute, Véronique, he has saved, converted, and with whom he had been living in desperate chastity in recent years. He writes her that if she doesn't save him, he will be her doom. He returns to find that she has acquitted herself admirably in this regard in a manner to which I shall return. Thereafter she will wax alternately mystic and psychotic, and will eventually be interned. But the novel's climax is the dinner party which proves Caïn's downfall. The circumstance is as follows: the protagonist, whose excesses had resulted in his being effectively blackballed from the world of journalism, nevertheless remained so admired for the brilliance of his style that an effort was made to hire him as leading journalist of an important paper. He is given *carte blanche* by editor-in-chief Properce Beauvivier and invited to read his first article at a dinner party.

Concerning that gathering, the following observations:

1. Properce Beauvivier is a surrogate for Catulle Mendès, who himself is generally regarded as the bad-smelling "Quelqu'un" (cápital Q) who intrudes on the dinner – just when the pigs return home – at the end of the tale with which we began, "Propos digestifs."[17] The host at this dinner is the untimely intruder at the other; he happens to be a Jew.

2. Caïn is horrified to find the guests at the dinner to be all the mediocrities castigated in passing in the article he has been

asked to read. He asks for (and is given) a separate table. The term used by Bloy to describe such mediocrities (including the Bourget-surrogate) is *porchers* – swineherds.[18] Whereas in the dinner of "Propos digestifs," Bloy was able to unleash his *porcs* on the powers that be as in an assault from the unconscious, here his alter ego finds himself surrounded (or besieged) by their tenders.

3. The principal subject of conversation at the dinner – although no names are named – is the notorious duel between Edouard Drumont, author of *La France juive*, and Arthur Meyer, his Jewish challenger. Drumont had been wounded, but in Bloy's version, he is killed. Caïn, the guest of honour, is asked to comment. He senses a trap: "Ils veulent me faire bramer" (p. 261). He decides to dead-pan it, commenting in a tone, he says, fit for ordering tripe in a restaurant. What would *he* have done in Drumont's place? Strike down Meyer with the nearest stick handy – *sans phrase et sans colère* (p. 262). Why? Because a duel is "an exploit befitting a gentleman, and *we* are boors." Years later, Bloy would find himself fired from the journal *Gil Blas* precisely for having acted on the opinion voiced at this dinner, and refusing to accept a challenge to duel.[19] The episode is elaborately evoked in his book, *Léon Bloy devant les cochons*.[20] Pigs again ... That title, in fact, epitomizes the persecutory scenario in Bloy's work. But it will be sensed just how far removed we are from the insidious *porcs* investing the surface of bourgeois identity at the dinner in "Propos digestifs." Simultaneously within and without, they were precisely that *before* which one could not be. He who would insinuate his herd into the previous dinner here finds himself guest of honour in the House of the Pig. But it is also the house of Beauvivier-Mendès, the house of the Jew.

4. Caïn reads his article, in which all are duly castigated, but with such scatological brilliance and vigour that they are transfixed. Led by their host, they emerge from their stupor to applaud – thunderously. Whereupon there follows Caïn's downfall. His host, at a loss for words, congratulates him: "Mais ... je ne vous connaissais pas cette force tragique, qui m'étonne encore plus, je vous assure, que votre talent d'écrivain ... C'est à se demander pourquoi vous n'êtes pas au théâtre. Vous en deviendriez le

maître et le Dieu ..." (p. 267). Caïn-Bloy stuns all assembled by reacting to these words of praise as though they were a slap in the face. They ask him to explain, which he does:

> La vocation du théâtre est, à mes yeux, la plus basse des misères de ce monde abject et la sodomie passive est, je crois, un peu moins infâme. Le bardache, même vénal, est du moins, forcé de restreindre, chaque fois, son stupre à la cohabitation d'un seul et peut garder encore, – au fond de son ignominie effroyable, – la liberté d'un certain choix. Le comédien s'abandonne, *sans choix*, à la multitude, et son industrie n'est pas moins ignoble, puisque c'est son *corps* qui est l'instrument du plaisir donné par son art. L'opprobre de la scène est, pour la femme, infiniment moindre, puisqu'il est, pour elle, en harmonie avec le mystère de la Prostitution, qui ne courbe la misérable que dans le sens de sa nature et l'avilit sans pouvoir la défigurer. (p. 267)

The passage astounds Caïn's hosts and will lead in short order to his definitive exclusion from their company. But its affinities with paranoia go further yet. Bloy here all but invents the scenario of his own unmanning. His conclusion is virtually Schreber's: they want to use my body like a strumpet's.[21] Similarly, to be on stage is to find one's body divided among and invaded by a multitude. It is the very multitude of pigs needed to exorcise the Gerasene demoniac in Apemantus' seminar returning here as the nightmare of a "corps morcelé."

What is most striking in the episode, however, is the final phrase about a prostitute, however debased, not being able to be disfigured, *défigurée*. For we are now in a position to return to the means used by Véronique, the former prostitute with whom Caïn-Bloy was living, to save her saviour from the temptations of the flesh. In a rather grueling episode, she stunts his desire, by first selling her hair, and then using the money to pay for her own disfiguration (*défiguration*). She hires out a villain (who is modeled on none other than the Arthur Meyer who had just fought Drumont in a duel) to remove all her teeth. As Caïn's friend informs him: "Tu as écrit une lettre insensée à Véronique et la pauvre fille s'est *défigurée* pour te dégoûter d'elle" (p. 160). The madness, that is, has been joint, dual: Caïn, through his letter, has extinguished his desire, in effect unmanned himself, in the materiality of Véronique's flesh; his unmanning is hideously visible in the gaping toothless mouth of her disfigured face. The episode is a crucial step on the path to the undoing of the protagonist. The other is the disastrous dinner culminating in Caïn's rage at the suggestion that he take to the stage, a sequence, we have seen, that contains a bizarre reference to the impossibility of "disfiguring" a prostitute ...

Consider, then, that the entirety of *Le Désespéré* might be interpreted in terms of a conflict between "prefiguration" and "disfiguration." On the one hand, the articulation of a theology of irreducible prefiguration: the world as the eternal return of those "iterative prefigurations of a catastrophe" whose impotence to materialize itself is best metaphorized as "eunuchdom." On the other, the collapse of that theology in the catastrophic materiality of a disfigured face and the (self-)destructive path down which it takes Bloy's protagonist. That "disfiguration," which effects the "unmanning" of Caïn, might be read, I would suggest, as a disengagement from the figural *per se*. The specific impotence of the (pre-)figural, the metaphorics of eunuchdom, has returned in reality as the actual unmanning of the paranoid protagonist.

Enter Jacques Lacan with his discovery in Freud of a defence mechanism specific to psychosis: as opposed to repression (*Verdrängung*), foreclosure (*Verwerfung, forclusion*). In "The Wolf Man," for example: "the third current, the most archaic and deepest one, which had purely and simply repudiated (*verworfen*) castration and in which it was not yet a question of its reality, was still capable of being reactivated. I have related in a different paper a hallucination that this patient had had at the age of five ..."[22] The specific traits of *Verwerfung* – in its opposition to repression – may be observed in that brief passage. The signifiers (of castration) are not integrated into the subject's unconscious. They constitute, in fact, what Lacan calls a gaping hole in the signifier (*un trou dans le signifiant*).[23] And they return not from "within," but at the heart of reality, characteristically in the form of hallucinations.[24] Consider now the relation between that "trou dans le signifiant" and the gaping, toothless mouth thematized as the disfiguration of Véronique. That disfiguration is a breach in the existence of our theologian of the irreducible *préfigurant*. It separates him from the virility he draws from his access to the meta-phorical "eunuchdom" whose impotence is the regulating prin-ciple of the *préfigurant per se*. But in casting such "eunuchdom" out, it effects, in its hallucinatory presence, (1) a stunting of his desire, his virtual unmanning: the threatening gap in the other is construable as the absence of his phallus; and (2) the paranoid episode of the dinner during which he imagines quite extrava-gantly that the suggestion that he appear on stage is tantamount to an emasculating disfiguration.[25]

Having earlier elaborated all that joined Lacan's psychoana-lysis of the *signifiant* and Bloy's theology of the *préfigurant*, we can now add that the relation between repression and foreclosure in Lacan finds a homology in that between prefiguration and disfiguration in Bloy. Somewhere in between the two, late in *Le Désespéré*, Véronique lapses into madness and is interned at Sainte-Anne, the very clinic at which Lacan would begin his career with an important thesis on paranoia. "L'Eglise est écrouée dans un hôpital de folles," Caïn intones mystically, in *Le Désespéré*, in apparent anticipation of that internment: the Church is bolted into a hospital for madwomen (p. 223). The above analysis has been offered in the suspicion that Lacanian psychoanalysis in crucial respects may be understood historically as a protracted effort to effect its liberation.

Somewhere in the first volume of his *Seminar*, Lacan proposes a parable of the emergence – or re-emergence – of human speech that is at once so pregnant with the future evolution of his thought and so suggestive of the antecedents suggested in this essay, as to function as something of a summary of my argument. The circumstance evoked is that of Ulysses' companions trans-formed – for reason of their "insidious penchants" – into swine.[26] The question raised is that of the linguistic status of the grunts they emit to the extra-porcine world. Lacan deciphers: "Nous re-grettons Ulysse, nous regrettons qu'il ne soit pas parmi nous, nous regrettons son enseignement, ce qu'il était pour nous à travers l'existence."[27] The message is ambivalent, since Ulysses, we are told, had been a rather "irritating" (*gênant*) guide, but the point of the fable, Lacan insists, is that the grunts take on linguistic reality only through the presence of someone posing the question of their meaning. On the one hand, then, a kind of primordial de-centering of discourse, constituted (from the "silken rustling" of the pigs) by its transit through an expectant other. On the other, something of a primal scene (or seminar) of the emergence of human speech: an irritating teacher casts his followers in the role of the swine that have excluded him – *Jacques Lacan*, if you will, *devant les cochons*.

It would be tempting to derive the whole persecutory history of Lacanian psychoanalysis – the "split" of 1953, the "excommu-nication" of 1964 – from that latter scenario.[28] It would take us right down to the dissolution of the Ecole Freudienne in 1980, interpreted as an acting out of Lacan's Circean fantasy: leaving his disciples with a "nostalgia" for Lacan substantially no dif-ferent from the one for Ulysses indulged by the Homeric swine ...[29] But the references in the remainder of that session of the *Seminar* to "transference" – the reviviscence, in a "temporal parenthesis," of a "former discourse" in a "present" one – incline one rather to read the fable as a reminiscence of Bloy. "Qu'il suffise d'un qui s'en aille pour que tous soient libres, c'est dans mon noeud borroméen, vrai de chacun, il faut que ce soit moi dans mon Ecole ..."[30] Thus Lacan, topologizing his depar-ture. And Bloy, only half ironically, to his publisher at the begin-ning of *Belluaires et porchers*: "Je suis celui qu'il faut lâcher."[31] The *Seminar* continues with a genealogy of the term transference (*Übertragung*) in Freud. Its initial sense turned on *Tagesreste*, daytime residues, "errant forms" shorn of their sense and free to be invested with lost meanings.[32] And what if the "psychoana-lysis" on which Lacan alighted were itself a "daytime residue" of the "days" of surrealism, an "errant form" free to be secretly in-vested with lost cultural signification? In the penultimate volume of his *Seminar* (*Encore*), Lacan's early fascination with extrava-gantly self-punitive female paranoiacs resurfaced as an interest in the great female mystics of Christianity. As though his writings were stretched taut between the two possibilities incarnated by the Véronique of Bloy's *Le Désespéré*. It was in that context that Lacan proffered a thought too chancy, perhaps, for inclusion in the text proper, too pressing to be consigned to a footnote, and which these reflections have attempted to endow with sufficient substance to justify its quotation in this context as a conclusion: "Ces jaculations mystiques, ce n'est ni du bavardage, ni du verbiage, c'est en somme ce qu'on peut lire de mieux – tout à fait en bas de page, note – *Y ajouter les Ecrits de Jacques Lacan*, parce que c'est du même ordre."[33]

CHAPTER II

The Holocaust comedies of "Emile Ajar"

Throughout the 1970s, a period during which American academics seemed poised to absorb from France ever more "radical" doses of what was called literary "theory," the readership of France itself was unwittingly embarked on an unprecedented literary experiment, of remarkable speculative import, under the tutelage of a French man of letters so apparently conventional as to identify his years of service as French consul general in Hollywood as a high point of his career.[1] For these were the years during which Romain Gary published a series of three tonally innovative novels under the pseudonym "Emile Ajar": *Gros-Câlin* (1974), *La Vie devant soi* (1975), and *L'Angoisse du roi Salomon* (1979). The critical success of the books was such that attempts were made, beyond what all took to be a fabricated biography on the book jacket of *Gros-Câlin* (a *pied noir* physician and sometime abortionist, living in Latin America, in flight from French authorities), to identify the actual author of books that were emerging as *the* literary achievements of France in the 1970s. Press speculation concerned only the highest echelon of the French literary pantheon: Raymond Queneau and Louis Aragon.[2] Ajar's publisher, Mercure de France, as much in the dark as everyone else, prevailed on its author, through an intermediary, to grant an interview to the press. Gary requested his "nephew," one Paul Pavlowitch, to play the role of Ajar in an interview with a journalist from *Le Monde*, in an apartment in Copenhagen, and to do so on the condition that his "actual" identity not be divulged.[3] Pavlowitch, however, revealed enough of his own life for an old acquaintance to be able to identify him as Ajar. When that (astute, but erroneous) attribution surfaced in the French press, shortly after "Ajar" himself, in what seemed to many a parody of Sartre's rejection of the Nobel Prize, refused the Prix Goncourt for *La Vie devant soi*, Gary's sublime reaction was to write *Pseudo*, the unrelenting memoirs of Pavlowitch, *alias* Ajar, now revealed to be a psychotic, writing for reasons of therapy, and paranoiacally obsessed with his uncle, referred to only as Tonton Macoute, and the nefarious designs that relative seemed to have on "Ajar" 's emerging career.

With *Pseudo*, the Ajar enigma appeared to be solved. What France seemed to be witnessing was a twentieth-century replay of Diderot's *Neveu de Rameau*: a wildly talented and unstable nephew venting his rage against an all too established uncle. *Romain's Nephew*, as one critic called it, seemed additionally to infuse the Diderot scenario with a tone oddly akin to the paranoid Céline's: it was not for nothing, apparently, that "Ajar-Pavlowitch" wrote from Denmark.[4] The paradox, of course, lay in the fact that what was received as the nephew's book about the uncle was in fact the uncle's unrelievedly self-denigrating book about the nephew. There were, of course, ample reasons not to suspect that Gary was Ajar: not only did Gary continue to write and publish at his usual pace during the Ajar years, but he even managed to publish a novel, *Les Têtes de Stéphanie* (1974), under a *different* pseudonym, which was soon revealed to be such. Plainly, criteria of rate of productivity alone seemed to militate against any attribution of the Ajar books to Gary – even as that motif came to be inscribed as a principal obsession of what all failed to see was Gary's most daring creation: the heteronymous couple, Ajar-Pavlowitch.

Finally, the entire fabrication was revealed as such in a manuscript left behind by Gary, at the time of his suicide in 1980, *Vie et mort d'Emile Ajar*.[5] In that work, Gary revealed his motivation as a desire to escape from his going image as a successful professional. Given the laziness of prevailing habits of reading, only a mystification such as the one he put together would allow his recent books, allegedly by Ajar, to be read with the sense of excitement (or novelty) without which he would not have written them. And yet all of Ajar, he claimed, was already present in one of his first novels, *Tulipe*.[6] Pity the author for having to make do with so sclerotic a reading public. And allow him, now that the demonstration had been completed, now that the whole Ajar "phantasm" had unfortunately nested in another subject ("nephew" Paul), to exit as diplomatically as possible from the premises. In the last published (posthumous) words of the author: "Je me suis bien amusé. Au revoir et merci."[7]

Gary's claim that all of Ajar is already in Gary, however, makes short shrift of a tonal rift between the two that can be ignored only at the expense of the piquancy of the entire project. Consider two instances. During the Ajar years, Gary published a strikingly titled novel about the onset of sexual impotence in an aging French businessman. That title, *Au-delà de cette limite votre ticket n'est plus valable* (1975), is a witty recall of the ominous signs announcing one is leaving the Parisian *métro* system, and that one's ticket will no longer be honored: such, metaphorically, would be the plight of the sixty-year-old protagonist, Rainier, in Gary's novel. Compare that to the following observation by Cousin, the sympathetically portrayed lost soul of an incipiently psychotic narrator, toward the end of the first Ajar novel, *Gros-Câlin*: "A la sortie du métro, le ticket ne me jeta pas et me garda la main avec sympathie, il savait que je passais par des moments difficiles."[8] A certain invalidity upon leaving the *métro* is the stuff of both images, but the expertly chosen metaphor in Gary has become an unthinkable scramble, a dream image, in which a nightmarish loss of agency is experienced as the premise of an episode that can only be construed as comforting. Ajar here appears to have subjected Gary to all the poetic potential of what Freud called the "primary process." Or take the following line from Gary's *récit*, *La nuit sera calme*: "Les types des chaînes de télévision américaines se marraient comme des baleines."[9] We are invited to savor the grotesqueness of the convulsed and blubbery producers – sympathetically. Toward the end of the final Ajar novel, *L'Angoisse du roi Salomon*, we read: "Là on s'est vraiment marrés comme des baleines qu'on extermine."[10] Here the appended phrase adds to the sympathetically grotesque image the twin motifs of human cruelty (extermination) and a measure of delusion hard to fathom: laughing just *that* hard at one's own destruction. The Ajar version, that is, in a burst of laughter, manages to shatter the very value the Gary image seemed to be advancing.

It is as though Gary and Ajar during the 1970s were two distinct literary personalities: one the mature man of letters, obsessed
with the waning of his own energies, finding no more appropriate
setting for the beginning of one of his better novels of the period
than Venice in the process of going under; the other, at once
more desperate and funnier, the first and most distinguished literary harvest of the libertarian (and anti-psychiatric) excesses of
May 1968.[11] Whence the interest, in the literary-"theoretical"
context evoked above, of the longest passage of his work quoted
by Gary in *Vie et mort d'Emile Ajar*. It is a page Gary published in
1971 about a ninety-six-year-old Spaniard of Toledo, whose speci-
alty, in the shadow of the Alcazar, is sculpting statuettes of Don
Quixote for the tourist trade, and who has the quixotic habit of
seeing a fortune teller every day for news about his future. Gary
quotes it as a blunder of his, since he unwittingly incorporated
that very episode, with minor changes, in Ajar's *L'Angoisse du roi
Salomon*: "C'est exactement le chapitre XV, où monsieur Salomon
va consulter une voyante!"[12] Now the reference to Don Quixote
is eloquent, for these were the very years in which Borges' celebrated fable on the speculative interest of erroneous attribution,
"Pierre Menard, Author of *Don Quixote*," was settling in as a *locus
classicus* of literary "theory." Borges invites us to imagine how different our interpretation of the Spanish novel would be if we
could think of it as the achievement of a man of a very different
generation: the meaning of a brief paragraph is variously analyzed by the narrator according to its assumed authorship (by
Cervantes or by the Nîmes Symbolist Menard).[13] But the entire
Ajar experiment executed Borges' quixotic wager on a far grander
scale. Readers were forced to assess the interpretative consequences of reading three major novels and a pseudo-memoir by
Gary as though they had been written by an entirely different
author – and then, after Gary's death, to reverse themselves. It is
one thing, that is, to read of the mix of revulsion and tenderness
experienced by the young narrator of *L'Angoisse du roi Salomon*
upon sleeping with a sixty-five-year-old female has-been and to
interpret those sentiments in terms of the narrator's status as surrogate for the novel's young author. It is another to be forced into
the realization that the actual author, Gary, not only was busy

writing about the travails of becoming a has-been, but was the exact age of the woman in his book at the time of its writing.

Now nowhere is the shift in readerly perspective resultant from the attribution of Ajar's works to Gary more telling than with regard to the persistent reference to Jewish tragedy throughout the pseudonymous works. And it is to a reading of those works (and specifically to their treatment of Jewish suffering during the Occupation), within the space of the reversal effected by their attribution to Gary, that these pages are devoted.

But first a word on the end, then the beginning of the Ajar experiment. "Je me suis bien amusé. Au revoir et merci," as we have seen, is Gary's own final line on the project. The appearance of consummate urbanity – *au revoir*, indeed! – is belied by the suicide apparently prerequisite to a revelation designed to be posthumous. Moreover, the very terms of the project's end seem menacing: "Je m'étais *dépossédé*. Il y avait à présent quelqu'un d'autre [Pavlowitch] qui vivait le phantasme à ma place ... le rêve était à mes dépens ..."[14] With the discovery that (one's own) fantasy is crucially the province of an other, that one's dreams are perhaps essentially constituted at the expense of ego or self, the resolutely anti-Freudian Gary appears, through "Ajar," to be edging undogmatically toward particularly unsettling insights. The name Lacan is perhaps by now too associated with scholastic recastings of his thought to capture the sinister freshness of the discovery Gary, on the eve of his suicide, seems close to backing into here, and yet, we shall attempt to demonstrate, one is hard put to adduce a better one.

Romain Gary, we have said, invented "Emile Ajar," ultimately, in his words, at his own expense. But that formulation, or statement of origin, overlooks a consideration that most readers of Ajar in the 1970s no doubt had already forgotten: namely, that "Romain Gary" itself was a *nom de plume*. Before being a pen name, however, it was a *nom de guerre*, the name assumed by our (future) author upon joining the Free French as an aviator in 1940, and one later officialized in 1951. Romain Gary, by the time the Ajar books began appearing, was a well-known, even notorious figure. A member of the Resistance decorated by de Gaulle; the author of the book (*Education européenne*) Sartre had described as perhaps the best novel of the Resistance; a winner of the Prix Goncourt in 1956 (*Les Racines du ciel*); a diplomat both at the United Nations and in California; the husband of Jean Seberg; the figure of the successful professional novelist ... There was, of course, a downside to almost all these aspects: loyalty to de Gaulle seemed by the late 1960s to be a mark of political "incorrectness"; a lingering affection for his old aviator's jacket aroused suspicions of "fascist" leanings; the Jean Seberg affair, the pro-American tendency, seemed to cast him in the role of a sub-Arthur Miller to Jean Seberg's Marilyn ... Add to that his authorship, in 1965, of *Pour Sganarelle*, a somewhat heavy-handed essay attacking both Sartre and the *nouveau roman*, and the figure of the consummate "reactionary," to resort to the idiom of the day, seems complete.

The forging of Romain Gary's identity is, in fact, the subject of one of the author's most striking books, *La Promesse de l'aube* (1960). It is something of an autobiography of the author in the form of a recounting of the dreams of his unmarried mother, Nina Kaccw, a Russian Jew, first in Vilnius, then in Warsaw, for the future of her son. A worshiper of French values, she conceived in Lithuania the extravagant dream that her son, Romain, would some day be a great French diplomat and writer. And the book is Gary's record of his fidelity to that delirious project: "Ma mère me parlait de la France comme d'autres mères parlent de Blanche-Neige et du Chat-Botté et, malgré tous mes efforts, je n'ai jamais pu me débarrasser entièrement de cette image féerique d'une France de héros et de vertus exemplaires. Je suis probablement un des rares hommes au monde restés fidèles à un conte de nourrices." We observe Romain literally "becoming" the laughter of those Polish acquaintances jeering at Nina's Francophilic projects for him; making his way, with his impoverished mother, to Nice; observing her physical decline; reacting to de Gaulle's fabled call to resistance of 18 June, 1940, as though it were ventriloquized by his mother; and finally returning, something of a military hero and already an author, to Nice at war's end. As the War proceeds, something of a fusion takes place between mother and son: "Je crois vraiment que c'était la voix de ma mère qui s'était emparée de la mienne, parce que, au fur et à mesure que je parlais, je fus moi-méme éberlué par le nombre étonnant de clichés qui sortaient de moi ..."[16] Then: "en vérité, ce n'était pas moi qui errais ainsi d'avion en avion, mais une vieille dame résolue, vêtue de gris, la canne à la main et une Gauloise aux lèvres, qui était décidée à passer en Angleterre pour continuer le combat ..."[17] The Gauloise in the second example, the clichés in the first are useful illustrations of just how effective Gary is in the difficult business of eschewing sentimentality.

The tempo of the book, in its last third, is dictated by the author's realization that if he is to fulfill his apparent destiny, to be Nina's "happy end," his life must be a race against the clock.[18] For she has already begun falling prey to hypoglycemic comas, a harbinger of imminent death. The rush is thus on to turn her, through his talents, into the "great artist" she had always dreamed of (his) being.[19] It is largely through the encouragement brought him throughout the War by his mother's impassioned letters that he is able to bring his (or her) dreams to fruition. And it is thus with a particular sense of shock that "Gary," returning home to Nice at war's end, learns that his mother had in fact died three and a half years earlier, toward the beginning of the War, but had written on her deathbed 250 letters which she had arranged to have sent to her son, in weekly installments, from Switzerland.

Consider now the configuration informing *La Promesse de l'aube*. For the east-European (half-?)Jew Romain Kacew to become "Romain Gary" meant becoming the "happy end" of his abandoned mother insofar as it was imaginable as a figure of exemplary Frenchness. That such a figure was fundamentally imaginary is underscored by the unreal (because posthumous) epistolary underpinning of the author's entire wartime phantasia. Exemplary Frenchman, military hero, and above all a hallucination of his abandoned mother's "happy end," the "Romain Gary" of *La Promesse de l'aube* figures nothing so much as what Lacan called the maternal phallus.

Enter Emile Ajar, in the guise of the narrator of his first novel, *Gros-Câlin*. For if *La Promesse de l'aube*, as we have seen, presents a certain mythology of imaginary integration into the French community, Cousin, Ajar's protagonist-narrator, seems to be characterized above all by his total alienation from the France in which he lives. The novel's plot is relatively simple: Cousin, a statistician working in Paris, has two obsessions, his pet python and his barely articulated love for a black co-worker in his office, Mlle. Dreyfus. A series of episodes, at once hilarious and sad, concerning the python, culminates in Cousin's panic at hearing that Mlle. Dreyfus has quit her job to return to Guyana, his subsequent chance meeting of her during one of his regular visits to a brothel, and his decision to donate his python to the zoo. At novel's end, Cousin himself seems to be metamorphosing into his abandoned pet.

If *La Promesse de l'aube* records an imaginary integration into "France," *Gros-Câlin*, it would seem, all but depicts a reversal of that process. Here the key figure is Cousin's nemesis, the "office boy," whose knowing airs are regularly evoked (or hallucinated) as a dreamt-out dream of *francité*: "C'était surtout le garçon de bureau et ses grosses moustaches démagogiques vieil-ouvrier-de-France qui m'énervait avec ses airs entendus et racoleurs, lorsqu'on se rencontrait dans les couloirs ou sur le palier … Un jeune mec de vingt-cinq ans qui fait dans le genre vieille France avec nappe en toile cirée à carreaux blancs, gros rouge, velours cotelé et imprimerie à l'intérieur, c'est fini, tout ça, ça a déjà été fait."[20] With his caricatural Frenchness ("des coups d'oeil malins à la francaise, avec lueurs d'ironie"), he is the precise obverse of Cousin and many another of Ajar's narrator-surrogates.[21] And to the extent each of those apparent surrogates figures a manner of expulsion from the French community, a virtual disintegration of the achievement named "Romain Gary" in *La Promesse de l'aube,* is it not, we may already wonder, as though the anti-Gary named "Ajar" were at some level the return of the East European Romain Kacew, whose very repression it may have been the purpose of the name Gary to consolidate?

"Romain Gary," in *La Promesse*, as Lacan's maternal phallus: the suggestion is sustained by one's realization that *Gros-Câlin* offers nothing so much as the incipiently psychotic confessions of a man turning into a pet python which is confused throughout the book with a male organ. Consider the case of the Portuguese cleaning lady (who, like the python itself, is referred to, untranslatably, as "l'immigration sauvage"). Here is Cousin's description of her first encounter with the serpent: "A côté de ma table de travail, il y a un grand panier pour mes lettres d'amour. Je les jette toujours là, après les avoir écrites. J'étais occupé de chercher sous le lit, lorsque j'entendis la Portugaise pousser un hurlement affreux. Je me précipite: mon python s'était dressé dans la corbeille à papier et oscillait aimablement en regardant la brave femme."[22] The serpent's arousal, out of the evidence of Cousin's affective misery, has its inevitable effect on the cleaning lady. She rushes off crying to the police: "monsieur sadista, monsieur exhibitionnista." Other examples of the python-phallus confusion abound.[23] What is striking is just how maternal a phallus Gros-Câlin, as he is called, proves to be: his great skill is not penetration but embrace, envelopment: *il s'enroule*. And the great dilemma he imposes on the narrator is less genital than oral: pythons eat only live flesh, and Cousin spends most of the novel agonizing over whether to feed his snake his pet mouse, Blandine. So this enveloping and de-vouring male organ is the most maternal of phalluses. Toward whom Cousin, in a striking "ajarisme," waxes touchingly (because idiotically) maternal: "Enfin, les pythons ne ronronnent pas, mais j'imite ça très bien pour lui permettre d'exprimer son contentement. C'est le dialogue."[24] And it is this maternal phallus into which Cousin, traumatized in his love life, metamorphoses at the end of the novel. Having given his python over to the zoo, he is found popping down mice and slithering around his apart-ment.[25] It is all as though the unconscious subtext of *La Promesse de l'aube* – "Romain Gary," Frenchman *par excellence* and/as maternal phallus – had decided to speak – and undo – itself in a quasi-Kafkan fable by "Emile Ajar": the maternal phallus bespeaks the humiliations of its life as a pseudo-Frenchman (or bogus human) and slithers off into clandestinity.

Cousin's would-be *fiancée*, whom he discovers, in the novel's climax, working in a brothel, is named Mademoiselle Dreyfus: "C'est une Noire de la Guyane française, comme son nom l'in-dique, Dreyfus, qui est là-bas très souvent adopté par les gens du cru, à cause de la gloire locale et pour encourager le tourisme. Le capitaine Dreyfus, qui n'était pas coupable, est resté là-bas cinq ans au bagne à tort et à travers, et son innocence a rejailli sur tout le monde."[26] It was, in brief, in the interest of any black family to adopt the name Dreyfus as a kind of protective ploy: "Comme ça, personne n'ose les toucher." Gary had already forged an ironic link between the tragedy of the Jews and anti-black racism in *Tulipe* (1946), a not very successful treatment of the adventures of a Buchenwald survivor living in Harlem. The more interesting connection between the Ajar-surrogate Cousin's aspirations toward (Mlle.) Dreyfus and the work of Gary, however, is to be made rather by way of *La Promesse de l'aube*. For that work contains its own degraded miniature of the Dreyfus Affair. Just prior to World War II, Romain Kacew entered the French air force academy at Avord: the prospect of at last attaining his (mother's) goal or end ("but"), returning to Nice in a French officer's uniform, seemed imminent. And yet out of a graduating class of nearly three hundred, Kacew was alone in not receiving an officer's commission. Informally, he is given two reasons: first, that his French naturalization is too recent ("mais, je suis français"); then, more unanswerably: "C'est à la cote d'amour qu'ils t'ont baisé."[27] Thus does the young East European Jew come face to face with the forces of intolerance in the very citadel of the French military he had been taught to adore. Invoking a god out of his imaginary pantheon, he writes: "Mais, c'est surtout Filoche, le dieu petit-bourgeois de la médiocrité, du mépris, et des préjugés que je reconnaissais et ce qui me crevait le coeur, c'est qu'il avait revêtu pour la circonstance l'uniforme et la casquette galonnée de notre Armée de l'Air."[28] One could imagine these words, suitably transposed to another branch of the military, as being pronounced by a more sensitive and astute version of Captain Alfred Dreyfus. What is striking, in *La Promesse de l'aube*, however, is that no sooner are they pronounced than the author retreats from the Dreyfus-like role into which French prejudice seems to have cast him. First, a pirouette: from the time of that incident on, he writes, he felt more French than ever. Why? "Il m'apparut enfin que les Français n'étaient pas d'une race à part, qu'ils ne m'étaient pas supérieurs, qu'ils pouvaient, eux aussi, être bêtes et ridicules – bref, que nous étions frères, incontestablement."[29] Then a vow: what was to be spared injury, at whatever cost, was his mother's image of France as the homeland of justice.

And finally, a petty lie: he tells his mother that if he was denied his commission it was only because he had seduced the wife of the academy's commandant. His humiliation, in brief, was to be chalked up to his virility. The identity of "Romain Gary," maternal phallus and/as exemplary citizen of France, is thus forged out of the denial of another identification which circumstances had imposed on the young Romain Kacew: one with Alfred Dreyfus.

Returning now to *Gros-Câlin*, we can perceive the significance of the humiliation which Mlle. Dreyfus, whose very name is born out of the degradation of the exemplary saga of Alfred Dreyfus, inflicts on poor Cousin. To the extent that Ajar-Cousin is a return of all that was repressed by "Romain Gary," the return of the half-Jew Romain Kacew, it is fitting that it be "Dreyfus," his own shunted identity in *La Promesse de l'aube*, that should effect his undoing. As though Cousin were telling us, in the voice of Ajar: I, "Romain Gary," maternal phallus, declare myself to be such, and hereby come undone, declaring my bankruptcy as human, through a disintegration of the Dreyfus Affair, [Mlle.] Dreyfus in a brothel. I *am* Gros-Câlin, "python juif."[30]

La Vie devant soi, Ajar's next novel, attains a kind of zero degree of political correctness. It is the desperate love story of an Arab orphan, Momo, and Madame Rosa, the former prostitute and inmate of Auschwitz, a Jew who has made it her clandestine business, in old age, to take care of the children of prostitutes in her apartment in the Belleville section of Paris. The novel's pathos comes in large measure from Madame Rosa's confusion, in her advancing senility, between the Nazis, who had threatened her life during her youth, and the welfare-medical establishment of contemporary France, which seems intent on using inhuman means to extend a life she no longer thinks worth living. But the book's piquancy is entirely a function of Momo's narrative voice, for he is condemned to recount what he would never think of calling his love for the decrepit Jewess in the only idiom at his disposal: the street clichés of prostitution and anti-Semitism. Here, for instance, is Momo on the infamous "Orléans rumors," reports of a white slave trade run by Jews out of the dressing rooms of

Orléans retail shops: "Les rumeurs d'Orléans, c'était quand les Juifs dans le prêt-à-porter ne droguaient pas les femmes blanches pour les envoyer dans des bordels et tout le monde leur en voulait, ils font toujours parler d'eux pour rien."[31] Wherein the debunking of an anti-Semitic "rumor" turns into new grounds for resenting the Jews. Or consider Momo's marvelously wrong-headed response to news that Madame Rosa is no longer receiving funds for his support: "Vous pouvez compter sur moi [Madame Rosa]. Je vais pas vous plaquer parce que vous recevez plus d'argent."[32] Here love and loyalty, against all economic sense, speak the only language available to them: that of the pimp. Such are the bizarre stylistic turns which make *La Vie devant soi* a particularly powerful tool for challenging the canons of what is currently termed "political correctness."

Momo, then, is one more slightly crazed narrator in the Ajarian series beginning with *Gros-Câlin*'s Cousin: fundamentally estranged, in his beleaguered muti-racial ghetto, from what he calls "les quartiers français."[33] The relation between *La Vie devant soi* and *La Promesse de l'aube* is particularly striking. As Momo, in terror, attends to the dying – and irredeemably grotesque – Madame Rosa, hiding her corpse in the cellar retreat she has prepared in the event of a return of the Gestapo, dousing her body with cheap perfume to abate the stench, it is as though he were performing a labor of mourning which we have seen *La Promesse de l'aube* deny to "Romain Gary." Whereas the mother-son dyad of the Gary book seemed to culminate in an imaginary integration into the community, "Ajar," on the contrary, repeats the scenario of the earlier work only to undo it: his Momo emerges as fundamentally excluded.

There is a passage toward the beginning of *La Promesse de l'aube* whose displaced repetition in *La Vie devant soi* offers an instructive illustration of the relation between "Gary" and "Ajar." The earlier work relates a trauma that so galvanizes its young protagonist into a sense of his role in the world as to be construable as a veritable *cogito*. During Romain Kacew's adolescence in Nice, it was a matter of honor for his struggling mother to serve him a daily beefsteak at noon. She herself ate only vegetables, claiming that meat and its fat were strictly forbidden her, for medical reasons. Then one day, he finds her in the kitchen, wiping up the greasy bottom of the pan on which his steak had been cooked with a piece of bread and eagerly downing it. He understands the reasons for her vegetarian diet and breaks down in tears, formulating shortly thereafter "une farouche résolution de redresser le monde et de le déposer un jour aux pieds de ma mère ..."[34] Such would be the rather sentimental origin of the militant humanism of the *belle âme* – or "bleating idealist (*idéaliste bêlant*)" – which Gary, in his more ironic moments, knew himself to be.

Toward the middle of *La Vie devant soi*, Momo is told by Madame Rosa's physician, Dr. Katz, of the principal consequence of his guardian's rapidly hardening arteries: her brain will no longer receive sufficient oxygen and blood. "Elle ne pourra plus penser et va vivre comme un légume."[35] Madame Rosa emerges from her catatonic state just long enough to pick up a word or two and later asks Momo what the doctor said about vegetables. Momo's sublime response: "Il faut bouffer beaucoup de légumes pour la santé, Madame Rosa ..."[36] By which point we have come full circle. The maternal lie about eating vegetables, which so traumatized the protagonist of *La Promesse de l'aube*, is here repeated as a lie, this time *to* the mother figure, in *La Vie devant soi*. In mid-course, the sentimental image of the mother caught giving the lie to her own vegetarian loyalties is grotesquely recast as the mother(-figure) transformed into a vegetable. It is as though the vegetables of *Promesse* were here being shoved back down the throat of the mother who had dared lie to her son about them. But with the scenario of Ajar undoing or dismantling precisely what Gary had been intent on consolidating, we encounter anew a configuration characterizing the Gary-Ajar relation from the beginning.

Late in *La Vie devant soi*, there occurs an episode one is tempted to call the hidden center of Ajar's literary production. It concerns the sudden arrival, after many years, of Kadir Youssef, Momo's father, bearing a receipt for his child, at Madame Rosa's door. Having recently been released from a psychiatric hospital, where he had been interned after murdering his prostitute wife, he now wants to see (and perhaps reclaim) his son. Madame Rosa snaps out of her near-comatose (or vegetable) state long enough to concoct a saving stratagem. She is willing to reunite father and son, she says, but, after consulting her stash of (forged) papers, pretends that through a clerical error, she had confused two children left to her on that same day in 1956, and as a result has raised the son of Kadir Youssef ("Youyou pour les infirmiers"!) as a Jew: Kashrut, Bar Mitzvah, and all.[37] She thereupon calls on "Moïse," the only other child beside Momo (Mohammed) left in her declining enterprise, to embrace his father. The Arab's reaction at finding his son a Jew is one of sheer horror. Upon seeing "Moïse," and just before succumbing to a heart attack, he utters, in one of Ajar's most memorable formulations, "une chose terrible pour un homme qui ne savait pas qu'il avait raison: 'Ce n'est pas mon fils!' "[38] The self-dramatizing performative the father believes he is delivering is rendered splendidly beside the point by its constative validity: Moïse, the other child, is indeed not his son. Whereupon the father collapses and dies.

One imagines the pleasure taken by Gary, caught up in the adventure of forging a new identity for himself, in this tale of false papers. More significant, however, is the obvious subtext of the episode: the judgment of Solomon. For in the celebrated sequence in the first Book of Kings (chapter III), Solomon resorts to a ruse (agreeing to cut a live child in two) in order to determine who his natural and rightful parent is. Here we also have a dispute among would-be "parents" (Madame Rosa and Kadir Youssef), a confusion between children (Momo-Mohammed and Moïse), and a ruse invoked to arrive at a just settlement: Madame Rosa, that is, plays not only the rightful "parent," but King Solomon himself. Moreover, even as the Biblical dispute is between "harlots," the Ajar sequence pits an ex-prostitute against a pimp. Now what makes the passage in *La Vie devant soi* nodal in Ajar's *oeuvre* is that the author's next and final novel, after the pseudo-psychiatric memoir *Pseudo*, is *L'Angoisse du roi Salomon*. As though the final novel itself had arisen from the sequence just discussed. *Angoisse* – be it anxiety or anguish – is, of course, not wisdom, and it may indeed be suggested that the function of wisdom may in fact be to repress such anxiety. Nevertheless, at the conclusion of *L'Angoisse du roi Salomon* we find an oddly displaced recasting of our episode in *La Vie devant soi*, a version so

oblique that it would be impossible to trace it back to Biblical Solomon's judgment had it not been for the Madame Rosa episode.
And yet the overdetermined "Solomonic" bond between the two
sequences leads one to speculate on the sequence's final version as
hidden *telos* of the entire Ajar experiment.[39]

It will be helpful to sketch the plot of *L'Angoisse du roi Salomon*,
Ajar's second and final Holocaust comedy, at this juncture. It is
narrated by Jeannot, a young cab driver and autodidact of
vaguely *gauchiste* sympathies. In the course of the novel, he is
engaged by a retired and supremely ironic philanthropist,
Salomon Rubenstein, the retired "pants king," an eighty-year-old
dandy of astonishing vigor. "King Salomon" has an almost Virgi-
lian sense of the sadness inherent in the passing of time, runs a
switchboard service ("S.O.S. Bénévoles") to comfort a variety of
desperate souls, and hires out Jeannot to deliver presents to one
Cora Lamenaire, *chanteuse réaliste*, a would-be Edith Piaf whose
brief but promising career seems to have come to an end during
World War II. In the course of the novel, Jeannot is stunned to
learn that Salomon had been Cora's lover before the War, had
refused to make use of a visa to Portugal so that he might stay in
hiding in a "cellar" on the Champs-Elysées and be with her. No
sooner had the Nazis invaded, however, than Cora fell in love
with Maurice, a handsome thug working for the Gestapo on
"Jewish matters." During the War, she thus neither visited
Salomon – nor mentioned him. For which reason, it befell King
Salomon to testify on her behalf at her trial for collaboration: her
silence had indeed "protected" a Jew during the War. Such is the
source of Salomon's sense of the bitter irony – or vanity – of
things. After the War, he makes money, and takes pleasure in be-
stowing some of it on an impoverished Cora – as punishment. If
he has sent Jeannot her way, it is because he is the physical
double of Maurice, her former collaborationist lover. Jeannot too
has a measure of Salomon's "piety" (as opposed to pity) – and
ends up sleeping with Cora out of sheer rage at what life (or time)
has done to her. The novel comes to a happy end when Jeannot
brokers a marriage between Cora and Salomon, who then take
off to Nice, leaving Jeannot to his newfound love for a bookseller
friend, named Aline.

The episode which displaces the sequence in *La Vie devant soi* harking back to the judgment of Solomon occurs toward the end of *L'Angoisse du roi Salomon*. Jeannot feels it is his destiny to reunite Cora and Salomon; he tells her of his own love for Aline. Shortly thereafter, word comes to Salomon and Jeannot that Cora has attempted suicide. Salomon's only response is to ask whether the suicide was because of Jeannot or because of himself: "pour lui ou pour moi?"[40] Such is the content of his anxiety. Jeannot realizes that all will depend on her answer. Cora's suicide note is too ambiguous to be of use, and so he secretly destroys it. He then enters into elaborate negotiations with her to get her to rewrite the note, as though her suicide had been dictated by unrequited love for her old *beau*, Salomon. She can't quite bring herself to produce such a self-forgery, but ten days of negotiations between Cora and Salomon are sufficient to hammer out a nuptial agreement. The only condition stipulated in the marriage arrangement is that their wartime misadventure never be mentioned by either of them.

If we superimpose this sequence on the episode from *La Vie devant soi*, we find Cora, with her would-be forged document, in the position of Madame Rosa; the nearly indistinguishable twins Jeannot/Maurice in that of Momo/Moïse; and paternal Salomon in that of Kadir Youssef. In graphic distribution, the configuration would be as follows:

Mme. Rosa	Momo/Moïse	Kadir Youssef
Cora	Jeannot/Maurice	Salomon

It will be seen that whereas the earlier sequence seemed to be concerned with eliminating a father (to protect a child), the later one is intent on marrying off a mother (to protect a child). In fact, in *La Vie devant soi*, that possibility had already been broached. For there is another "Arab father," aside from Momo's natural one, in the earlier novel: Monsieur Hamil, a senile sage who has increasingly begun confusing lines of the Koran with those of Victor Hugo, and whom Momo dreams of marrying off to Madame Rosa. Moreover, he too, like Salomon, bears the affective wound of an abandonment by a beloved woman as a determining event in his life. So that once one adds the name of

Monsieur Hamil to the paternal column, it begins looking as though *L'Angoisse du roi Salomon* has succeeded in carrying off a project which the irredeemably pre-Oedipal earlier novel could not: Madame Rosa and Monsieur Hamil were too old and senile (if not comatose), and Momo too young to bring it about.[41]

Ultimately both episodes bring us back to the Gary *Urtext, La Promesse de l'aube.* For there we find a sequence that combines our two motifs of saving the child and marrying off the mother. A painter, Monsieur Zaremba, enlists Romain's aid in convincing his mother to marry him. With a Gauloise hanging from her lips and an air of "goguenarde bienveillance," she dismisses him in tones as castratory as those used by Madame Rosa with Kadir Youssef.[42] What is striking in the case of Zaremba, however, is his reason for wanting to marry Nina Kacew: "Sous son apparence de grand seigneur dans la force de l'âge, M. Zaremba cachait un orphelin qui n'avait jamais reçu sa part de tendresse et d'affection, et qui a été saisi d'espoir et peut-être d'envie à la vue de cet amour maternel qui brûlait d'une flamme sous ses yeux. Manifestement, il avait décidé qu'il y avait de la place pour deux ..."[43] Thus Zaremba fits simultaneously into the columns of the rejected father and the twin sons. Our schema may be completed as follows:

La Promesse de l'aube:		
Nina	Romain/Zaremba	Zaremba
La Vie devant soi:		
Mme. Rosa	Momo/Moïse	Kadir Youssef
		(Monsieur Hamil)
L'Angoisse du roi Salomon:		
Cora	Jeannot/Maurice	Salomon

It is only in Ajar's final novel that the project of defending the child by marrying off the mother is carried off. The broader significance of that project, and specifically the chiasmus that has Jews (Madame Rosa, Salomon) and anti-Jews (Kadir Youssef, Cora) switching positions between Ajar's two Holocaust comedies remains, however, to be gauged.

L'Angoisse du roi Salomon comes replete with its own equivalent of a Greek chorus: Monsieur Tapu, the vilely Poujadist concierge of

Salomon's apartment house. He is, to be sure, also an anti-Semite and allows Jeannot in to see the man he refers to as "le roi des Juifs" only because he is certain, in his cynicism, that Jeannot will eventually murder his employer. That observation is particularly precious because it allows us to link Ajar's last novel to a major work by Gary during the same period, *Au-delà de cette limite votre ticket n'est plus valable* (1975). In that work, Ruiz, a chauffeur and the would-be murderer of the protagonist, Rainier, serves to fuel the latter's erotic imagination, thus forestalling a threat of psychic impotence. Simultaneously, the novel develops a meditation on France being revived by the energy and grace of the third world: in Gary's heterosexual revision of a Gidean motif: "les châteaux de la Loire rêvent de travailleurs africains . . ."[44] But that observation allows us to align Rainier scouring the streets of la Goutte d'or section of Paris in search of a fantasy of Ruiz with Gary's similar search in the same neighborhood for the fantasies of "Emile Ajar."[45] Ruiz is thus to Rainier as Ajar is to Gary, and the onslaught against uncle Romain (referred to ominously as "Tonton Macoute") in *Pseudo*, the pseudo-memoir by Ajar-Pavlowitch, confirms the point emphatically. But that superimposition, we have seen, may in turn be superimposed on the figures of Jeannot and Salomon as imagined by Monsieur Tapu. Which is to suggest that his vile ramblings implicitly contain a speculation about the Ajar project in its entirety.

Tapu is the consummate figure of what the French call a *con* – a jerk. Whence the special *frisson* felt by Jeannot upon beholding him. Jeannot's experience with Tapu is commented on by a friend: "Chuck dit que si je suis tellement ému devant la Connerie, c'est parce que je suis étreint par le sentiment d'éternité et il m'a même cité un vers de Victor Hugo, *oui, je viens dans son temple adorer l'Eternel.*"[46] Chuck indeed suggests that the fact that there are no theses being written on the sacred potential of "la Connerie" is a sure index of the decline of Western spirituality. Now perhaps the most striking aspect of Ajar's – or Chuck's – quip is that the line said to be by Victor Hugo is in fact by Racine. For whatever the importance of Hugo to Ajar's project – Momo dreams of writing the only book worth the effort, which he calls, in touching lower-case, "les misérables," and Salomon imagines himself a latter-day Booz – the line of verse quoted is in fact a slight modification of the beginning of *Athalie*: "Oui je viens dans son temple adorer l'Eternel."

Now the significance of the Racine line is that *Athalie*, like our novel, pits a Jewish patriarch, Joad, against an aged woman, Athalie, guilty of causing Jewish suffering. For the queen in fact is the architect of a policy of Jewish genocide that ultimately comes to ruin at the play's end with her death. During World War II, I have argued elsewhere, Giraudoux revives the *Athalie* scenario only to reverse it: the Madwoman of Chaillot, at play's end, sets a trap for the "President" and his alien "race" of speculators and lures them to their doom.[47] The "President," moreover, is a character borrowed from Giraudoux's own play of 1938, his modern-dress transposition of the Song of Songs, entitled *Cantique des cantiques*. He is, that is, a surrogate for King Solomon. (But the "President" of the 1938 play is in significant respects derived from the arch-Jewish banker Moïse, in Giraudoux's 1927 novel, *Eglantine*: the alien "race" of speculators to be exterminated in the 1943 play, that is, is at some level the Jews.) Thus whereas Racine, in his last play, has his genocidal *vieillarde* (as Giraudoux called her) done in by the Jews, and Giraudoux, at the end of his career, reverses the scenario and has his mad old lady lure a Salomon-surrogate and his alien race to their doom, "Ajar," in *his* final novel, succeeds in marrying off *his* Salomon to Cora, the mad old lady who during the War had abandoned him for a French agent of the Gestapo.

Salomon's marriage to Cora could be arranged, we have seen, only upon agreement that the wartime experiences of the two never be mentioned. For the compulsively Gallic ex-songstress (a would-be Piaf) and the Jewish patriarch, the marriage was thus in a broader sense an act of amnesty: the end of the Holocaust. At the same time, we have seen, the imaginative marrying off of an intrusive "mother" (Nina, Madame Rosa, Cora ...) is the successful culmination of a project that we have observed since *La Promesse de l'aube*. The Oedipalization of the plot here coincides with an amnesty for collaboration. Rarely has the forgetting or repression of "castration" received a more striking political content.

Gary himself had written a novel of the Holocaust in 1967: *La Danse de Gengis Cohn*. On its final page, Gary and Jean Seberg appear under their own names to evoke their strange trip, Gary's return to Warsaw in 1966. Gary, upon approaching the ghetto, fainted and proceeded to mutter in Polish. In the book, his wife explains to his astonished hosts that he had in fact done his "humanities" in the ghetto. Their response: "Ah! Nous ne savions pas qu'il était juif ..." Hers: "Lui non plus."[48] It is tempting to see the Ajar project as being born in that swoon. Kacew returns, against the myth of "Romain Gary," as Ajar. In *Gros-Câlin*, the maternal phallus bespeaks his plight, relives the repressed humiliations of his own Dreyfus Affair. In *La Vie devant soi*, the memory of Auschwitz presides over the brilliant unraveling of all that had been *forged* in *La Promesse de l'aube*. *Pseudo*, allegedly by Pavlowitch, stages a "half-Jew" 's onslaught against an imaginary "Gary." And finally the *drive* energized by that "half-Jew" or "partial object" is integrated or symbolized in an act of Oedipalization which is also a form of amnesty: the end of the Holocaust, but also the end of "Emile Ajar."[49]

CHAPTER 12

Pour Sainte-Beuve: *Maurice Blanchot,* *10 March 1942*

In response to a manuscript meditating his contributions to the 1930s fascist journal *Combat* and the distance he would have had to traverse from the margins of Action Française to the "passivity beyond all passivity" of his later excursus on literature, Maurice Blanchot, in a letter of 1979, zeroed in on what he called an "exemplary" error in the text I had sent him.[1] It turned on a footnote that quoted first Claude Roy on Blanchot's transition from "Maurrassian nationalism" to the Resistance, then a passage from Léautaud's *Journal* in which Drieu la Rochelle – in May 1942 – is heard on the subject of the editorial assistance at the *Nouvelle Revue française* he has received from Blanchot during a period in which he was overworked. Blanchot, in his letter to me, had eyes only for the Léautaud entry and insisted on setting the record straight. He recounted how he had in fact turned down an offer from Drieu to assume "free" editorship of the journal (with Drieu himself retaining nominal authority as a safeguard). Blanchot, in consultation with Paulhan, first stalled, then came up with a list of "great writers" for a new editorial committee. Given their anti-Nazi sympathies, Drieu declined. Thus Blanchot in his letter of 26 November 1979.

The most striking aspect of the letter was less the correction of Léautaud's second-hand account, about which I myself had expressed doubts, than its marginality to the principal subject of my essay. I wrote back to that effect, offering Blanchot a fantasy, whose vulgarity no doubt sealed the conclusion of our brief correspondence: a great work of fiction by Blanchot, which he would no doubt never write, registering the return of a "phantasm" of February 1934 in the heart of May 1968. Its title, I suggested, might be *Les Evénements.* I have since come to the conclusion that Blanchot, in 1948, came quite close to having written just such a work – half in memory, half in anticipation – under the title of *L'Arrêt de mort.*[2] The principal elements of the demonstration are as follows: Given the fact that *Le Très-Haut* (1948) is, as Foucault intuited, Blanchot's idiosyncratic treatment of the Orestes myth, and given the fact that Louise, the Electra, of that novel reappears as the sister of J. in *L'Arrêt de mort,* mythological consistency would cast J. in the role of Iphigenia . . . condemned to death. Moreover, given the fact that the action of *L'Arrêt de mort* is said to coincide with the "most somber days of the Munich pact" in October 1938, the stalled mobilization of the French army at that time in anticipation of a bad war corresponds precisely to the situation of Agamemnon's army in the Greek myth. At which point the best candidate for superimposition on Iphigenia in 1938 would be precisely Blanchot's own investment in fascist ideology, embraced, no doubt, out of French nationalism, and now sacrificed, in the face of a looming fascist enemy, for the very same reason. Finally, if *Iphigenia at Aulis* is the subtext of the first (J.) segment of Blanchot's *récit,* one is hard put not to assign to the second (Nathalie) segment *Iphigenia among the Taurians* as subtext. In 1948, Blanchot dreams a future return of Iphigenia 38, the receding fascist investment, in some ecstatic future encounter: Nathalie or May 1968. Philippe Ariès, moreover, has reported just such a fantasy – the anti-democratic right of the 1930s returning on the anti-parliamentarian left in May 1968.[3]

I recount my interpretation to underscore the oddity of its genesis: I had challenged Blanchot to write a book which I then proceeded to convince myself he – thanks to my interpretation – had already written. My intention, in these pages, however, is to return not to the utopian response I imagined my early text eliciting – *Les Evénements* or *Iphigenia 38* – but to the actual response it received: the zeroing in on the question of Blanchot's relations with Drieu and the spectre of collaboration Blanchot sought to dispel. It is remarkable that literary history has retained not Blanchot's account of declining Drieu's offer but rather the fact of his service with the wartime *NRF.* Thus Pascal Fouché writes: "En avril 1942 Maurice Blanchot est venu assister Drieu en assurant le secrétariat général de la revue."[4] And Pierre Hebey, in *La NRF des années sombres: 1940–1941*, refers to Paulhan's introduction of Blanchot onto the staff of the collaborationist *NRF* and quotes a Paulhan note to Drieu about increasing Blanchot's role: "Peut-être pourrait-on demander à Blanchot d'organiser la partie notes. (Mais le voudrait-il? D'après ses écrits, je le trouve intimidant . . .)"[5]

For Hebey, however, the collaborationist *NRF* was a shield or lightning rod whose collaborationism protected the (relative) independence of the Gallimard publishing house. That circumstance would make Blanchot the Resistance's ambassador to the Collaboration, a delicate situation indeed. Pierre Andreu and Frederic Grover, whose biography of Drieu is a principal source for both Fouché and Hebey, refer, in the conditional, to the proposed new organization of the review mentioned by Blanchot in his letter to me of 1979: "Drieu accepterait d'être directeur en titre . . . Mais il est bien entendu que le plus gros du travail serait fait par un secrétaire (Maurice Blanchot), et par Paulhan qui serait chargé officiellement d'assurer la liaison entre le comité directeur et Drieu."[6] Once again we find Blanchot's projected role as that of liaison between the collaborationist Drieu and the *résistant* Paulhan, the vehicle of their collaboration with each other.[7]

But that eventuality, the official renewal of an independent *NRF* – conveyed by the conditional of Grover and Andreu's formulation – never materialized. Thus we are left with the past tense of Fouché's and Hebey's account: Blanchot's service for an *NRF* that remained Drieu's organ of collaboration, the intellectual pride of Abetz's and Heller's Paris.

One's sense of Blanchot being stranded in the collaborationist *NRF*, moreover, is confirmed by Paulhan's recently published wartime correspondence. On 9 June 1942, he sent a note to Drieu: "Au fond rien ne me fait croire, ni ceux que j'interroge, que les temps de la réconciliation soient déjà venus. Ne pensez-vous pas que le provisoire, que nous allons tenter d'établir avec Blanchot, pourrait très bien durer?"[8] That is: the Resistance writers will not work with you, but perhaps we can work out an arrangement with Maurice Blanchot, more or less in anticipation of a reconciliation which nonetheless seems unforeseeable. A day later, Paulhan writes to Drieu that in view of the failure of the newly projected *NRF*: "le plus 'sage' est sans doute que vous repreniez la revue ... Là-dessus que faire? Peut-être simplement, pour vous et pour moi, aider Maurice Blanchot du mieux que nous le pourrons à diriger la revue apolitique que vous lui avez remise."[9] Within a day, the future conditional has given way to the past tense. Blanchot appears to be stranded, the bearer of Paulhan's pipe dream of apoliticism, in an *NRF* fundamentally under the control of Drieu.

It is in this context of Blanchot between Drieu and Paulhan, the Collaboration and the Resistance, that I would like to examine a text written by Blanchot for the resolutely Pétainist *Journal des débats*. Blanchot was a cultural critic for that paper, which had settled in Clermont-Ferrand, during much of the War. His column, which was called "Chronique de la vie intellectuelle," first appeared on 16 April 1941, and seems, for the most part, supremely disengaged from the torment of the War in which much of the world was engaged. Many of the columns in the *Journal* appeared *tel quel* in *Faux pas* when that volume was published by Gallimard in 1943. Blanchot, that is, who was about fifteen years Paul de Man's senior, had a job during the War not all that different from the one Paul de Man had accepted with *Le Soir* in Brussels.[10]

Blanchot's articles, appearing regularly, at a few days' distance, in the *Journal*, were generally consigned to the third page of the abbreviated wartime newspaper. On 10 March 1942, however, Blanchot crafted a long first-page article headlined "La Politique de Sainte-Beuve." It was a review of Maxime Leroy's volume of the same name, which had appeared at Gallimard in 1941, and was to all appearances a rousing endorsement of the book.[11]

For anyone interested in the role of politics in the life and work of Blanchot, arguably France's pre-eminent critic of the twentieth century, this article on the politics of France's pre-eminent critic of the nineteenth century cannot but be of central interest. But that circumstance cannot, of course, have accounted for the prominence accorded the Blanchot article. Such pride of place, I shall argue, may best be explained by the special opportunity an article on Sainte-Beuve's politics afforded its author to take a stand on the issue of intellectual collaboration with the Vichy regime. For Sainte-Beuve attained notoriety in the Romantic generation as the one major figure from its ranks to have wholeheartedly embraced the 2 December *coup d'état* of Louis Bonaparte: Paul Guth, in his sprightly literary history, has captured the ignominy of Sainte-Beuve's career as the nineteenth century's nearest approximation to what the next century would call a collaborator: "Il veut tirer du nouveau régime tout ce que les précédents lui ont refusé."[12] At a time when Marx was writing *The Eighteenth Brumaire of Louis Bonaparte* and Victor Hugo, in exile, *Napoléon le Petit*, Sainte-Beuve was justifying the bloody December *coup* in these terms: "La plénitude du principe monarchique, entendue selon la libre et nationale interprétation, elle est là où apparaissent deux restaurateurs de la société à cinquante ans de distance, deux conducteurs du peuple remettant la France sur un grand pied et, sans trop se ressembler, la couronnant également d'honneur."[13]

Worse yet, on 23 August 1852, Sainte-Beuve published a "lundi" under the title "Les Regrets." Its subject was the foolishness of any intellectuals who chose to resist the regime whose brutal seizure of power was still fresh in all minds: "je ne viens pas ici conseiller d'épouser le pouvoir, mais simplement de ne pas le nier avec obstination, de ne pas bouder la société qui l'a ratifié, le fond et le vrai de la société de notre temps."[14] All resistance was assimilated to a variety of "ressentiment":[15] "Le danger, aujourd'hui, pour quantité d'esprits distingués, atteints dans leurs habitudes, dans leur symbole politique, et qui ont à se plaindre des choses, serait de se fixer dans une disposition habituelle de rancune, d'hostilité sans grandeur, de jugement ironique et satirique: il en résulterait une altération, à la longue, dans le fond même de leur esprit et de leur jugement."[16] The central fact about the new regime for Sainte-Beuve was that it secured "order and the guarantees of civilization."[17] The issue of censorship was dismissed as a red herring.[18] All calls toward resistance were "sentimental," appeals for pity on the part of men "whom no other unconsolable misfortune has befallen than that of no longer governing me."[19] In the face of such sentimentality, the critic writes, better simply reset one's watch and commit oneself to living in the present.[20] Sainte-Beuve's argument, then, sets up something of a primal scene of intellectual collaboration with an unpopular military regime. Sainte-Beuve nonetheless took wounded pride in his political incorrectness and referred to the scandal it provoked and above all to Cuvillier-Fleury's "refutation" in *Le Journal des débats* as proof that it was on target.[21] The author of *Port-Royal*, meanwhile, was being cast by the intelligentsia in the role of the complete opportunist – or conformist. Appointed professor of Latin poetry at the Collège de France in 1854, he was forced to resign his post because he was regularly jeered – as a collaborator – by his would-be students: "Vous déshonorez la poésie. Vous n'êtes qu'un historiographe du *Moniteur* [the regime newspaper]."[22] At the Ecole Normale, where he was subsequently appointed to a position in French literature, he was widely distrusted. In the words of Charles Bigot, in his *Souvenirs de l'Ecole Normale*: "Il avait beau nous prodiguer ses aperçus les plus ingénieux, ses plus piquantes anecdotes ... Il s'était rallié à l'Empire, cela suffisait, il était jugé."[23] Even after entering into mild dissent *vis-à-vis* the orthodoxy of the regime, he would be characterized by the Goncourt brothers in their journal as: "le souteneur autorisé du régime." Moreover: "son courage ne lui est venu qu'avec son traitement d'inamovible et ces palmes de sénateur gagnées à servir avec de la mauvaise foi de prêtre toutes les viles rancunes du 2 décembre."[24] With the cartoon of the complete collaborator in place, it would not be long before a literary historian (Paul Guth) could feel authorized to risk the following comparison in his *Histoire de la littérature française* with reference to Sainte-Beuve's late and mild dissidence toward the regime he had championed: "En lui faisant [à l'Empire] une opposition limitée, il prépare l'avenir, comme les '*collaborateurs*' de la dernière guerre qui, au moment où l'occupant commençait à faiblir, aidaient les résistants."[25]

Now lest the leap from 1852 ("Les Regrets") to 1942 (the date of Blanchot's "La Politique de Sainte-Beuve") be regarded as too precipitous, we shall make a stop midway – at the Dreyfus Affair. Such a pause between Bonapartism and Nazism, at the anti-Semitic riots of the Affair, is of course a staple of the anti-fascist treatment of the genealogy of the Hitler phenomenon. Hannah Arendt saw the Dreyfus Affair as a "dress rehearsal" for the ensuing genocide of the Jews, and evoked the abortive *coup* attempt of Jules Guérin, criminal hero of the subproletarian mob, in terms reminiscent of Marx's classic treatment of Louis Bonaparte.[26] Our own pause in the Affair, this time to observe the anti-Dreyfusard camp, will be to read Charles Maurras' "capital" work of 1898, *Trois idées politiques: Chateaubriand, Michelet, Sainte-Beuve.*[27]

Maurras, Blanchot's early master, to whom he could not but make reference, as we shall see, in any discussion of Sainte-Beuve's politics, came up with an ingenious and artfully crafted argument. The right, he claimed, had made a grave error in thinking that Chateaubriand was its ideal standard-bearer, even as the left was completely mystified in promoting Michelet to ideological prominence. Moreover, once those errors were dispelled, a case could be made that the figure best suited to unite both (republican) left and (royalist) right would be (to general surprise) the (Bonapartist) Sainte-Beuve: "Si les partis de droite pouvaient oublier ses passades d'anti-cléricalisme; si, à gauche, on savait ce que parler veut dire et qu'on y cherchât, où elle est, la liberté de la pensée ... eh bien! l'oeuvre, le nom, la moyenne des idées de ce grand esprit, sans oublier ce prolongement naturel, leurs conséquences politiques, feraient le plus beau lieu du monde où se grouper dans une journée de réconciliation générale."[28] Maurras, in fact, proposes – in 1898 – a national *fête* consecrated to Sainte-Beuve, of the sort, no doubt that Jeune France, the Vichy cultural machine on whose literary committee Blanchot served, briefly, during the War, would assiduously plan.[29]

Now before considering the substance of Maurras' argument, it should be observed that its conclusion, a reconciliation of right and left in a new political and cultural synthesis was at the heart of fascism. *Ni droite ni gauche*, as Zeev Sternhell phrased it, in a study of fascism in the 1930s that found its best definition in a programmatic political statement, perched between nationalism and socialism, by Blanchot himself.[30] If Maurras' 1898 text, moreover, concludes with a fascist gesture, superseding the division between extremes of left and right, it begins with an epi-

graph by Paul Bourget which is as chillingly and precisely anticipatory of fascist doctrine as anything in Maurras: "Nous devons
chercher ce qui reste de la vieille France et nous y rattacher par
toutes nos fibres, retrouver la province d'unité naturelle et hér-
éditaire sous le département artificiel et morcelé, l'autonomie
administrative, les Universités locales et fécondes sous notre Université officielle et morte, reconstituer la famille terrienne par la
liberté de tester, protéger le travail par le rétablissement des cor-
porations, rendre à la vie religieuse sa vigueur et sa dignité par
la suppression du budget des cultes et le droit de posséder libre-
ment assuré aux associations religieuses, en un mot, sur ce point
comme sur les autres, défaire systématiquement l'oeuvre meur-
trière de la Révolution française."[31] Here then was an early call
for the program which would be attempted under Vichy's "national revolution": reactionary corporatism or fascism intent on
rolling back the political culture of the French Revolution.[32]
And the most remarkable feature of all, from our perspective,
was that this reactionary revolution, according to Maurras,
might well culminate in a national holiday or festival dedicated
to Sainte-Beuve.

What then of the substance of Maurras' argument? For all of
his much vaunted royalism, Chateaubriand was too much the romantic, devoted to an isolation in heroism substantially unrelated
to the solidarities of the *ancien régime*. His royalism, moreover, was
for the most part masochism: he may have been horrified by the
advent of modern times, but the truth was that he loved his
horror. No self-respecting monarchist, in brief, can have any
truck with a man more interested in mourning monarchy,
however clegiacally, than restoring it. On the left, Michelet, on
the other hand, for all his interest in emancipation, is too weak a
thinker to emancipate anyone: "Michelet a donné ce scandale
d'un très grand écrivain français dont la pensée est molle, l'ordre
nul, la dialectique sans nerf."[33] If education is the road to emancipation, Michelet, according to Maurras, is too intent on elevating
every "rudiment of a general idea" to the dignity of a divine principle to serve as anyone's mentor. A man without nuance, Michelet and the cult his centenary in 1898 had become were as
much an error on the left as the Chateaubriand cult, revived on

the occasion of the fiftieth anniversary of his death in 1898, was on the right.

Enter Sainte-Beuve, whose "empirisme organisateur" is seen by Maurras as the new left-right solution to the dilemma Chateaubriand's "anarchy" and Michelet's "democracy" had never come close to resolving. Maurras' own *pour Sainte-Beuve* is curiously synchronized with Proust's brief against the critic. He quotes Nietzsche on the pettiness of the individual only to make a very Proustian distinction between the man and his work: "Mais qu'est-il nécessaire que son personnage nous plaise! En oubliant le peu que fut cette personne, il faut considérer l'essence impersonnelle de l'esprit pur."[34]

With Sainte-Beuve, according to Maurras, we are freed from the sentimental narcissism of his age: "Un jour arriva promptement que Charles-Augustin Sainte-Beuve sut préférer la vérité à son coeur ... Quand il s'occupa des écrivains d'un autre siècle que le sien, il cessa de chercher ... sa propre ressemblance au fond de leurs oeuvres."[35] No more self-dramatizing projection, then, but what Maurras calls the constitution of a Museum of partial truth: *un Musée de la vérité partielle.*[36] And if a preference for the partial or component dimension over totalizing self-reflection seems precociously analytic, such is precisely the term chosen by Maurras for Sainte-Beuve: "le plus analyste des hommes" in the sense, we read, that analysis "decomposes" in the interest of providing the "elements of a recomposition."[37]

Ultimately what characterizes Sainte-Beuve's thought is its refusal of sentimental utopianism, an empiricist's sensibility that has him "organizing" tangents of ideality, *échappées sur l'idéal,* against what Maurras calls l'*imaginaire*, on the basis of the given. And it is that refusal of utopian rejection of empirical reality which dictated Sainte-Beuve's collaboration with the second Bonapartist regime. "Bien que fort jaloux des libertés de la plume, Sainte-Beuve se sépara des hommes de la seconde République pour se ranger à la contrainte impériale ... Puisque, en effet, l'ordre public est la condition même de la durée de la science ... comment la science pourrait-elle hésiter à céder à l'ordre public? On ne scie point une branche sur laquelle on se trouve assis."[38]

To this thoroughgoing realism, Maurras opposes a "scientific fanaticism" which threatens science itself. "Il perdrait un Etat pour tirer des archives et mettre en lumière un document 'intéressant.'"[39] The reference to the subversive curiosity of intellectuals is a reminder that Maurras was writing in the middle of the Dreyfus Affair, and lest anyone miss the point the founder of Action Française supplies us with a telling metaphor: what Sainte-Beuve (along with Maurras) is opposed to "consiste à remplacer le dieu des Juifs par la Curiosité, dite improprement *la Science*, mise sur un autel au centre du monde, et revêtue des mêmes honneurs que Jéhovah."[40] Thus just as Sainte-Beuve, under Maurras' tutelage, is welcomed into the anti-revolutionary ranks of, first, Renan and Taine, then the ultra-Catholic de Maistre and Bonald, anti-Beuvianism is associated metaphorically with the Jews.

But let us now return to what Maurras would no doubt call our own fanatically searched out document, Blanchot's front page column, in the *Journal des débats* of 10 March, 1942, on the politics of Sainte-Beuve. What we have provided is a frame for that centerpiece, which it would be important not to turn into a frame-up. The frame consists of the established tradition which saw in Sainte-Beuve (by virtue of "Les Regrets") the intellectual "collaborator" *par excellence* with a dictatorial regime and (by way of Maurras) the anti-Semitic right's surprise choice, at the time of the Dreyfus Affair, as intellectual standard-bearer. The centerpiece was a test: Blanchot, we have seen, was to be – and, to a certain extent, was – Paulhan's man in Drieu's *NRF*, the Resistance's ambassador to the Collaboration. It is as though he, the ex-militant fascist, were being asked, in reviewing Leroy's *La Politique de Sainte-Beuve*, to take a stand in a literary code the Germans themselves may not have understood, on the whole vexed question of intellectual collaboration and/or resistance.[41]

Leroy's *La Politique de Sainte-Beuve*, the subject of the Blanchot evocation or *tableau* we have just framed, offers itself as an apology for the political itinerary of the man Leroy calls, in 1941, "our contemporary."[42] For the famous critic was not only "one of the two or three major intelligences of the nineteenth century,"[43] according to Leroy, but a figure whom it would be an error to consider as fundamentally literary in his interests: "son fond me paraît être ailleurs."[44] And that elsewhere lay in a series of social preoccupations which would bring him closer to us.

Now the heart of any political apologia for Sainte-Beuve would of necessity lie in justifying his rallying, after the *coup d'état* of Louis Bonaparte, to the Second Empire. And this is in many ways the principal aim of the book. Leroy's is an effort to free Sainte-Beuve from the detestable epithet "renégat," to restore a measure of integrity to a figure who, given his support for the insurgents of February 1848, was subsequently branded a traitor to their cause. Leroy, in 1941, confesses his "astonishment" at the hatred provoked in 1852 by "Les Regrets," Sainte-Beuve's broadside against the anti-imperial resistance. The critic's notorious humiliation and forced resignation under political pressure from his own students at the Collège de France in 1855 is characterized as "une émeute à huis clos" and a "lâcheté" on the part of its perpetrators.[45]

How, then, does Leroy's defense proceed? The brief is pursued on two apparently contradictory fronts. On the one hand, we find an anti-utopian tendency in Sainte-Beuve which ultimately culminates in what might be called the Maurrassian defence. The rationalizing "orgy" of the eighteenth century had led to a series of disappointing revolutions erupting every fifteen years in France. Sainte-Beuve appears to have had his fill of revolutions after 1830, which he supported, but which initiated a regime whose corruption he analyzed with considerable venom and eloquence.[46] By 1852, his position was one of "organizing empiricism," a label of Maurras' that Leroy, who refers to Maurras only once, fully endorses. Better to reshape what is already there than to pretend to "invent" a new regime ... The simple necessities of civilized life necessitate the minimum of order that Napoleon III alone can provide, or, in Sainte-Beuve's own words: "L'acclamation universelle par laquelle la France a salué son président en 1852 et l'a sacré empereur a été, entre autres choses, un acte de haut bon sens."[47]

All of this, however, what might be called the skeptical, anti-utopian proto-Maurrassian side of Leroy's book, that is, of Blanchot's *subject*, is familiar to us as a motif from the ornate frame we have erected for Blanchot's *tableau*. (To clarify the painterly analogy: my earlier comments on Sainte-Beuve's notoriety in the nineteenth century and Maurras' effort to rehabilitate him at the time of the Dreyfus Affair constitute a *frame* for Blanchot's *tableau* or evocation, the March 1942 article, whose *subject* is Leroy's book *La Politique de Sainte-Beuve*.) We turn now to the other front in Leroy's apology for the critic's stance in 1852, one that is far more original, and which will undergo a curious displacement in Blanchot's own version of Sainte-Beuve. For Leroy devotes his longest and most substantial chapter to what might be called a left-wing defense of Sainte-Beuve. Around the time of the July Revolution, Sainte-Beuve served a year's stint as a Saint-Simonian fellow-traveler. Disillusionment with the theological and erotic antics of Saint-Simon's disciples was not long in coming, but Leroy leans particularly strongly on the critic's link to that productivist utopia in order to present his later rallying to the Second Empire as a residually Saint-Simonian outflanking of the Republican left *on its own left*.[48] In Leroy's most succinct formulation: "Si [Sainte-Beuve] est césarien, il l'est en socialiste."[49]

If, then, (*côté Maurras*) there is a rightist evolution – from abortive revolution to abortive revolution – of Sainte-Beuve's thought toward support of the December *coup*, there is, on the left, something less on the order of an evolution than a surprise return of the repressed. For it should not be forgotten that the Saint-Simonian leader Enfantin greeted the advent of the Empire as "providential," something on the order of what Maurras himself, in June 1940, called a "divine surprise."[50] For Leroy, the belated return of the "socialist" or Saint-Simonian in Sainte-Beuve was in fact of a piece with the critic's admiration for and interest in the work and person of Proudhon. Toward the end of his life Sainte-Beuve was at work on an unfinished biography of Proudhon, a "masterpiece," and for Leroy it as though the two nodes of Sainte-Beuve's leftward political itinerary were the early sojourn with the Saint-Simonians and the later work on Proudhon.[51]

Now concerning Proudhon, Leroy insists at length on the fact that he was an early left supporter of the Empire. As a convinced anti-parliamentarian and anti-democrat, he was more concerned with social than political reality. And Sainte-Beuve's positions are said to be essentially those of Proudhon. In Leroy's words, "*La Ré-volution sociale démontrée par le coup d'Etat* de Proudhon est très exactement le pendant des *Regrets* de Sainte-Beuve."[52]

In the France of the young Blanchot, the name Proudhon was highly charged. In *Combat*, the journal for which Blanchot had written in the late 1930s, an effort was made to mythologize a pre-World War I group, the Cercle Proudhon, as Europe's first authentic attempt at a fascist group. Under the name of (the rabidly anti-Semitic) Proudhon, (Maurrassian) royalists and (Sorelian) syndicalists had come together in their shared contempt for democracy.[53] It was in that context, no doubt, that Leroy felt comfortable anachronistically imagining Sainte-Beuve's "disabused smile" at finding a "striking justification for his own political empiricism" in a passage he proceeds to cite from Sorel.[54]

Leroy's 1941 apologia for Sainte-Beuve's collaboration with the Empire thus is twofold: Maurrassian on the right and Proudhonian-Sorelian on the left. As such it discreetly captured the two components of France's *ur*-fascist formation as mythologized in Blanchot's own milieu in the 1930s. But perhaps that extremist left-right fusion was already in germ in the Saint-Simonianism that Leroy seems so intent on assigning a formative role in Sainte-Beuve's political thought. For there is persistent reference to the paradoxical centrality of the thought of Joseph de Maistre (as well as Bonald and Ballanche) in the organic social vision of the Saint-Simonians. De Maistre, of course, was the reactionary ideologue whom Isaiah Berlin has discussed most recently as being at the wellspring of fascism. Berlin: "He was the first theorist in the great and powerful tradition which culminated in Charles Maurras, a precursor of the Fascists ..."[55] And for Sainte-Beuve, in his *Nouveaux lundis*, "le saint-simonisme rendit à l'esprit français d'alors cet éminent service d'implanter dans le camp de la révolution et du progrès, quelques-unes des pensées élevées de M. de Maistre et de les y naturaliser en bonne terre et d'une manière vivante."[56] Thus Leroy's Sainte-Beuve of 1941 moves from the extreme left-right fusion of Saint-Simon and de Maistre to that of Proudhon (or Sorel) and Maurras. *Ni droite ni gauche*, in Sternhell's phrase. Which is to say that no thinker could make as much claim to being "our contemporary" during the Nazi occupation – in a France intent on proving, in defeat, its own autonomy or centrality – as Leroy's Sainte-Beuve, who draws on an extreme left-right ideology in rallying to the brutal putsch of a military dictator.

If Saint-Simonianism lay at the heart of Sainte-Beuve's rallying to the Empire (for he is alleged to have claimed that Napoleon III was Saint-Simon on horseback),[57] it becomes of some interest, in this context, to note one of the defining idiosyncrasies of the movement as evoked by Leroy. As a social movement, Saint-Simonianism veered into a religion, but the particularity of that religion, we are told, "si singulier que le fait paraisse," is that it itself was the development of an esthetic doctrine.[58] Society, stripped of class conflict, is an exercise in harmony, an endless performance of "la vaste symphonie sociale."[59] The esthetic sense, that is, is the matrix out of which and toward which Saint-Simonian politics registers its appeal.

But the "estheticization of politics" is, of course, Walter Benjamin's celebrated formula for the essence of fascism. It is therefore entirely fitting that Benjamin should attend to Saint-Simonianism at some length in his own archeology of the nineteenth-century dream world out of which fascism eventually emerged, The Arcades Project. In that massive and unfinished work, Benjamin is particularly alive to the pseudo-socialistic dimension of the movement. Based on the proposition that workers and capitalists together formed but "a single industrial class," the movement ended up, in Thibaudet's formulation, as "profoundly *grand bourgeois.*"[60] It was this illusory harmony, moreover, that opened up the esthetic wellsprings Leroy's Saint-Simonians seemed intent on exploiting. Or, as Benjamin puts it in a lapidary phrase: "On the notion of the total art work in Saint-Simon [Zur Idee des Gesamtkunstwerks, nach Saint-Simon] ..."[61] In their willful estheticization of socio-political reality, that is, Benjamin's Saint-Simonians are already proto-Wagnerians.

That fact is of special import when one recalls that Blanchot's chosen guide through the morass of the recent debate over Heidegger and Nazism was Philippe Lacoue-Labarthe's *La Fiction du politique.*[62] For Lacoue-Labarthe's central point was that the heart of Nazism was an estheticization of politics. Nazism, in his phrase, was above all a "national-esthétisme" or, more succinctly, "le modèle *politique* du national-socialisme est le *Gesamtkunstwerk*..."[63] We have moved, then, without ever leaving Benjamin, from the proto-Wagnerian Saint-Simonians to the deutero-Wagnerian Nazis, each with their vision of society as a total work of art. But we have done so in an effort to gauge Blanchot's daunting subject on 10 March 1942, his apparent response to a call to take a stand on Leroy's apologia for and analysis of the Saint-Simonian or "socialist" impetus behind Sainte-Beuve's eager rallying to a dictatorial regime...

Thus far we have dealt with what I have called the frame of Blanchot's *tableau*: Sainte-Beuve's role as collaborationist bogeyman of the liberal intelligentsia, his coronation by Maurras during the Dreyfus Affair. And we have dealt with its subject: Leroy's two-pronged apologia for Sainte-Beuve's politics, "empiricist" with Maurras, "socialist" with Saint-Simon and Proudhon. But we have yet to read a word − or stroke − of Blanchot's piece. Which is to say, perhaps, that we have been engaging in a form of hyper-structuralism, sketching out the contours or even generating the only text, as yet unread, that might satisfy the various constraints − of frame and subject − we have adduced. Structuralist, indeed: were one to examine the space the *Journal des débats* accorded Blanchot's article − front page, double column, flush right − diachronically, we would find it was earmarked for cultural justifications for adhering to Pétain's policies. A week earlier (4 March 1942), Gaetan Sanvoisin, in the same space, issued a long and laudatory comparison between Richelieu and Pétain ("Un rapprochement s'impose. En ce qui concerne le double souci de l'unité nationale et la noblesse du vocabulaire, comme Richelieu le maréchal Pétain se sert d'une langue impeccable pour définir les lois essentielles de notre sauvegarde territoriale.")[64] So much for diachrony. Synchronically, Blanchot's article would appear to form a diptych with a front-page editorial the same day hailing Pétain as "the only man able to lead us."[65] Such at least must have been the expectation of Blanchot's editors. That those expectations were decisively thwarted, even at the cost of a misreading of Leroy's argument, strikes me as a precise gauge of Blanchot's political honor. It is to that topic, as mediated by Blanchot's article, that we now shall turn.

The piece begins ominously enough with a statement of admiration for Leroy's identification with his subject. Leroy, we are told, seems to have wanted to become "tout semblable" to Sainte-Beuve. Indeed Leroy's sympathetic insinuation into the critic's mind is compared to Sainte-Beuve's own identification with the Catholic mystic and monarchist Ballanche in an essay that so "shocked" (Blanchot's word) Sainte-Beuve's liberal friends that Leroy uses the word "treason" to characterize their assessment of it.[66] At stake in Blanchot's article, in brief, is an identification with the Sainte-Beuve whose own political identifications opened him up to accusations of treason on the part of the liberal intelligentsia. And that chain of identifications, moreover, which admits no reservation, is what joins the situation of Leroy in 1941 (and potentially of Blanchot in 1942) to Sainte-Beuve at the time of the *coup d'état* of 1851. In Blanchot's words: Leroy "ne consent à aucune réserve. Il trouve le meilleur dans le pire. Et ce parti-pris d'apologiste, grâce à une extraordinaire entente des circonstances cachées, ne donne que rarement l'impression de troubler un regard perspicace." The extraordinary "entente" or affinity, concealed though it may be, and to which Blanchot feels empowered to allude in the most discreet terms, is precisely the one which we have attempted to shed some light on in our preceding comments.

The subject, in brief, will at some level be, Blanchot suggests, collaboration and its apologists in the France of 1941. And Blanchot's tone in his first paragraph implies that Leroy's apology is a remarkably impressive feat – without quite implying that it is a politically or ethically justified one. At this point Blanchot turns to the whole side of Sainte-Beuve's career which led Irving Babbitt to suggest that the best motto for the critic might well have been "Enthusiasm and repentance."[67] In 1830 and in 1848, he was a sympathizer with the insurgents, but one who soon found himself disappointed and occasionally overwhelmed by the cause he had championed. There is at times here a quite Blanchotian sense that the repentance is so much stronger than the initial enthusiasm as to have left nought but an extreme nihilism in its wake. Thus this quotation from Sainte-Beuve (in a letter to Adam Mickjewicz) as early as 1833: "Vous vous dites pèlerins et bannis, et nous aussi, nous sommes bannis de la révolution que nous avons aimée et que nous avons faite: nous sommes expulsés de nos espérances." It is hard not to imagine Blanchot, the ex-apologist for fascist terrorism, the ex-bureaucrat of Jeune France, not feeling addressed by that assessment.[68] Yet Leroy's Sainte-Beuve retained a certain positive wisdom of disillusion and it was precisely that dimension that brings Blanchot to Leroy's endorsement of Sainte-Beuve's rallying to the Empire: "M. Maxime Leroy justifie longuement Sainte-Beuve d'avoir accepté le 2 décembre et de s'être rallié à l'Empire. Il montre que son goût de l'autorité, formé à l'école de Saint-Simon, trouve dans le nouveau régime plus à louer qu'à blâmer." Yet curiously Blanchot does not approach the heart of Leroy's enthusiasm for what he regards as Sainte-Beuve's own enthusiasm for the Empire: the Saint-Simonian or "socialist" heart of the program, the possibility of outflanking the liberals on their left. Blanchot does all he can to mitigate Sainte-Beuve's enthusiasm, to inscribe the rallying to the Empire under the rubric of "repentance" or disillusionment: "Il y a beaucoup de retenue et un certain mépris dans son ralliement..."

But this confronts Blanchot with a second embarrassment, the fact that the slope of repentance in Babbitt's imagined motto leads Blanchot precipitously to Maurras' own essay on Sainte-Beuve's "empiricism." For it would be more than a mere pun to read the authoritarian Second Empire back into Maurras' vision of the critic's empiricism. Now the paradox, in this chess game that Blanchot seems to be playing with Leroy (or his own editors) on the front page of the *Journal des débats* is that the "empiricist" culmination of Sainte-Beuve's disillusionment (or repentance) in the endorsement of Maurras forces Blanchot to confront, in Maurras, the very enthusiasm, on the margins of Action Française, he was then – in 1942 – desirous of shunting off if not repenting for.

At this point Blanchot appears to flinch. No sooner has he discussed the politically explosive precedent of rallying to the Empire than we read: "On sait que M. Charles Maurras a donné

le nom d'empirisme organisateur à la methode d'observation politique qu'a appliquée Sainte-Beuve et qui l'a conduit, dans un
siècle dévoré de systèmes, d'idéologie, de passions abstraites et de
frénésie instinctive, à se soumettre à la loi des faits et des résultats.
C'est là la principale leçon de cet esprit sinueux, instable, religieux au fond, inquiet et blessé, sur qui l'intelligence, en accord
avec une sensibilité perpétuellement soucieuse d'harmonie, a
étendu l'empire le plus large, le plus étranger aux bornes."
Sainte-Beuve's itinerary in disillusionment or repentance, that is,
has culminated in the object of Blanchot's enthusiasm, his endorsement of Maurras' analytic endorsement of Sainte-Beuve. That
Blanchot's endorsement, moreover, all but repeats our pun,
moving from "empirisme organisateur" to "empire," puts it in
painful contiguity with the whole subject of collaboration, the presumed reason Blanchot's Pétainist editors had reserved pride of
place on the first page of their newspaper for him. Blanchot
would appear to have all but fallen into the trap.

Whereupon he performs an about-face, engages in his own palinode: "Il va de soi que les limites d'un tel réalisme ne sont pas
facilement supportable. Sainte-Beuve lui-même ne les a pas sup-
portés. Il s'en est sans cesse affranchi et il a porté en lui des rêves
qu'éveillait le mouvement d'une croyance opiniâtre." Now on the
path to this shunting off of the Maurrassian reading that has just
been endorsed, it is significant that the principal landmark is the
critic's Saint-Simonianism: "Saint-Simonien dans sa jeunesse, il a
consacré une partie de lui-même à des espérances vagues et con-
solantes, à une sorte d'optimisme dévot que nulle déception n'est
parvenue à effacer." Such is Blanchot's principal reference to
Saint-Simon in the article, the starting point for a renunciation of
what had been consolidated around the endorsement of Maurras.
Yet we have seen that for Leroy, Sainte-Beuve's Saint-Simonianism (refracted through Proudhon) as well as his "empiricism"
or proto-Maurrassianism were not in conflict but in fact fused as
the two strands – left and right – of what Blanchot's own generation had learned to champion as fascism. So that the pitting of a
dreamy Saint-Simonianism against a hard-nosed Maurrassianism
is totally at odds with the Sainte-Beuve of whom Leroy writes:
"s'il est césarien, il l'est en socialiste, comme Enfantin ou

Proudhon, ralliés a l'Empire."[69] In a flagrant and glorious mis-reading of Leroy's book, Blanchot has pitted the two ideological dimensions of what would unite as fascism against each other in a patently anti-collaborationist move.

Where does this take him? The sole further reference to Sainte-Beuve's Saint-Simonianism is a quotation from the Goncourt *Journal*, denying the perpetuity of "literary property." Sainte-Beuve's Saint-Simonianism, that is, becomes a first step toward the domain of radical dispossession characteristic of what would later be called *l'espace littéraire*. The next anti-Maurrassian salvo is by way of the Abbé Brémond: "La foi dont l'abbé Brémond a voulu lui faire présent [à Sainte-Beuve] dans son livre, *Roman et histoire d'une conversion*, se réfracte ainsi à travers une âme obscure où l'inquiétude, la déception, le désir d'aimer, des élans sans cesse contrariés entretiennent une insatisfaction qui nourrit sa recherche, mais qui lui fait briser secrètement le réalisme tranquille auquel il s'attache." The "realism" or "empiricism" or attachment to the Empire is again thwarted, shattered, by religious faith. The Brémond book is a curious tale of Sainte-Beuve's role as consoler and confessor in the conversion of his friend Guttinguer.[70] It was an experience that saw both men writing novelistic versions – each named *Arthur* – of their joint ordeal and which brought Sainte-Beuve himself to the brink of religious conversion. What is most striking in the present context is that in Blanchot's article, Sainte-Beuve has moved from illustrious predecessor in the byways of collaboration with a reviled military dictatorship to confidant in an experience of conversion. But for anyone who has followed Blanchot's writing from the margins of Action Française to the extreme "passivity" characteristic of "literary space," is it not as though what were at stake were something in the order of a conversion? Blanchot, that is, would have written himself into the role of Sainte-Beuve's confidant and convertee Guttinguer.

Consider, in that light, the fact that Guttinguer's conversion was in large part triggered by the flight of one of his mistresses, Rosalie, to a convent on the rue Picpus, and was haunted by his desire to murder the woman he referred to in his correspondence (in italics) as *"la religieuse."*[71] Guttinguer's conversion would at some level entail the sacrifice of "la religieuse." Let us pause to imagine that proposition, from the book adduced (against collaboration) by Blanchot, resonating in the critic's mind. Diderot's own *Religieuse*, the novel, he may have known, was said by its author to have been inspired by the myth of Iphigenia.[72] The fact becomes illuminating when one recalls, as evoked above, that Blanchot's own allegory of his sacrifice of an investment in fascism in 1938 was written up after the War, as his own version of the myth of Iphigenia, *L'Arrêt de mort*. Here we find Blanchot, in flight from the specter of collaboration, in flight from his own Maurrassian past, in concealed flight as well from Leroy's reading of Sainte-Beuve, inviting his readers to dream a tale of conversion informed, by implication, by the myth that would later haunt him, that of Iphigenia.

After Saint-Simon and the expropriation of the author, after the abbé Brémond and his tale of conversion, Blanchot leaves us with a final marker for situating "the politics of Sainte-Beuve," the abbé Sieyès. Having gutted whatever positivity may have been left of Sainte-Beuve's proto-Maurrassian empiricism, having evoked the "desperation" such a view would entail, he concludes: "Il est naturel d'évoquer, à son propos, comme l'a fait M. Leroy, l'étrange retraite de Sieyès qui, poussé par la désillusion, renonça à lui-même et s'enferma dans le silence. L'extrême incrédulité, quand elle s'accepte, conduit à une netteté désespérée qui interdit toute distraction, rend vaine la possession d'aucun trésor et raye enfin la nuit." Here one senses the eloquent nihilism of Blanchot's maturity, but what interests me is its links to the retreat from Pétainist collaboration which I take the article on Sainte-Beuve's politics to be. There is, of course, good reason for adducing Sieyès as a prototype for Sainte-Beuve's behavior. For the author of *Qu'est-ce que le Tiers Etat?* was notorious for having both ushered in the Revolution and drawing it to a close: he was a principal coconspirator with Bonaparte in the first 18 Brumaire. Such, I assume, was Leroy's reason for linking him with Sainte-Beuve, who managed to be a man of both 1848 and 1851: Sainte-Beuve, or the second time as farce, if one likes. Blanchot, however, is less interested in the political maneuverer than in the long-lived survivor of political catastrophe. In the 1830s, it has been said, "they thought him another Daniel delivered from the burning fiery furnace; the hair of his head had been singed, the smell of fire had passed upon him; and [people] drew back a little from his touch."[73] At the end of "La Politique de Sainte-Beuve," that is, we find ourselves somewhere between *La Part du feu* and *L'Ecriture du désastre*. The Sieyès of his retirement or "philosophical silence," as he called it, was a man become, in his own words, "entièrement négatif," committed to absolute silence on the subject of what he had been through. Sainte-Beuve, in his own *Lundi* on Sieyès, evokes his silence, has him interrupting his every discourse: "Je ne trouve plus le mot, il se cache dans quelque coin obscur."[74] Translated into Blanchot's post-War idiom of 1948: "Un récit? ... Non, pas de récit, plus jamais."[75] The War is over; the *récit* is not forthcoming; and it remains perhaps for us to piece together the fragments of what it might have been.

CHAPTER 13

Flowers of evil: Paul Morand, the Collaboration, and literary history

Accablé de fatigue et de bienfaits, Daniel eut de la peine
à contenir sa rage. Mais il appartenait à une génération dés-
armée devant les fleurs, devant l'Europe nouvelle, et qui n'a
jamais su dire non.

Paul Morand, *L'Europe galante* (1925)

In 1921, Marcel Proust, in the last months of his life, chose to
excuse himself from what he called a temporary lodger who had
taken up residence in his brain, a foreigner (*étrangère*) he identified
as Death, and set pen to paper to write a rambling preface to
Tendres stocks, a volume by the young Paul Morand.[1] Perhaps the
most significant aspect of Proust's text is his opening reference to
an observation – on style – by his "master Anatole France."[2] For
France, of course, had prefaced Proust's early volume of stories,
Les Plaisirs et les jours.[3] Here then was a legacy: in identifying
Morand as "le nouvel écrivain original" *par excellence*, Proust was
inscribing him in the grand tradition he no doubt felt he himself
had joined, at the beginning of his career, with the blessings of
France. And as if such a godparent were not sufficiently auspi-
cious, *Tendres stocks* would soon be set into English, under the title
Fancy Goods, by none other than Ezra Pound.[4] The next generation of the West's literary pantheon would weigh in with even
more forceful votes of confidence. Céline opined that in the year
2000, Morand and (to be sure) he himself would be the only two
contemporaries still being read.[5] And Sartre, in *Qu'est-ce que la littérature?*, let it be known, in pages on how "speed" in Morand had
come to play the role of the "paranoiac-critical method" in the
Surrealists, that whatever "literature" was in 1947, it transited
Morand's *oeuvre* in telling manner.[6]

That *oeuvre* is slashed in two by the fact of Morand's collaboration with the Vichy government. A diplomat stranded in London during the fall of France, he snubbed de Gaulle's historic call to resistance of June 18 (which had, in fact, been typed by a member of his own staff), and, along with eighty percent of the French then in London, requested repatriation to Vichy France.[7] In 1942, he would serve as Vichy's chairman of the Commission de Censure Cinématographique; in 1943, he would assume the post of Vichy's ambassador to the royal court of Romania.[8] The wartime years, it has been observed, introduced a thematic break in Morand's work as well. Whereas the pre-War period saw the author making use of the modernist motif of speed to effect a series of telling short-circuits between nations and cultures, the post-War period saw a newly constrained Morand, living in Swiss exile, effecting his short-circuits in time.[9] To take the case of two works we shall be examining, if *L'Europe galante* (1925), as Sartre put it, represents the "nullification of countries by the railroad," *Le Flagellant de Séville* (1951) effects an unexpected (apologetic) link between the Spanish collaboration with Napoleon and the French collaboration with Hitler.[10]

In April 1958, Morand became the focus of a scandal when he attempted to secure election to the Académie Française. François Mauriac and Jules Romains regarded his candidacy as a provocation and led a bloc in drafting a letter of protest to the academy's acting director, observing that whatever Morand's literary credentials, "his name and his role during the last war remain associated with memories and grievances whose nature is such as to revive old controversies and conflicts better settled by the passage of time."[11] Romains went so far as to claim that the election of Morand would be tantamount to "the revenge of the Collaboration."[12] Passions were inflamed and it was not until de Gaulle himself intervened – with a negative opinion – that Morand withdrew his candidacy. He would eventually be elected in October 1968.

Meanwhile Morand had become (with Céline) something of a symbol of the Collaboration. It is instructive to compare the virtual omission of his name from the classic literary manual *La Littérature depuis 1945*, published by Bordas, with the lavish treatment he is accorded, as one of the "great figures of the century," in that volume's sequel, *La Littérature française depuis 1968*.[13] Plainly the amends the authors of the later volume seek to make is the reflection of a change of climate. Finally, the promise Morand seemed to hold for Proust reappears as fulfilled in the remarks of the French writer best attuned to the nuances of literary climate, Philippe Sollers. In a recent preface to Morand's *New York*, the editor of *L'Infini* writes of Morand: "C'est sans doute le meilleur écrivain français du XXme siècle, en retrait de Proust et de Céline, bien sûr, – il a compris ses limites –, mais loin devant les autres dont l'inutilité s'accroît tous les jours."[14] Sollers treats us to a daydream about what the contours of French literature in this century might have been if, as he puts it, the Morand of *New York* had stayed on the other side of the Atlantic and the Céline of *Pont de Londres* had remained on the other side of the Channel. And yet we have the French literature that we have, one in which Sollers' utopian fantasy of a literature uncompromised by the disasters of French history remains just that.

My purpose in these pages is to dwell within the vexed status of Morand's magnitude as a writer, to rehearse the distinction that Proust and Pound intuited in him at the inception of his career and that Sollers attempted to restore to him posthumously, but without for a moment failing to acknowledge the ethical catastrophe whose centrality for any late twentieth-century reader cannot but radiate as a malignant source throughout Morand's *oeuvre*. What I propose, then, is a reading of three Morand texts, from both before and after World War II, with an eye to the paradoxical – even anachronistic – interdependence of their commanding esthetic achievement and the ethical stain which continues to permeate them: a small anthology, then, of flowers (*anthos*) ... but of evil. The first is the short story "Lorenzaccio," from the 1925 collection *L'Europe galante*; the second a major novel, published in 1951, *Le Flagellant de Séville;* the third, written midway between the two, a satirical novel of 1934, in the spirit of Gide's *soties, France-la-doulce*.[15] The fact, moreover, that these texts have been culled from both before and after the War affords a byway into the question of literary anachronism which shall as well offer us entry into the first of the Morand texts to be examined, "Lorenzaccio."

The very title is, of course, a reference to Musset's great romantic drama of Renaissance Florence, and the problems of interpretation – or anachronism – begin with Morand's apparent failure to follow through on the intertextual clue he has provided his reader. The editor of the Pléiade edition of Morand's works, for one, declares himself, nonplussed: "Par son titre, ce récit se réfère au drame de Musset et le lecteur s'attend que cette relation soit explicitée par la suite. Or, il n'en est rien."[16] Let us turn first, then, to the Musset plot to see what resonances it holds for an analysis of Morand. *Lorenzaccio* is the drama of Lorenzo di Medici, a young Hamletic idealist, who decides it is his destiny to free Florence from the tyranny of his debauched cousin Alessandro, a puppet dictator kept in power by the German soldiers installed in Florence by the Emperor Charles V. Lorenzo, in his plan to be a new Brutus, slaying a new Caesar, ingratiates himself with his would-be victim, becomes his procuror and partner in debauchery, and is perceived by all of Florence as "un lendemain d'orgie ambulant (a walking hang-over)."[17] We eventually learn that having plunged so deeply into Florentine corruption, Lorenzo has lost all faith in the effectiveness of the assassination he will nonetheless carry out, if only out of fidelity to whatever remains of the initial idealism that drew him to his abortive plan in the first place. He assassinates Alessandro, but no uprising occurs, and Lorenzaccio, in Venice, leaving the scene for a last stroll "on the Rialto," is himself murdered and dumped into the lagoon.

At the center of Musset's play, then, is an almost existential drama of absurdist heroism. Moreover, an additional layer of pathos is supplied by the ongoing ordeal of Marie Soderini, Lorenzo's mother. For she is visibly shattered by the life her son is leading. She dreams of awakening from an idyllic dream "dans les bras d'un spectre hideux qui vous tue en vous appelant encore du nom de mère."[18] Lorenzo himself seems obscurely aware that his choice will have disastrous consequences for his mother: "Que ma mère mourût de tout cela, voilà ce qui pourrait arriver."[19] Meditating his crime, he repeats his obsession: "Que ma mère mourût de tout cela, ce serait triste."[20] It is small surprise then that news of the mother's death follows directly on Lorenzo's murder of the tyrant, for it is almost as though the murder of Alessandro were at some level an oblique matricide. Indeed, in his major monologue of act IV, our would-be Brutus changes mythic identity: "Le spectre de mon père me conduisait-il, comme Oreste, vers un nouvel Egisthe?"[21] With Lorenzo-Hamlet become Orestes, the centrality of the matricide motif seems secure.

But with the motif of Orestes committing some version of matricide in order to free a very Parisian evocation of Florence from the tyranny of German occupation, it becomes clear that what we have beeen discussing by way of *Lorenzaccio* is Sartre's own allegorical reading of his classic drama of the Occupation, *Les Mouches*. Already in 1944, Sartre was writing: "Pourquoi faire déclamer les Grecs ... si ce n'est pour déguiser sa pensée sous un régime fasciste? ... Le véritable drame, celui que j'aurais voulu écrire, c'est celui du terroriste qui, en descendant des Allemands dans la rue, déclenche l'exécution de cinquante otages."[22] The guilt of any anti-Nazi terrorist, knowing that his every murder would result in the suffering (or death) of the innocent was, to be sure, not a subject which could be treated explicitly on the French stage during the German Occupation. But then neither was *Lorenzaccio*, Musset's drama of thwarted resistance against a very German occupation. It would have been unthinkable, for example, to include the anti-German rhetoric of act I, scene II ("Il en sort tous les jours de nouveau, de ces chiens d'Allemands, de leur damnée forteresse") in a stage version in the early 1940s.[23]

It is, of course, possible to argue that Musset's play was a significant influence on Sartre's, and that position surely carries some merit. When Lorenzo is exhorted: "que l'homme sorte de l'histrion"; when Lorenzo describes vice as a garment which has attached itself to his skin and can no longer be differentiated from it, it is as though the Sartrean critique of gestures, a central motif of *Les Mouches*, were being sketched by Musset.[24] Yet my point here is, in fact, the opposite: to argue the influence of Sartre on Musset. This is one of those effects of retroaction that T. S. Eliot used to delight in: an earlier text changing – releasing or withdrawing regions of potentiality – under the pressure of a more recent one. *Lorenzaccio* will have been the play whose unabridged performance remained impossible under the Nazi Occupation and whose existential treatment of the metaphysics of resistance would attain maximal clarity only by way of Sartre's allegorical reading, after the War, of *Les Mouches*. It is as though anachronism were the medium in which Musset's play demanded to be read, as though the commentators who have observed that the Rialto bridge onto which Lorenzaccio makes his final exit was in fact built some fifty years after the play's action (in 1537) had missed the point. The protagonist makes his final exit onto the scene of anachronism, and it is that scene which our reading of Musset's play has attempted to stage.

Morand's "Lorenzaccio," then, a story of 1925, read within the anachronistic coupling of *Lorenzaccio* and *Les Mouches* ... It is a gesture that is not without resonances in Morand's own *oeuvre*. In the newspaper *Candide*, in May 1928, he published a short piece titled "1958, choses prévues." It was a delightful bit of futuristic prose, quite wrong about what might be the case thirty years later, but which came with piquant instructions to the reader: "Mettez cet article au fond d'un tiroir et, si vous avez un soir à perdre, en 1958, relisez-le."[25] Morand's text, that is, was written within the esthetic mode of anachronism and derived its pungency from that circumstance. Our situating of Morand's "Lorenzaccio" within a constitutive (Musset-Sartre) anachronism is thus in keeping with one of the paradoxical tendencies of the author's own inspiration.

"Lorenzaccio," as if to confirm our gesture, comes with a subtitle, "le retour du proscrit," that seeems a premonition of Sartre's plot. For *Les Mouches* begins with the return of an exile, Orestes, returning to Argos and his family palace some twenty years after he was sent abroad, at age three, following the murder of Agamemnon. Morand's tale opens with the evocation of a long-awaited return home: "Bien que son attente durât depuis quinze mille soirs, c'est-à-dire depuis quarante-deux ans environ, Tarquinio Gonçalves était impatient de rentrer chez lui."[26] Whereupon the parallel in short order breaks down: Tarquinio is returning from political exile in London to Portugal, where he had had a career as a political leader and "man of order" under the Regency. He is in no way the would-be assassin of Musset's – then Sartre's – play. The editor of the Pléiade declares himself at a loss as to how to view Tarquinio as a "Portuguese Lorenzaccio."[27] But that is because he has failed to recall that Tarquinius is in fact an important – although erroneous – reference in Musset's play. In act II, scene IV, Lorenzo, who would assassinate a tyrant, confuses Brutus, assassin of Caesar, and a second Brutus who avenges the suicide of Lucretia, by forcing the overthrow of her rapist Tarquinius. Since there is a Lucretia figure in the play, the noble Louise Strozzi, sacrificed to Alesssandro di Medici's turpitude, Lorenzo's (or Musset's) error serves an esthetic end. From our own perspective, the important point is that Musset's plot pits Lorenzaccio-Brutus against Alessandro-Caesar-Tarquinius. But if Alessandro is Tarquinius, the implication is that Morand's Tarquinio, despite his role as protagonist of the tale, corresponds not at all to Lorenzaccio but to his would-be victim. Morand, that is, has served us up a concealed plot reversal of the sort that his sometime tutor and friend Giraudoux (himself the author of a paradoxical *Pour Lucrèce*) excelled in. But to effect a reversal of Musset's premonition of – Sartre's allegory of – anti-German resistance is presumably not without links to our perception of Morand's subsequent role as a wartime collaborator. In that perspective, we return to the plot of Morand's tale.

Tarquinio Gonçalves, we learn, was a politician who had squandered his life, something of a "Portuguese Gambetta." Anti-dynastic under the monarchy, briefly a head of government under the Regency, but too indifferent a democrat to succeed under the new republic, he had been reviled as an authoritarian under the new regime and ultimately sent into exile. Now years later he returns to Lisbon, one of the sun's "preferred cities," called back by a new political turn that sees one of his childhood friends named prime minister. Gonçalves' first stroll upon reaching the port is to his family mansion, a baroque palace which like many another in his neigborhood has been put up for rent under the new regime. He approaches, is surprised to find the principal door ajar, and cannot resist the familiar gesture of making his way into the hallway of his childhood. Whereupon a

"Levantine" gentleman in formal dress greets him with the words: "Monsieur a dû oublier sa carte. C'est dix réaux."[28] It is at this point that the "Dictator," as he had been called under the Regency, much as Gambetta had been suspected of caesarism in the early years of the Third Republic, realizes that his ancestral residence has been converted into a gambling casino.[29]

Gonçalves pays his way into the casino, takes in the full measure of Portugal's decadence, and suddenly finds himself accosted at the gaming table by the words: "Prêtez-moi de quoi souper, j'ai tout perdu." He turns to observe a very young sailor: "un de ces voyous flexibles et débauchés de la flotte qui, par leur mauvaise tenue et leur insolence, jouissent dans les arsenaux et aux postes d'équipage d'une autorité sans conteste."[30] Gonçalves responds by stuffing a bill into the sailor's jersey, turning around abruptly, and leaving the premises. Meanwhile, the political situation heats up: the republican ministry of the protagonist's friend fails, a communist-linked committee takes power, and Gonçalves, having retired to a life of gardening in his country residence, has nonetheless become the "man of order" rumored to be the center-right's one hope for redressing the situation. The left, though still in power, reacts by targeting the "Dictator" for assassination, and the chosen assassin turns out to be none other than the insolent sailor whose enigmatic beneficiary Gonçalves had been in the casino. Morand, however, was not rewriting "Androcles and the Lion," but *Lorenzaccio*. The protagonist proceeds to deliver his would-be assassin a brief but withering lecture on the decadence of the navy, tells him he would not mind being murdered by someone with a taste for killing, but that it is out of the question that he allow himself to be assassinated by someone who, plainly, doesn't love anything but has accepted his task for need of money. Whereupon, he waxes Charlus-like, tells the sailor that he gave him the money for his beauty, and proceeds in short order, exploiting his overwhelming discursive advantage, to bugger the humiliated sailor. He then dismisses his victim (*la victime*), watches him or "her" (*[il] la regardait*) pull up his trousers, and tossing him a rose, metonym for this first of our flowers of evil, delivers what he would like to be the moral of

Morand's tale: "l'assassinat de Tarquinio de Gonçalves ne se traite pas à l'entreprise."[31]

Morand has written flippantly of the story that it is an effort to treat pederasty as "one of the modes of the Portuguese baroque."[32] From our own perspective, as seen from within the Musset-Sartre intertext already elaborated, it is clear that Morand shunned the Orestes motif adopted from the play by Sartre in order to adopt, but also reverse, Musset's Tarquinius subtext. Tarquinius (or Tarquinio) is Alessandro di Medici, which would leave the insolent sailor with the role of Lorenzaccio. But the sense of futility of this twentieth-century Lorenzaccio would be so pronounced that not only will he not carry out his assassination, but he will be unmanned in the process. Now to the extent that Lorenzaccio was fighting against a German occupation, to the extent that his mission would always already have been that of Sartre's World War II Orestes, it is as though Morand were already declaring the bankruptcy of the anti-German resistance in his 1925 tale of the sodomization of Lorenzaccio. Pressing Alessandro's derisive sobriquet for the character – "Lorenzetta" – to the extreme, Morand, as *macho* as Sartre in his way, seems to be answering the latter's characterization of the effeminate collaborator, eager for submission, with an image of the sodomized *résistant* every bit as demeaning. That the *anti-résistant* (or proto-collaborationist) "Dictator," Gonçalves, should be compared by Morand to Gambetta, who in fact was a leader of the resistance to a very different German occupation of France, in 1871, is an irony – lure or trap – of history whose victim Morand, in retrospect, appears to have been.

"Lorenzaccio," then, as an anachronistic blueprint for the hopelessness of resistance against the German Occupation in 1940 ... The speed with which the author of *L'homme pressé* left London in July 1940, shortly after de Gaulle's arrival, and made his way to Vichy, regular lunches with Laval, and the disastrous series of assignments he subsequently accepted, seems very much that of a reader (or writer) who has drawn the lesson of *L'Europe galante*'s reading of Musset's plot. As Morand put it in a letter to a friend in 1945: "Je ne suis pas resté à Londres parce que je sentais qu'un monde était à sa fin, qu'il fallait chercher ailleurs ..."[33] Morand's principal statement on his years as a collaborator, however, occurs not in his correspondence but in literature, in the characteristically oblique and anachronistic novel, written in Swiss exile, and published in France in 1951, *Le Flagellant de Séville*. It is to that work, the longest work of prose fiction ever authored by Morand, that we now shall turn.

Seville was already something of a code word for readers of Morand. The author's last significant allusion to the city was in "Le Festin de pierre," a denunciation of the mendacity of Third-Republican political life cast as a moralizing reading of the punishment of Don Juan and published in December 1940 in the inaugural issue of Drieu la Rochelle's *Nouvelle Revue française*: "Don Juan apparaît comme le type du démagogue ... Orage sur la forêt, tempête sur la Pologne, coup de tonnerre hitlérien, et le Vengeur apparaît ..."[34] The masochistic flagellant of Seville, in 1951, does indeed appear to be paying for Morand's treatment of the legendary *burlador* of that city in 1940. But the principal literary subtext of Morand's novel lies elsewhere, as a brief consideration of the lineaments of its plot will make clear.

Le Flagellant de Séville is set in the period of the Napoleonic occupation of Spain. Its protagonist is one Don Luis de Almodóvar, an enthusiast of Enlightenment values and the French Revolution, who gradually commits himself to supporting the puppet Bonapartist regime of Napoleon's brother Joseph, become King of Spain, in the name of just those values. Don Luis' family discourages him in his career as a collaborator, and his principal adversary is in fact his cousin Blas, a kind of Nietzschean *Untermensch*, "un homme de *mala digestión*," who has joined the Resistance underground and is said to maintain contacts with the British. Meanwhile, Luis' adored wife, Marisol, accompanies him, dolorously, in what they both suspect is his moral decline (and social ascension) from Seville to Madrid. Nonetheless, she nurses secret dreams of being his salvation. To this end she befriends and to all appearances becomes somewhat enamored of an anarchistic terrorist affiliated with the Resistance, one Marcos. Her hope is that by secretly spying *against* the French, she will be able to accumulate the kind of credit with the Resistance that will allow her to buy the well-being of her husband should things turn against him politically. Luis meanwhile has become a police spy for the French, and in that capacity, after a bizarrely sketchy encounter with a tightly outfitted and seemingly effeminate *majo*, said to be part of the Resistance underground, leads the French to ambush the *majo* and his network. The result is a small massacre in the course of which, unbeknown to Luis, Marisol, who had joined the network out of love for him, is killed. When he subsequently learns of his responsibility for his wife's death, he waxes Oedipal, goes into exile in Bordeaux, there befriends a similarly disillusioned Goya, and finally, under an assumed name, joins a group of flagellants in Seville for their annual rite of masochism.

Morand, it will be sensed, has given us an oblique account of the plight of the collaborator in World War II, and has done so with a virtuosity in anachronism which we have yet to assay. Our first task, however, will be to observe the ingenuity with which the author has offered us this, his tale of collaboration, as though it were a rewriting of *the* great French novel of the nineteenth century, *La Chartreuse de Parme*. As if to say: we may have been wrong, but we have taken the French novel, perhaps French literature itself, with us in our error. *La Chartreuse*, after all, is the story of a young nobleman of a Mediterranean country occupied by Napoleon, who sides (too late) with Napoleon against the benighted pettiness of the indigenous rulers, subsequently allies himself with Comte Mosca – a Napoleonic enthusiast become suave adept of *Realpolitik* and (if need be) mass-murder – and who lives long enough to withdraw in disillusionment to the ecclesiastical retreat of the Charterhouse.[35] The Carthusian of Parma, that is, has known a life not all that different from that of the flagellant of Seville.

In *Monplaisir . . . en littérature* (1967), Morand published a preface to *La Chartreuse*, in which he evokes the "milieu italien familier de l'armée française, à la fois patriote et collaborateur, adorateur de Napoléon," and goes on to wonder what the Fabrizios of today would have to say about the state of Europe.[36] The backdrop for an answer is all but provided by his tourist's observation that American planes have pulverized Parma's Teatro Farnese. For that answer, ingeniously transposed westward, is, I would suggest,

Le Flagellant de Séville. True, the musty court of Parma, centered on the *opera buffa* figure of Ernesto Ranuccio, is anti-Napoleonic, and the similarly grotesque court of José Bonaparte, is the creation of the Emperor. But the key element of continuity in the Stendhal novel is the urbanely anti-American Mosca, whose Napoleonic allegiances are never forsworn, not even when he orders the army to fire on the people, and writes to his beloved Duchessa: "je vais me battre et mériter de mon mieux ce surnom de Cruel dont les libéraux m'ont gratifié depuis si longtemps."[37] Mosca, then, figures a surprising idealization of the path from Napoleonic fervor to brutal dictatorship ...

La Chartreuse, of course, even as it recounts the decline and decimation of the Napoleonic epic, pits that historical evolution against the Oedipalized sentimental history of Fabrizio. (Indeed the famous Waterloo episode refloats the myth of Oedipus even as it pretends to demystify the myth of heroic valor.)[38] Specifically, the novel relates Fabrizio's not entirely successful transition from a debilitating fixation on his glorious maternal surrogate, the Duchessa of Sanseverina, the character, it has been said, with whom more literary critics have fallen in love than any other, to a melancholic contemporary, Stendhal's answer to Racine's Aricie, the jailer's daughter, Clelia Conti.[39] The transition may be characterized as not entirely successful, not merely because Stendhal precipitates Fabrizio's relation with Clelia to its ruin once the protagonist escapes from prison, but because that relation itself, for all its rapture, seems so characterized by overt forms of perversion. Fabrizio's is a peep-hole form of sexuality: "Tout à coup un morceau d'abat-jour, plus grand que la main, fut retiré par lui ... elle se retourna rapidement vers ses oiseaux et se mit à les soigner; mais elle tremblait au point qu'elle versait l'eau qu'elle leur distribuait ..."[40] One need not be a Freudian to sense that somewhere, on one side or the other of Fabrizio's furtively crafted aperture, we are witnessing an ejaculation. A similar transgressiveness characterizes both the lie Fabrizio tells his beloved in order to make her yield and the peek-a-boo trysts that find them meeting in the dark lest Clelia break her vow never again to see her beloved. The transition from mother (surrogate) to non-incestuous love object, then, has been anything but successful, and so little survives the special circumstances of the prison cell named "Passive Obedience" that we may wonder whether or not the true end or goal of Fabrizio's progress was not that set of circumstances itself.

At this point, however, it suffices to recall Stendhal's life-long admiration for the Idéologues, or, more specifically, his oft quoted remark to the effect that "these days you must read Bentham and Ricardo,"[41] to open up the possibility that the deeper subject of his novel may well be that transition to a "disciplinary" society of the sort Michel Foucault has placed under the tutelage of Bentham and the exemplary institution of the (panopticon) prison.[42] The ultimate defeat of the Duchessa would be tantamount to the repression of all those extravagant energies Stendhal associated with the Italian Renaissance and which Fabrizio, under the rubric of "Passive Obedience," has learned, in his rapture over the melancholic jailer's daughter, to dismiss.

But how might this development relate to *Le Flagellant de Séville?* Don Luis, after all, has but a single female love, Marisol, for whose death he ultimately finds himself responsible. Yet no sooner does the protagonist cast his dilemma in allegorical terms than we find him split in his affections between a mother (surrogate) and a beloved contemporary: "L'Espagne est ma mère, se dit-il, elle est vieille et je l'aime. La France est ma fiancée, elle est neuve, je ne l'ai pas encore touchée; si ces deux amours se combattent et me déchirent, que ferai-je?"[43] And in Morand, as in Stendhal, the move from mother (substitute) to fiancée is botched. Beyond that split and its failed resolution, *Le Flagellant* appears to treat its heroine, Marisol, and her downfall, in terms reminiscent of Stendhal's heroine, the Duchessa. Indeed to the extent that the Duchessa's extravagance or generosity of emotional commitment has been thematized by critics as her *espagnolisme,* it may be suggested that Marisol figures an attempt at a more essential (because more Spanish) Duchessa.[44] Like the Sanseverina, Marisol plots an extravagant act to save her beloved: "[elle] comprit qu'il lui faudrait accomplir un acte grand, dangereux, mémorable pour que son mari fut sauvé." And just as the Duchessa's act of illegality entails a decisive encounter with an esteemed terrorist, Ferrante Palla, so Marisol becomes a close ally of Marcos, with whom she is last seen, in fact, riding off on horse-back. "Elle faisait jouer une serrurerie compliquée, l'esprit de Marcos ..."[45] Nowhere does Morand, who as a traveler in Italy had written of "le plaisir de mettre mes pieds dans ceux de Fabrice," seem to be following Stendhal more closely than in aligning the relation between his heroine and Marcos with that of the Duchessa and Ferrante Palla.[46]

Marisol's plans, however, like Gina's, come to nought, and it is worth observing the terms of her failure against the Stendhalian backdrop. Luis, accompanying a British prisoner whom the French have consigned to him, comes upon a somewhat effeminately garbed *résistant* haranguing his associates: "L'inconnu était vêtu comme un *majo*, culotte de soie très ajustée, boléro à boutons rapprochés, serrant un torse flexible de danseur pris dans un gilet et dans une veste garnie de galons ..."[47] There are several enigmatic flashes of recognition surrounding the episode. The British prisoner seems so intently interested in the *majo* that Luis wonders whether he might be homosexual. Meanwhile Luis himself believes he recognizes the contour of one of those listening to the harangue – just before he slips underground. The general impression created by the episode is one of grave importance slightly out of focus. It is not until close to the novel's end that Luis realizes that in tipping the French off to the meeting place of the *majo* and his band, he has implemented the murder of his wife. At that point his only resort is retreat to the masochistic rituals of la Confrérie de la Grande Discipline. The progress (or regress) then has been from an unfocused flash of homosexuality to the murder of the wife to the male brotherhood of – "disciplinary" – flagellation. One need not be an entirely convinced reader of James Miller's study of Michel Foucault to observe that if the fiasco of Fabrice, enraptured by the "Passive Obedience" of his prison cell, calls for understanding in terms of the argument of *Surveiller et punir*, the fate of Don Luis, retreating to his own masochistic discipline, similarly begs interpretation in terms of the erotic subtext Miller claims to have discovered in Foucault's great work on prisons.[48] "Attends qu'on te frotte (Aguarda que te unten)" is the tag from Goya with which Morand titles his second chapter, all but reminding us of the erotics of flagellation.[49] "Des dartres sombres, des gerçures violettes fleurirent sur les épaules, les avant-bras."[50] Luis' wounds are so many flowers of evil.

There are, to be sure, other significant links between the two novels. Both Fabrizio and Luis are pitted, in their enthusiasm for Napoleon, against a brother (or cousin) whose resentful opposition to the new order is said to be a function of inferior moral fiber: Ascanio in Stendhal, Blas in Morand. Lest Morand's change of venue escape the reader, Luis opines early in the novel: "les Italiens sont de faux fous; leurs extravagances démasquent toujours au dernier moment un robuste bon sens ... Les Espagnols, au contraire, sont d'authentiques insensés ..."[51] Better, then, to transfer the novel's action to a site where it can be played out to the limit. Finally, it may be observed that the Queen of pre-Napoleonic Spain, referred to in the novel, is none other than Marie-Louise de Parme, which happens as well to be the name of the widow of Napoleon at the time she is visited by Stendhal, in a brief scene sketched by Morand in *Monplaisir ... en histoire*, in search of permission to embark on the subject of *La Chartreuse*.[52]

But if *Le Flagellant de Séville* was to be a transposition – westward – in space of the action of *La Chartreuse de Parme*, it was simultaneously to be a transposition – backward – in time of the French experience of collaboration in World War II. (When Morand sought to write up his disgrace after the War, it was, then, no accident that he should end up writing the story of the humiliation of Fouquet at the hands of Colbert: for "Fouquet est un personnage de Stendhal"; whereas "Colbert est un héros de Balzac.")[53] It remains for us to establish the parameters of the short-circuit in time Morand attempts to establish between Spain 1808 and France 1940. That linkage, it should be noted, was not unique to Morand. In *D'un château l'autre* Céline, recalling the *josefín* backers of José Bonaparte, describes himself, by analogy, as a *adolfín*.[54] The parameters in Morand pertain to a certain simultaneity between categories of repetition and difference. For on the one hand, the author invites his readers to savor a situation which is a mirror reversal of that of 1940: France the occupied becomes France the occupier. Indeed, the reader is forced to enter into the mind and discourse of a character whose collaborationism is inseparable from a love of France. Morand, that is, would have his reader entertain a situation symmetrically opposite to the one obtaining in 1940 and put his sense of justice to the test.

On the other hand, however, the reversal or difference between 1808 and 1940 is shot through with a significant number of repetitions, and it is the counterpoint between that difference and those repetitions which constitutes the esthetic and/or heuristic achievement, such as it is, of the novel. Consider, for instance, the fact that Blas, having gone underground into the Resistance, is assumed to have ongoing contacts with the British. For if Morand's evocation of 1808 reverses 1940, how is it that the principal ally of the Resistance in 1808 is the same as in 1940? Similarly, in 1808, when Juan-Bautista, a Spanish Napoleonic diehard, announces that he is about to fight in Russia with the Joseph-Napoléon regiment of the Spanish Legion, the reader, recalling the Légion des Volontaires Français of the 1940s, finds the episode dislocated between the contrary pressures of repetition – another invasion of Russia – and difference: the occupier become occupied. And what of the British decision, scornfully reported by Luis, to sink a portion of the Spanish fleet lest it end up in French hands? The episode was, of course, repeated at Mers el-Kébir in 1940 *by the British* – all of which again raises the question of how repetition that apparently precise can subsist amid so complete a reversal.

Were one to search out a philosophical or critical guide to the resonances of Morand's temporal short-circuitry – the sudden flash of resonance established between two lost generations, present and past, and the redemptive potential of the twin catastrophes thus aligned – one would inevitably and paradoxically end up confronting the "Theses on the Philosophy of History" of Walter Benjamin.[55] The historian for Benjamin "grasps the constellation which his own era has formed with a definite earlier one. Thus he establishes a conception of the present as the 'time of the now' which is shot through with chips of Messianic time."[56] It was in this sense, it would seem, that *Le Flagellant de Séville* constitutes what one would have to call an exemplary case of a "tiger's leap into the past" in Benjamin's sense.[57] If one hesitates to adduce the name of Benjamin in this context, it is, of course, because the circumstances at stake, the sinister tragedy of French collaboration with the Nazis, were the very ones attendant on the critic's suicide in 1940 at the Spanish border. The irony of history, one wants to think, cannot have been that vicious that it would be left to an unapologetic collaborator like Morand to perform the critical move espoused by Benjamin. The extent to which such a paradox or heterogeneous constellation – Morand-Benjamin – may be sustained, however, is one of the more surprising upshots of a reading of the broader context of *Le Flagellant de Séville*, and it is to its elaboration that the final section of this essay is devoted.

In establishing its oscillation between 1808 and 1940, *Le Flagellant* simultaneously effects a displacement in space: the reader is expected to register a tragedy on France's western border as an allegory of a tragedy on its eastern border. Indeed the west for east displacement furnishes a key measure of that difference within which repetition wreaks, within the novel, those effects of disorientation apt to result, in a period of purges, in the kind of mistrial the French call *non-lieu*.[58] It is, moreover, just that displacement which will take us deeper into the more devastating levels of the Morand-Benjamin alignment just posited.

Consider the key episode closing the second section of the novel, the battle of Vitoria. In flight from Spanish insurgents, the "intruder king" and his cohort make their way back to the French border, bearing with them as much booty as they have been able to pillage. Amidst the ignominious retreat, the French come to experience a humiliation greater than defeat itself. As their sacks of booty break open over the battlefield, the combatants know a demeaning cessation of hostilities. Here is how it is described by a French officer, Poupard: "On s'est surtout battu autour du trésor: imaginez, mon cher, un sac troué par où tout le blé foutrait le camp. Il n'y avait qu'à se baisser pour faire fortune. [. . .] En Egypte un chamelier m'a raconté que les lions, les gazelles, tous les animaux du désert, quand ils se retrouvent au bord d'une mare, font la trêve de l'eau. Eh bien, à Vitoria c'était la trêve de l'or; cent millions répandus par terre et, autour, les soldats, les nôtres et ceux de l'ennemi, remplissant leur musettes et leurs sabretaches. Je vous fous mon billet que personne ne songeait à se battre! Sans âge ni grade! Ça ramassait, ça butinait! Quelle jolie cueillette!"[59] By chapter's end, the description veers toward the Célinian: "Ah! Les salauds, dit-il, les cajoleurs de gros sous! Jamais, jamais on n'avait vu cela! Ça, une bataille? Ça un champ d'honneur! Ah! merde! Une guerre comme celle-là, c'est la fin de tout!"[60] With the battle stalled for reasons of pure greed the historical sequence evoked in the novel has attained something of a nadir.

For readers of Morand, the breakdown of the battle of Vitoria, with its "truce of gold," is oddly and obliquely resonant with another interrupted battle on the French-Spanish border evoked elsewhere by the author and which lapses into frenetic inactivity for reasons of greed. For such is the case of the abortive film version of the *Chanson de Roland*, shot on location in the Pyrenees, in Morand's *sotie* of 1934, *France-la-doulce*.[61] Indeed the constellation jointly formed by *Le Flagellant de Séville* and *France-la-doulce* takes on additional coherence when one realizes that in both works, the battle on France's western border serves as a metaphor for an equally disastrous invasion that has occurred on France's eastern border. In the post-War novel, it is a matter, as we have seen, of the German Occupation of France being displaced onto the French occupation of Spain. In the pre-War novel, France's defeat at Roncevaux, or rather the defeat of the project to film it under the title "France-la-doulce," is a displacement of what Morand took to be France's defeat at the hand of the (largely Jewish) immigrant hordes submerging it from the East. To graft the 1934 tale onto the 1951 novel, that is, is to open the web of *Le Flagellant* to a historical dimension it comes close to ignoring: the Jewish question and the antithetical relation to it of Napoleon and Hitler.[62]

France-la-doulce is in many ways a *sotie* or ironic fiction in the tradition of Gide's *Les Caves du Vatican*.[63] Just as the Gide text dealt with the derealizing experience of a conventional French provincial at the hands of a band of particularly deft impostors, so Morand, in a novel about the motion picture industry, deals with the discomfiture of an upstanding Breton lawyer at the hands of the international gang of speculators pretending to turn out films on the basis of a dubious stash of bank drafts: "des traites, des retraites, des traites de traites."[64] The plot is relatively simple.

Jacobi and his crew of foreigners set out to make a film with minimal investment of cash. They find a subject in the public domain – or the "fosse commune," as they call it: *La Chanson de Roland.* They even come up with a single investor, one Comte de Kergaël, who squanders his family's last two farms in order to invest in the film. Meanwhile one Max Kron, age forty, a Jewish refugee from Nazi Germany, arrives in the "new Zion" of Paris and sets out in search of work. He makes his way to the Champs-Elysées and is drawn to the "arid and offensive luxury" of the dying Arcades, where he observes the merchants issuing "distress signals, as they clutch their unsellable bric-a-brac (*camelote*)."[65] In the upper reaches of the Arcades, he notes the existence of dream factories: "des firmes cinématographiques éphémères et sans nationalité avaient installé leurs bureaux prétentieux ..."[66] Before long, he meets up with Jacobi, and, doing nothing to disabuse the latter as to his limited experience in motion pictures, he is signed on as director of the underfinanced superproduction of "France-la-doulce." Production begins in the Pyrenees; investor Kergaël dies; and his provincial lawyer, an exemplar of French probity aptly named Maître Tardif, comes across the record of his late client's investment in the film: "une bande de papier blanc couverte d'écritures, d'adresses, de chiffres, de tampons humides et de timbres de diverses couleurs: c'était une traite augmentée d'une rallonge, avec un protêt en annexe."[67] It should be said that for the modernist Morand, it is the generative capacity of this textual monstrosity – the fact that a whole novel and the film within it might stem from such a value- (or meaning-) less wad of paper – which constitutes the core of his work. As he puts it in his preface, his subject is the "mésaventures d'une traite," the eloquence assumed by its "itinéraire misérable."[68] Somewhere between the purloined letters of Poe and Lacan, then: Morand's dubious draft.

Maître Tardif, armed with his French probity, takes off to the Pyrenees and observes first hand the incompetence and dishonesty of the cosmopolitan camp which cannot seem to get its plans for a film version of the French masterpiece off the ground. Morand is eloquent on Tardif's esthetic and financial disorientation in the age of mechanical reproducibility:

Il était le seul à s'étonner, à vivre avec ahurissement dans ce cauchemar d'une superproduction où tous semblaient à l'aise, paisibles fonctionnaires de l'absurde, installés dans l'éphémère, vivant dans le faux; ce n'était même plus le trompe-l'oeil du théâtre, monde de cartonnages, de fleurs artificielles, de planches poussiéreuses et de velours rouge gansé d'or; c'était une dimension nouvelle, sans épaisseur, d'où la logique, les formes, les rapports normaux avaient disparu, tour de Babel à jamais inachevée où les mots s'étaient une fois pour toutes vidés de leur sens, et les idées les plus simples, celles qui servent chaque jour aux hommes à communiquer entre eux, de toute substance. Le mot *argent*, seul, était capable de réveiller cet univers international et enchanté. Mais pas pour longtemps; sur l'argent aussi, la malédiction pesait; cette notion lourde et puissante, que Me Tardif avait, par sa profession, accoutumé de trouver au fond de l'âme des hommes, au bout de chaque affaire, à la pointe de chaque sentiment, aux conclusions de chaque procès, il la voyait, depuis deux semaines qu'il s'occupait de *France-la-doulce*, se vaporiser sous ses yeux. A force d'être maniée par chiffres astronomiques, disloquée par des imaginations orientales et diaboliques, déformée par des fictions financières monstrueuses, elle devenait une monnaie d'échanges irréels, un moyen de paiement pour comptes de fantômes.[69]

But Tardif is not alone in perceiving the catastrophic breakdown of the cinematographic encampment in the Pyrenees. Jacobi and his speculators realize to their embarrassment that the Max Kron they have hired to direct the film is not at all the renowned Kron they believed they were dealing with. "Kron n'est pas *Kron*," as one of the speculators, in a line reminiscent of Gide's about the pope not being the pope, puts it.[70] Whereupon arrangements are made to have him deported as an undesirable. Kron, however, anticipating his firing, secretly escapes to New York with the sole completed fragment of *France-la doulce* under his arm. In New York, a baroque series of accidents results in his coming into a small fortune, which turns out to be exactly what Jacobi's syndicate, in search of an "angel" and never bothered by its own inconsistencies, is desperate for. Kron buys his way back into the picture, back into France, and is even able to enjoy the satisfactions of wreaking a kind of architectural revenge on the country that had had him deported as an undesirable. He is able to host the Prime Minister of France at the launching of his own theatre, the Ciné-Triomphe, an "orgy of architectural styles" characterized by an ostentatious use of glass. "Le Ciné-Triomphe était une cristallisation géante; cet édifice colossal, on le sentait d'une fragilité atroce."[71] The novel's last line finds an exultant Kron offering a concluding toast: "La France, Monsieur le Président, c'est véritablement le camp de concentration du Bon Dieu!"[72] And such, in fact, would be the title of the German translation of the book brought out in short order in Hitler's Germany: God's Own Concentration Camp, *Der Konzentrationslager des guten Gottes.*[73]

But it is at this stage of our analysis that the third of our anachronisms – after Sartre in Musset, France 1940 in Spain 1808 – begins wreaking its devastating effects. For however much Morand's contemporaries may have felt he was offering them a reinvigorated version of a Gidean *sotie*, it is hard for us to summarize Morand's plot without feeling that we have been served an uncanny anticipation of the course of Walter Benjamin's life from the perspective of anti-Semitic France. It is as though Morand in 1934 had been given the elements of Benjamin's remaining years and then redreamt them in the grotesquely distorted guise of *France-la-doulce*. In a drama about the defeat of French probity at the hands of Ashkenazi corruption, a tale that seems to act out one strand of Giraudoux's treatise *Pleins pouvoirs* (1939), Kron, like Benjamin, makes his way from Paris to Berlin, is drawn to the dying Paris arcades, taken with the dream potential of its more secret recesses.[74] Eventually he escapes from France, by way of the Pyrenees, with the unfinished draft of a "great" Germano-Jewish summa on a certain essence of France under his arm: Benjamin's Arcades Project, sometimes known as "Paris the Capital of the Nineteenth Century" has been replaced by *France-la-doulce*: France the Capital of Ninth-Century Christendom, if one likes. But by this point the dreamlike redistribution of terms, the manic reversal of fate has begun to operate. Benjamin, of course, never made it through the Pyrenees to New York but committed suicide in flight from the Nazis in 1940. His phantasmagoria of redemption and saving angels has here turned into the tawdry dream of playing the "angel" to a corrupt movie syndicate desperate for funds. Finally, instead of the completed Arcades Project, Benjamin's projected elaboration of all that was at stake in the nineteenth century's first significant stab at building with glass, Morand's Kron inflicts on Paris "une cristallisation géante," the architectural monstrosity of his newly acquired Ciné-Triomphe.

It is, in sum, as though Morand had been gifted with prophetic insight in *France-la-doulce*, an insight that saw far more than others, but which somehow saw it backwards. Granted an uncanny premonition of the end of Benjamin's career, the closest the twentieth century has come to a saga of intellectual martyrdom, Morand got things so *precisely* wrong that one is hard put to decide whether the significant element is the precision or the error. As he put it elsewhere, in what is no doubt his most infamous line: "En ce moment, tous les pays tuent leur vermine sauf le nôtre ... Ne laissons pas Hitler se targuer d'être seul à entreprendre le relèvement moral de l'Occident."[75]

Our entry into *France-la-doulce* with its stalled filming of the battle on the Franco-Spanish border was by way of *Le Flagellant de Séville*, a novel featuring its own stalled battle on the very same border: the infamous "trêve de l'or." The decision to graft one (deferred) battle onto the other, to splice the 1934 text on film into the 1951 novel of Napoleon, was further justified by the fact that in each case the enemy on the western front was a figure for an adversary to the east: Sarrasins for Jews in 1934; Spaniards for Germans in 1951. The reason for that splicing was the imperative of restoring to Morand's virtuoso alignment of Spain 1808 and France 1940 the heterogeneous blot which all but shatters it : the unmentioned but contrary stands on the "Jewish question" of Napoleon and Hitler. That *Le Flagellant de Séville*, a consummate exercise in what Benjamin might have called dialectical imagery, an episode or scene of the past flaring up to redeem a contemporary catastrophe, should be sustained (or shattered) by a fantasy – *France-la-doulce* – in such proximity to the pressures surrounding Benjamin's own death, is an irony sufficiently bitter, sufficiently odd for us not to want to imagine any resolution capable of blunting or blandishing its sting.

Appendix

The following letter by Maurice Blanchot was read by Roger
Laporte, with the agreement of the author, to the Blanchot colloquium at the Univerity of London on 8 January 1993, following
my presentation (Chapter 12 of this volume), *"Pour Sainte-Beuve:
Maurice Blanchot, 10 March 1942."* The circumstances of that
reading are evoked in the Introduction.

24 décembre 92
Cher Roger Laporte,
   Merci de m'avoir envoyé ce texte (et merci de l'avoir retrouvé). Je
n'en avais gardé aucun souvenir et doutais qu'il eût jamais été écrit.
   Je vais tout de suite au pire. Qu'en mars 1942, on nomme Maurras
(alors, en plus, que rien n'appelle ici un tel nom), c'est détestable et sans
excuse. Je sais bien qu'il ne s'agit pas du personnage malfaisant de
l'époque, mais du lointain disciple d'Auguste Comte, qui – trente ans
plus tôt – se recommande, à l'imitation de son maître, d'une observation
des faits sociaux, étrangère à tout dogmatisme, et proche de la science
ou d'une certaine science.
   Il reste que le nom de Maurras est une tache indélébile et l'expression
du déshonneur. Je ne me suis jamais approché de cet homme, à quelque
époque que ce soit et toujours tenu à l'écart de l'Action Française,
même quand Gide par curiosité allait le voir.
   Que dire encore? Ce texte, non simple, voire embrouillé, a le mérite
de rester en dehors du temps et en tout cas de n'apporter nul secours ni
espérance au régime qui règne encore et déjà s'écroule.
                                                    Maurice Blanchot

P.S. On me suggère – vous connaissez la censure: celui qui est désigné
ici, ce n'est pas le personnage encore puissant, c'est le positiviste
médiocre condamné par l'Eglise.

Notes

I INTRODUCTION

1 *A Structural Study of Autobiography: Proust, Leiris, Sartre, Lévi-Strauss* (Ithaca: Cornell University Press,, 1974); *Revolution and Repetition: Marx/Hugo/Balzac* (Berkeley: University of California Press, 1977); *Cataract: A Study in Diderot* (Middletown: Wesleyan University Press, 1979).

2 "Orphée scripteur: Blanchot, Rilke, Derrida," *Poétique 20* (1974), detects a phantom phonograph (from Rilke's prose fantasy "Ur-Geraüsch") lodged within the presumably primal voice of (the poet's sonnets to) Orpheus, and allows its "floating stylus" to establish an articulation between Blanchot's *Espace littéraire* and the writings of Derrida.

3 *Legacies: Of Anti-Semitism in France* (Minneapolis: University of Minnesota Press, 1983).

4 *Les Années 30, MLN* 95, (1980).

5 Bernard-Henri Lévy, "La gauche, telle quelle" in *Le Matin*, 22 June 1982.

6 Mathieu Bénézet, "Maurice Blanchot, Céline, and *Tel quel*" in *La Quinzaine littéraire*, 1–15 July 1982.

7 *L'Infini* (January 1983).

8 Jean Laplanche, *Life and Death in Psychoanalysis* (Baltimore: Johns Hopkins University Press, 1976), translated with an introduction by Jeffrey Mehlman.

9 My translation of Lacan's "Seminar" first appeared in *French Freud, Yale French Studies* 48 (1973); subsequently in *Aesthetics Today*, ed. P. Gudel (New York: New American Library, 1980) and *The Purloined Poe*, ed. W. Richardson and J. Muller (Baltimore: Johns Hopkins University Press, 1987).

10 "On Tear-Work: l'*ar* de Valéry," *Yale French Studies* 52 (1976), had attempted to wrest a series of para-Freudian surprises from the poetry of the self-described "least Freudian of men," and, in so doing, to

advance the Freudian analysis of Valéry's poetry beyond Charles Mauron's "psychocritical" readings. In delineating the functioning of a disruptive agency I called "tear-work" (on the model of Freud's "dream-work"), the analysis pretended to open the poems to the kind of heterogeneity Derrida had extracted from Valéry's prose in *"Qual quelle*: les sources de Valéry," *Marges de la philosophie* (Paris: Minuit, 1973).

11 "Mallarmé/Maxwell: Elements," *Romanic Review* 71: 4 (November 1980), expands an insight of Jean Hyppolite according to which *Un coup de dés* would have as its secret subject the exorcising of Maxwell's demon. The essay is plainly indebted to the tutelary thinker of *Cataract*, Michel Serres: a metaphorics of astronomy gives way to one of meteorology, and the dream of a perpetual motion machine endlessly (and uncannily) generative of its own constitutive difference – in Mallarmé's terms, *le hasard vaincu mot par mot* – seems on the way down what is not simply a metaphorical drain . . .

12 "Poe *pourri:* Lacan's Purloined Letter," *Semiotext(e) 3* (1975), predates Derrida's "Facteur de la vérité" and is considerably less hostile to Lacan's text than Derrida. (The critique of the dubious "bedrock" of castration, that is, seems more feasible by way of the analytic matrix opened up by Lacan's "Seminar" than through opposition to it. Cf. my *Revolution and Repetition,* pp. 93–103). Concerning Derrida's reading, it may be noted that in claiming that the "purloined letter" finds its castratory destination in the lap of the Queen, Derrida overlooks Lacan's statement that the letter's "address" is "à la place précédemment occupé par le Roi, puisque c'est là qu'elle devait rentrer dans l'ordre de la Loi." But in so doing, Derrida stages an allegory of his own pseudo-gallant gesture of restoring the allegedly purloined argument of Lacan's text to its presumed source (and destination), Marie Bonaparte.

13 J. Derrida, *Parages* (Paris: Galilée, 1986).

14 J. Paulhan, *De la paille et du grain* in Paulhan, *Oeuvres complètes* (Paris: Cercle du Livre Précieux, 1970), p. 329.

15 Concerning the circumstances surrounding that attribution, see my translation of J.-D. Bredin, *The Affair: The Case of Alfred Dreyfus* (New York: Braziller, 1987).

16 The Sabbatians' reaction, in the seventeenth century, to the news that the man they believed to be the Messiah, Sabbatai Zevi, had converted (under duress) to Islam was to affirm that at this stage of the redemptive process, the Messiah would have to enter into evil in order to vanquish it *from within.* From this there emerged a full-scale antinomian theology, which instructed its adherents to violate the Law in order to fulfill it. The Jewish Enlightenment would be the

precipitate of this process – what remained of the cult of mystical transgression of the Law once its justification had been forgotten. Scholem's thinking on the "false Messiah" is intimately connected with Benjamin's speculations on the "*weak* Messianic power" with which every generation is endowed. See *Legacies*, p. 86. Scholem's views on Sabbatianism are also discussed in my *Walter Benjamin for Children: An Essay on His Radio Years* (Chicago: University of Chicago Press, 1993).

17 For further thoughts on "Jewish self-hatred," see my review of Sander Gilman, *Jewish Self-Hatred* (Baltimore: Johns Hopkins University Press, 1987) in *MLN* 102: 3 (1988), and my "Weininger in a Poem of Apollinaire," a reading of "La Chanson du mal-aimé," forthcoming in *Jews and Gender: Responses to Otto Weininger*, ed. N. Harrowitz and B. Hyams (Philadelphia: Temple University Press).

2 CRANIOMETRY AND CRITICISM: NOTES ON A VALERYAN CRISS-CROSS

1 Letter to Maurice Denis, reproduced in Valéry, *Oeuvres*, I, ed. J. Hytier (Paris: Pléiade,1957), p. 1623.

2 Page references in the text to Valéry's poetry are to the first volume of the Pléiade edition, hereafter cited as *O*.

3 J. Mehlman, "On Tear-work: *L'ar de Valéry*," *Yale French Studies*, 52 (1976), pp. 152–73.

4 Page references to "La Crise de l'ésprit" in the text are to the first volume of the Pléiade edition.

5 Valéry, *Oeuvres*, II, ed. J. Hytier, (Paris: Pléiade, 1960), p. 69: "Le fond de la pensée est pavé de carrefours." *Oeuvres,* II hereafter cited as *O* II.

6 H. Poincaré, *La Valeur de la science* (Paris: Flammarion, 1905), p. 183. The reference to Poincaré was first adduced in W. N. Ince, "The Sonnet *Le Vin Perdu* of Paul Valéry," *French Studies* 10 (1956), pp. 40–54. On Valéry's relation to physics, see also C. M. Crow, *Paul Valéry and Maxwell's Demon: Natural Order and Human Possibility* (University of Hull: 1972).

7 Poincaré, *La Valeur, p.* 180.

8 *Ibid.*, p. 184.

9 Quoted in W. Ehrenberg, "Maxwell's Demon," *Scientific American* (November 1967), pp. 103–10.

10 J. Hyppolite, "Le *Coup de dés* de Mallarmé et le message" in Hyppolite, *Figures de la pensée philosophique* (Paris: PUF, 1971), vol. II. I have discussed Hyppolite on Mallarmé in "Mallarmé/Maxwell: Elements," *Romanic Review* 71: 4 (November 1980), pp. 374–80.

11 "Mallarmé/Maxwell: Elements."
12 Page references in the text to "Une conquête méthodique" are to the first volume of the Pléiade edition. Valéry wrote of the circumstances that culminated in his writing the essay in "Souvenir actuel," included in *Regards sur le monde actuel, Oeuvres,* ii, pp. 982–86. It should be noted that Valéry's meditation on "German method" was written in the year following the publication of *L'Introduction à la méthode de Léonard de Vinci* (1895).
13 E. Williams, "Made in Germany," *The New Review,* 14: 80 (1896).
14 Valéry, "Souvenir actuel," p. 984.
15 *Ibid.,* p. 985.
16 Williams, "Made in Germany," pp. 20–21.
17 On Valéry and the esthetics of expropriation, see J. Derrida, *"Qual quelle:* les sources de Valéry," in *Marges de la philosophie* (Paris: Minuit, 1973).
18 Valéry, *Oeuvres,* ii, p. 629 and i, p. 483.
19 Valéry's apprenticeship in craniometry with Vacher de Lapouge is mentioned in the biographical sketch preceding *Oeuvres,* i. On Vacher in general, see G. Nagel: *Sozialdarwinismus in Frankreich: Georges Vacher de Lapouge, 1854–1936 (Freiburger Forschungen zur Medizingeschichte,* iv, 1975). On his contribution to the emerging doctrine of fascism, see Z. Sternhell, *La Droite révolutionnaire, 1885–1914: Les Origines françaises du fascisme* (Paris: Seuil, 1978).
20 O. Nadal in P. Valéry-G. Fourment, *Correspondance, 1887–1933* (Paris: Gallimard, 1957), p. 23.
21 On Vacher's renown, see Nagel, *Sozialdarwinismus,* pp. 63–68. In Germany, Wilhelm II was said to regard him as the "only great Frenchman." (Reported in L. Poliakov, *The Aryan Myth* [New York: New American Library, 1974], p. 270.)
22 Quoted from *Le Messager du Midi* in Sternhell, *La Droite,* p. 155.
23 Derrida, *"Qual quelle:* les sources de Valéry," p.363. The letter is reproduced in A. Gide-P. Valéry, *Correspondance, 1890–1942* (Paris: Gallimard, 1955), pp. 342–44.
24 *Ibid.,* p. 343.
25 *Ibid.,* p. 344.
26 Page references in the text to *Regards sur le monde actuel* refer to the second volume of the Pléiade edition.
27 G. Vacher de Lapouge, *L'Aryen: son rôle social (Cours libre de science politique professé à l'université de Montpellier, 1889–1890)* (Paris: Fontemoing, 1899), p. 1. On p. 2, Vacher claims the revival of the Linnaean term as his own initiative (hereafter cited as *L*).
28 Page references in the text to "Agathe" are to the second volume of the Pléiade edition.

29 Gide-Valéry, *Correspondance*, p. 427.
30 In *Race et milieu social* (Paris: Rivière, 1909), p. 177, Vacher defined "cephalic index" as the relation arrived at by multiplying the maximum width of the skull by 100 and dividing by the maximum length. The lower the index, that is, the better!
31 "Lois de la vie et de la mort des nations," *Revue internationale de sociologie*, 1894, p. 424.
32 See "Le Sélectionnisme pratique," for example, in *L'Aryen*, p. 506. "La castration me paraît inutile, elle comporte des succédanés qui pourraient être utilement appliqués aux sujets à éliminer. La sclérose de l'épididyme, determinée par une injection de chlorure de zinc, est parfaitement suffisante et sans danger."
33 S. J. Gould, *The Mismeasure of Man* (New York: Norton, 1981) (hereafter cited as *MM*).
34 In this context, it is worth observing that for Vacher, who was pro-American (for reasons of race) and anti-democratic (for the same reasons), the scientific "revolution" that he initiated in Montpellier was to have its ultimate horizon in the United States. *L'Aryen*, pp. 449–50: "Si les tentatives faites pour arrêter mes premiers débuts avaient réussi, et si je n'avais pas écrit une ligne, l'anthropo-sociologie aurait été fondée à Karlsruhe en 1890 par Ammon au lieu de l'être en 1886 à Montpellier, mais cette science n'en serait pas moins exactement au même point au moment où s'impriment ces lignes. Et quand, à l'heure actuelle où les sélectionnistes sont à l'oeuvre sur le globe entier, où le sélectionnisme est introduit dans la législation américaine sous ses formes les plus difficiles à accepter, j'assiste à ces vaines tentatives, j'ai plutôt pitié des pauvres arriérés qui dans leur ignorance essaient d'arrêter la mer montante avec de petits pâtés de sable!"
35 Charles Mauron argues as much in *Des métaphores obsédantes au mythe personnel* (Paris: Corti, 1963), p. 164.
36 In "On Tear-Work," pp. 162–66, I have expanded the reading of the "tear" in "Le Cimetière marin" from the retentive sea-eye of Strophe III, through the "strange savor of tears, but of tears repressed" that Gustave Cohen intuited in Strophes XV–XVI, to the repetition-in-difference of Achilles immobile amidst his strides (*à grands pas).*
37. Page references in the text to "Le Yalou" are to the second volume of the Pléiade edition. The text has been analyzed at length by S. Yeschua in " 'Le Yalou': Enigmes, forme, signification," in *Paul Valéry contemporain*, ed. M. Parent and J. Levaillant (Paris: Klincksieck, 1974).
38 Quoted in Yeschua, " 'Le Yalou,' " p. 112.

39 Mehlman, "On Tear-Work," p. 162.
40 Concerning Valéry's stand against Dreyfus, see *Cahiers*, 1 (Paris: Pléiade, 1973), ed. J. Robinson, p. 129: "Pas 'méchant' – c'est-à-dire souffrant de voir souffrir – toutefois je me sens un coeur brusquement impitoyable à l'égard de celui qui spécule sur mon apitoiement – ou qui veut parvenir à ses fins en usant d'invocations à la Justice, à l'Humanité etc ... Ceci m'explique mon attitude dans l'affaire célèbre." On Salazar, see "L'Idée de dictature" in *Regards sur le monde actuel*, pp. 971–76. Valéry's "Discours sur Bergson" appears in *Oeuvres*, 1, pp. 883–86.
41 Mauron, *Des métaphores obsedantes*, p. 32.
42 *Ibid.*, p. 182.
43 Mauron, *Psychocritique du genre comique* (Paris: Corti, 1964), p. 142.
44 *Ibid.*, p. 142.
45 Francis Galton, "Generic Images," *The Nineteenth Century* (July 1879), pp. 161–62.
46 See Vacher de Lapouge, "L'hérédité," *Revue d'anthropologie* (1886), pp. 512–21, and *Résumé des travaux scientifiques* de M. G. Vacher de Lapouge (Poitiers: 1909).
47 See Gould, *The Mismeasure of Man*, pp. 75–76.
48 Francis Galton, *Probability, the Foundation of Eugenics* (Oxford: 1907), p. 30.
49 Vacher de Lapouge, "L'Anthropologie et la science politique," *Revue d'anthropologie* (1887), p. 15.

3 LITERATURE AND HOSPITALITY: KLOSSOWSKI'S HAMANN

1 See in particular the letter of 26 January 1936 to Alfred Cohn and that of 30 January 1936 to Werner Kraft in W. Benjamin, *Briefe*, ed. G. Scholem and T. Adorno (Frankfurt: Suhrkamp, 1966), II, pp. 702, 705. An English translation by H. Zohn of "Das Kunstwerk im Zeitalter seiner technischen Reproduzierbarkeit" appears in *Illuminations*, ed. H. Arendt (New York: Schocken, 1969), pp. 217–52.
2 Page references in the text to *La Révocation de l'Edit de Nantes, Roberte, ce soir*, and *Le Souffleur* all refer to their collective publication as the trilogy *Les Lois de l'hospitalité* (Paris: Gallimard, 1965).
3 In both *Les Lois de l'hospitalité* and *Le Philosophe scélérat* (Paris: Seuil, 1967), p. 25, the oppositon is between an auratic tension of transgression (exemplified by Sade) and its loss in a "universal prostitution of beings" (exemplified by Fourier's phalanstery). In 1969, Klossowski evoked Benjamin's discourse as poised curiously between Marx and Fourier ("Entre Marx et Fourier" in Le Monde, 31 May 1969, repro-

duced in D. Hollier, *Le Collège de sociologie* (Paris: Gallimard, 1979), pp. 586–87.

4 It is reproduced in its two versions in G. Scholem's moving essay, "Walter Benjamin and his Angel" in *On Jews and Judaism in Crisis* (New York: Schocken, 1976).

5 *Ibid.*, p. 216.

6 For a discussion of Benjamin, Scholem, and Jewish antinomianism, see the conclusion of my *Legacies: Of Anti-Semitism in France* (Minneapolis: University of Minnesota Press, 1983).

7 Scholem, "Walter Benjamin and his Angel," p. 207.

8 W. Benjamin, "On Language as Such and on the Language of Man," in *Reflections*, ed. P. Demetz (New York: Harcourt and Brace, 1978), pp. 325, 330.

9 *Ibid.*, p. 321.

10 Letter to Benjamin of 30 March 1931 in *Briefe*, II, p. 526.

11 In de Man's introduction to H. R. Jauss, *Toward an Aesthetic of Reception*, trans. T. Bahti (Minneapolis: University of Minnesota Press, 1982), p. xxiii, Jauss' relation to Benjamin on the subject of allegory is viewed as a replay of Herder's conflict with Hamann.

12 Corbin's translation appeared in *Mesure* (January 1939). Klossowski refers to it in the preface to *Les Méditations bibliques de Hamann* (Paris: Minuit, 1948), p. 10.

13 *Ibid.*, p. 10.

14 *Briefe*, II, p. 753.

15 Hegel's essay originally appeared in *Jahrbücher für Wissenschaftliche Kritik* – 1828).

16 "On a d'ores et déjà l'impression que Hegel fait par anticipation le procès de son futur et puissant adversaire Kierkegaard, tout de même qu'on a l'impression que Hamann prépare par ses faits et gestes l'arsenal kierkegaardien," Klossowski, *Les Méditations bibliques*, p. 62. On Kierkegaard's debt to Hamann, see C. Jambet, "Kierkegaard et Hamann," in *Obliques : Kierkegaard* (Nyons: Obliques, 1981), pp. 149–62, as well as H. Corbin, "L'humour dans son rapport avec l'historique chez Hamann et chez Kierkegaard," in *Obliques: Kierkegaard*, pp. 163–65.

17 Page references in the text to Hegel's essay refer to Klossowski's translation in *Méditations bibliques*.

18 Page references in the text to Klossowski's introduction(s) are to *Méditations bibliques*.

19. J. G. Hamann's *Briefwechsel*, ed. W. Ziesemer and A. Henkel (Wiesbaden: Insel, 1955), I, p. 315.

20 *Ibid.*, p. 318.

21 G. Deleuze, *Logique du sens* (Paris: Minuit, 1969), pp. 325–50.

22 *Ibid.*, p. 344.
23 R. Rorty, *Consequences of Pragmatism* (Minneapolis: University of Minnesota Press, 1982), p. 93.
24 "Neue Apologie des Buchstaben h," in Hamann, *Schriften zur Sprache*, ed. J. Simon (Frankfurt: Suhrkamp, 1967) pp. 181–91.
25 Hamann, in defence of the silent *h*, suggests sarcastically (p. 184) that perhaps all double letters should be eliminated as well. That notion brings the text into contact with the London conversion experience which began with Hamann's abortive effort to correct a stutter. In the "Apologie" he speculates that should every dialect find its idiosyncratic spelling, as would appear to follow from Damm's reform no dam (*Damm*) would be capable of holding back the flood of chaotic print that would ensue. For a discussion of dams, floods, chaos, and print in a related eighteenth-century context, see my *Cataract: A Study in Diderot* (Middletown: Wesleyan University Press, 1979).
26 Hamann, *Schriften zur Sprache*, pp. 193–96.
27 *Ibid.*, p. 194.
28 For a related development see the discussion of Léon Bloy's *Le Salut par les Juifs* in chapter 11 of my *Legacies*. The motif – from John 4 – of "salvation from the Jews" (*"Das Heil kommt von den Juden"*) appears in "Aesthetica in Nuce," *Schriften zur Sprache*, p. 120.
29 J. Nadler traces the image of fist and open hand to the Stoic Zeno, who invokes it to convey the relation between dialectic and rhetoric. See Hamann, *Schriften zur Sprache*, p. 263.
30 The phrase also appears in Klossowski's discussion of Blanchot's *Le Très-Haut* in *Un si funeste désir* (Paris: Gallimard, 1963), p. 174: "C'est pourquoi Sorge dit a Bouxx: 'Je vous supplie de le comprendre, tout ce qui vous vient de moi n'est pour vous que mensonge parce que je suis la vérité.' *Dei dialectus solecismus.*"
31 E. de Fontenay, in *Diderot: Reason and Resonance* (New York: Braziller 1982), pp. 74–81, has recently attacked Klossowski, Bataille, and those she calls the *merveilleuses* and *incroyables* of the Sadean revolution in a consideration of the political implications of devoting a cult to Sade in France during the period Hitler was consolidating his power in Germany. Without following her in her global denunciation, I am nevertheless tempted to make the following remarks: (1) Klossowski's Sade in 1947 praises "Nature" for periodically "causing entire populations to perish … through the acts of selected criminals (*scélérats*)," (*Sade mon prochain* [Paris: Seuil, 1947], p 120). (2) The crucial Sadean goal – in Klossowski's reading – of a morality of apathy (p. 132) finds an eerie historical echo in Hitler's achievement. See R. Rubenstein's important book on the extermination of the Jews, *The Cunning of*

History (New York: Harper and Row, 1975), intro. William Styron, p. 27: "It was only possible to overcome the moral barrier that had in the past prevented the systematic riddance of surplus populations when the project was taken out of the hands of bullies and hoodlums and delegated to bureaucrats." (3) The will – of Klossowski's Sade – to "strike down the law of the propagation of the species" (Klossowki, *Le Philosophe scélérat*, p. 32) through acts of perversion enters into odd resonance with the Nazi effort to destroy "surplus populations" through programs of mass-sterilization (Rubenstein, *The Cunning of History*, p. 52).

32 See E. Erikson, "The Fit in the Choir," in *Young Man Luther* (New York: Norton 1958), pp. 23–48. The occasion of the crisis was a reading of Christ's *ejecto a surdo et muto daemonio* (Mark 9: 17), the cure of a man possessed by a *dumb spirit*. One is tempted to situate the episode in relation to Hamann's "fit" at Damm's effort to eradicate the silent *h* .

33 German and Jew ... We approach here something of Foucault's sense of the core of Klossowski's thought (in "La Prose d'Actéon," *Nouvelle Revue française* [March 1964]) p. 444: "Mais si le Diable, au contraire, si l'Autre était le Même? Et si la Tentation n'était pas un des épisodes du grand antagonisme, mais la mince insinuation du Double?"

34 Deleuze, *Logique du sens*, p. 346.

4 LITERATURE AND COLLABORATION: BENOIST-MÉCHIN'S RETURN TO PROUST

1 This essay grew out of comments on a paper by Michael Weaver of Oxford University on "Right-wing Intellectuals and Racialism in the 1930s," delivered at a colloquium on *The Jews in Modern France* at the Tauber Institute of Brandeis University in April 1983.

2 D. Sibony, "Mais qu'est-ce qu'une histoire juive?" in *La Psychanalyse est-elle une histoire juive?: Colloque de Montpellier*, ed. A. & J.-J. Rassial (Paris: Seuil, 1981), pp. 142–43.

3 A *la recherche du temps perdu* (Paris: Pléiade, 1954), III, p. 952.

4 *Ibid.*, II, p. 1107. In *The Proustian Community* (New York: New York University Press, 1971), p. 205, S. Wolitz comments provocatively on this reference, but mistakenly locates it in *Le Temps retrouvé*. It occurs in *Sodome et Gomorrhe*.

5 *Avec Marcel Proust* (Paris: Albin Michel, 1977), pp. 53–54.

6 *Ibid.*

7 See M. Weaver's Brandeis manuscript (unpublished), p. 43.

8 R. O. Paxton, *Vichy France: Old Guard and New Order, 1940–1944* (New York: Norton, 1972), pp. 387–90.

9 *Ibid.*, p. 50.

10 See M. Weaver's manuscript.

11 Benoist-Méchin's most elaborate projects in European history were his *Histoire de l'armée allemande* (Paris: Albin Michel, 1936–38) and *Soixante jours qui ébranlèrent l'Occident* (Paris: Albin Michel, 1956). The tendentiousness of the second project, a history of Europe from 10 May to 10 July 1940, is severely criticized in P. Dhers, "Comment Benoist-Méchin écrit l'histoire," in *Regards nouveaux sur les années quarante* (Paris: Flammarion, 1970).

12 Benoist-Méchin was responsible for the serialization in *Paris-Match* of *Mein Kampf* during the 1930s. His *Eclaircissements sur "Mein Kampf"* (Paris: Albin Michel, 1939), p. 185, chose to avoid all "criticism" of or "personal commentary" on Hitler's positions.

13 Benoist-Méchin, *Avec Marcel Proust*, p. 134.

14 *Ibid.*, p. 127.

15 *Ibid.*, p. 167.

16 *Ibid.*, p. 171.

17 *Ibid.*, p. 170.

18 On the symbol of the *faisceau* – integrating nationalists and socialists – in the politics of the Marquis de Morès, see Z. Sternhell, *La Droite révolutionnaire: Les origines françaises du fascisme, 1885–1914* (Paris: Seuil, 1978), p. 180.

19 Benoist-Méchin, *Avec Marcel Proust*, p. 94.

20 On the emergence of such a "post-Marxian" socialism in the work of Henri de Man, see Z. Sternhell, *Ni droite ni gauche: L'idéologie fasciste en France* (Paris: Seuil, 1982), pp. 136–59. Concerning "la primauté de la collectivité sur les individus qui la composent" in emerging French fascism, see Sternhell, "Les Origines de l'antisémitisme populaire sous la IIIe République" (unpublished paper delivered at the Brandeis colloquium on *The Jews in Modern France*, April, 1982). Concerning Proust and "fascism," it may be noted that Benoist-Méchin's sole criticism of *La Recherche* is ultimately the same as the criticism lodged against France itself by Drieu la Rochelle in *Mesure de la France* (Paris: Grasset, 1964). Benoist-Méchin: "Aucune génération nouvelle ne vient assurer la relève de celle qui disparaît progressivement sous nos yeux, si bien qu'une fois morts tous les personnages du *Temps perdu*, la France serait dépeuplée" (pp. 131–32). Drieu la Rochelle: "La France n'a plus fait d'enfants. Ce crime d'où découlent les insultes, les malheurs qu'elle a essuyés depuis cinquante ans, elle l'a mûri à la fin du xixe siècle et consommé au début du xxe siècle" (p. 42).

21 For a discussion of this passage in a Lacanian context, see my *A Structural Study of Autobiography: Proust, Leiris, Sartre, Lévi-Strauss* (Ithaca: Cornell University Press, 1974), pp. 32–35.

22 Benoist-Méchin, *Avec Marcel Proust*, pp. 147–48.

23 *Ibid.*, pp. 150–51.

24 *Ibid.*, p. 151.

25 Proust *A la recherche du tenps perdu*, I, p. 38.

26 See my *A Structural Study of Autobiography*, pp. 20–31.

27 G. Deleuze, *Proust et les signes* (Paris: PUF, 1970), p. 97.

28 *The Origins of Totalitarianism* (New York: Harcourt Brace Jovanovich, 1951).

29 *Ibid.*, p. 80. Arendt borrows the phrase from J. E. van Praag, "Marcel Proust, témoin du judaïsme déjudaïsé," in *Revue juive de Genève*, 48, 49, 50. (1937)

30 Arendt, *The Origins of Totalitarianism*, pp. 107, 111. For a discussion of the textuality of *The Eighteenth Brumaire of Louis Bonaparte*, see my *Revolution and Repetition: Marx / Hugo / Balzac* (Berkeley: University of California Press, 1977), chapter 1.

31 Arendt, *The Origins of Totalitarianism*, p. 83.

32 *Ibid.*, p. 84.

33 Proust, *Contre Sainte-Beuve* (Paris: Gallimard, 1954), p. 137.

34 *A Structural Study of Autobiography*, pp. 20–64. The chapter in *Jean Santeuil* analyzed to this end is "Querelle de Jean avec ses parents" (part 3, chapter 7).

35 Proust, *Contre Sainte-Beuve*, p. 134.

36 *Ibid.*, p. 128.

37 Concerning Daudet, see P. Dominique, *Léon Daudet* (Paris: Vieux Colombier, 1964). Concerning his most successful novel, *Les Morticoles* (1894), E. Roudinesco, in her excellent *La Bataille de cent ans: Histoire de la psychanalyse en France* (Paris: Ramsay, 1982), p. 61, has written: "On trouve dans *Les Morticoles*, à l'état naissant, l'emphase, la redondance, la rhétorique accumulatoire, et le balancement de la parole alexandrine, qui vont caractériser, pendant tout le siècle suivant, le phrasé spectaculaire du pamphlet antisémite."

38 Proust, *Contre Sainte-Beuve*, pp. 439–40.

39 *Ibid.*, p. 440.

40 In the awkward blatancy of its contradictions, the sentence calls to mind Freud's statement in the famous letter (21 September 1897) to Fliess renouncing the theory of seduction: "It is curious that I feel not in the least disgraced, though the occasion might seem to require it. Certainly I shall not tell it in Gath or publish it in the streets of Askalon, in the land of the Philistines – but between ourselves I have a feeling more of triumph than of defeat (which cannot

be right)" *(The Origins of Psychoanalysis*, ed. M. Bonaparte, A. Freud, E. Kris [New York: Basic Books, 1954], p. 217). Much of psychoanalysis may be construed as a working through of those contradictions. One can only speculate on what Proust's novel would have been had he "worked through" the contradictions of the text on Léon Daudet.

41 Proust, *Contre Sainte-Beuve*, p. 441.

42 *Ibid.* For Daudet's evocation of Proust as a simpering Dreyfusard in the Restaurant Weber (Proust: "Vous comprenez, monsieur, monsieur, il peut supposer que sa force aux armes m'intimide. Il n'en est rien"), see his *Paris vécu* (Paris: Gallimard, 1969), p. 103.

43 The sequence is well discussed in J. Recanati, *Profils juifs de Marcel Proust* (Paris: Buchet/Chastel, 1979), pp. 54–56.

44 Proust, *A la recherche du temps perdu*, II, pp. 401–02.

45 On the role of a *manteau* (in *Jean Santeuil*) as anticipation of the *madeleine*, see my *Structural Study of Autobiography*, p. 61.

46 On Freud's relation to Judaism, see M. Robert, *D'Oedipe à Moïse: Freud et la conscience juive* (Paris: Calmann-Lévy, 1974).

47 See, for instance, my "Suture of an Allusion: Lacan with Léon Bloy," in *Legacies: Of Anti-Semitism in France* (Minneapolis: University of Minnesota Press, 1983) as well as E. Roudinesco, *La Bataille de cent ans*.

5 "PIERRE MENARD, AUTHOR OF *DON QUIXOTE*" AGAIN

1 G. Genette, "L'Utopie littéraire," in *Figures* (Paris: Seuil, 1966), pp. 123–32; J.-L. Borges, "Pierre Menard, Author of *Don Quixote*," in *Ficciones*, trans. A. Kerrigan (New York: Grove, 1962), p. 49.

2 It may be noted at this point that E. Rodriguez Monegal, in his *Jorge Luis Borges: A Literary Biography* (New York: Dutton, 1978), p. 123, acutely traces Borges' source in "Pierre Menard" to a text from Remy de Gourmont's *Promenades littéraires* (Paris: Mercure de France, 1916) dedicated to "Louis Ménard, A Mystical Pagan." De Gourmont was one of many who referred to Lazare in his response to J. Huret's celebrated *Enquête sur l'évolution littéraire* of 1891(Paris: Thot, 1982), p. 134: "je n'ai pas à parler specialement des poètes, ni de ceux, très hautains, qui se groupent autour des *Entretiens* où Bernard Lazare fait de la critique très excellente quoique un peu dure …" The best studies of Lazare are by N. Wilson: *Bernard Lazare: Antisemitism and the Problem of Jewish Identity in late Nineteenth-century France* (Cambridge: Cambridge University Press, 1978), and Jean-Denis Bredin, *Bernard Lazare: de l'anarchiste au prophète* (Paris: Editions de Fallois, 1993).

3 Charles Péguy, *Notre jeunesse* (Paris: Gallimard, 1957), p. 86: "Le prophète, en cette grande crise d'lsraël et du monde [the Dreyfus
Affair], fut Bernard-Lazare. Saluons ici l'un des plus grands noms
des temps modernes ..." Also, p. 90: "Il avait, indéniablement, des
parties de saint, de sainteté."

4 "Le Sacrifice," in *L'Ermitage* 1 (July, 1890), pp. 156–62.

5 The reference to an inaccessible virgin, modeled on Hérodiade, is
recurrent in Lazare's poetic prose. See, for instance, from "Inimica
Luna," the apostrophe to the moon: "– En d'autres nuits, Souver-
aine, tu ceins le diadème d'émeraude, et lorsque le désespoir me
saisit plus âpre, je crois voir aux empyrées le plateau de métal qui
échappa des mains blêmes de la courtisane quand le chef glorieux
du Saint s'exalta. – Et je voudrais voir aussi choir ma tête sur le
plateau d'Hérodiade – Hérodiade, moins cruelle que toi."

6 For a trenchant analysis of the voice of Borges' narrator in the
context of Argentine cultural history, see A. Borinsky, "Repetition,
Museums, Libraries: Jorge Luis Borges," in *Glyph* 2 (Baltimore:
Johns Hopkins University Press, 1977).

7 See Péguy, *Notre jeunesse*, p. 91: "En dehors de nous des cahiers, il n'y
a que M. Edouard Drumont qui ait su parler de Bernard-Lazare,
qui ait voulu en parler, qui lui ait fait sa mesure." From *La Libre
parole*, 5 September 1903: "Nous ne pouvons que souhaiter une
chose, c'est que les chrétiens se fassent de la grandeur et des devoirs
du nom de chrétien l'idée que Bernard-Lazare se faisait de la grandeur et des devoirs du nom de Juif."

8 *L'Antisémitisme: Son histoire et ses causes* (Paris: Stock, 1894).

9 Letter cited in Lazare, "Contre l'antisémitisme (Histoire d'une polémique)" (Paris: Stock, 1896), pp. 25–26.

10 See R. H. Feldman's introduction to H. Arendt, *The Jew as Pariah*
(New York: Grove, 1978), p. 32: "In terms of the perspective Arendt
displays, the importance of Lazare as a model of what it means to be a
political pariah is hard to overestimate." See also (p. 78) Arendt's evocation of the reasons for Lazare's ultimate failure: "the fact that when
he tried to stop the pariah from being a *schlemihl*, when he sought to
give him a political significance, he encountered only the *schnorrer*."

11 "Juifs et Israélites," in *Entretiens politiques et littéraires* 1: 6 (1890),
p. 177.

12 "La Solidarité juive," in *Entretiens politiques et littéraires* 1: 7 (1890), p.
230. For a speculative discussion of Giraudoux's anti-Semitism, see
my *Legacies: Of Anti-Semitism in France* (Minneapolis: University of
Minnesota Press, 1983), chapter III.

13. "De la nécessité de l'intolérance" in *Entretiens politiques et littéraires* 3: 21
(1892), p. 208.

14 See Lazare's preface to his *Figures contemporaines: ceux d'aujourd'hui, ceux d'hier* (Paris: Perrin, 1895), p. iv: "La haine est cependant, en littérature, comme en politique, comme en art, une passion primordiale et indispensable: celui qui ne sait pas haïr ne saura pas aimer ce qui, pour lui, est le beau …" On Lazare's propensity to negative affect, see as well André Gide, *Si le grain ne meurt* (Paris: Gallimard, 1954). p. 543: "Bernard Lazare, de son vrai nom Lazare Bernard, était un Juif de Nîmes, non point petit, mais d'aspect court et ineffablement déplaisant. Son visage semblait tout en joues, son torse tout en ventre, ses jambes toutes en cuisses. A travers son monocle il jetait sur choses et gens un regard caustique et semblait mépriser furieusement tous ceux-là qu'il n'admirait point. Les plus généreux sentiments le gonflaient; c'est-à-dire qu'il était sans cesse indigné contre la muflerie et la crapulerie de ses contemporains: mais il semblait qu'il eut besoin de cette muflerie et qu'il ne prit conscience de lui que par une opposition violente …"

15 Péguy's reproach to Clemenceau, in the *Cinquième Série* of the *Cahiers de la quinzaine*, is reproduced in Péguy, *Oeuvres en prose 1898–1908* (Paris: Gallimard, 1959), p. 1491: "Rien ne peut produire une aussi extrême indignation que cette primauté injustement attribuée à Zola: totale. Mon Dieu, nous savons tous que ce sont les musiques militaires qui gagnent les batailles, et que la grosse caisse, en particulier, fait plus que l'artillerie pour effondrer les carrés …"

16 M. Marrus, *Les Juifs de France à l'époque de l'affaire Dreyfus* (Paris: Calmann-Lévy, 1972), p. 203.

17 Lazare, "Les Quatre Faces," in *Entretiens politiques et littéraires* 1: 9 (1890), p. 290.

18 For Lazare's cult of Mallarmé, see *Figures contemporaines*, p 249: "Plus tard, ceux qui auront connu Stéphane Mallarmé dans leur prime jeunesse, ceux qui l'auront aimé comme un des plus purs, des plus désintéressés parmi les poètes, ceux qui l'auront entendu et qui auront chéri sa parole, raconteront sa vie comme le bon Xénophon raconta celle de Socrate. Fidèles, scrupuleux, ils commenteront vers par vers ses sonnets, et cela dans le but unique de révéler aux jeunes hommes de ce temps futur quel noble, profond et merveilleux artiste fut Stéphane Mallarmé."

19 A. Bertillon, "La comparaison des écritures et l'identification graphique" in *Revue scientifique*, 8: 25 (December 1897) and 9: 1 (January 1898). For an admiring study of Bertillon, see H. T. F. Rhodes, *Alphonse Bertillon: Father of Scientific Detection* (New York: Greenwood, 1956).

20 On the relations among questions of form, force, and structuralism, see J. Derrida's important critique of J. Rousset's *Forme et signification,*

entitled "Force et signification" in *L'Ecriture et la différence* (Paris: Seuil, 1967).

21 J. Starobinski, *Les mots sous les mots: Les anagrammes de Ferdinand de Saussure* (Paris: Gallimard, 1971), p. 23.

22 Mallarmé was a principal subject of four of Mauron's books: *Mallarmé l'obscur* (Paris: Denoël, 1941); *Introduction à la psychanalyse de Mallarmé* (Neuchâtel: La Baconnière, 1950); *Des métaphores obsédantes au mythe personnel* (Paris: Corti, 1963); *Mallarmé par lui-meme* (Paris: Seuil, 1964). The methods of "psychocriticism" were extrapolated from the second of these works.

23 For a discussion of Bertillon's relations – of mutual esteem – with Galton, see Rhodes, *Alphonse Bertillon*, pp. 191–92.

24 "Mémoire du Capitaine Dreyfus (30 janvier 1904)," reproduced in L. Leblois, *L'Affaire Dreyfus, iniquité et réparation: les principaux faits et les principaux documents* (Paris: Quillet, 1929), p. 130.

25 "Rapport de M. Bertillon, du 20 octobre 1894," reproduced in Leblois, *L'Affaire Dreyfus*, p. 124.

26 Deposition of Bertillon (4 February 1899) before the Chambre Criminelle, reproduced in Leblois, *L'Affaire Dreyfus*, p. 137.

27 "Mémoire de M. Painlevé, membre de l'Académie des Sciences," reproduced in Leblois, *L'Affaire Dreyfus*, p. 127.

28 *Une erreur judiciaire: L'Affaire Dreyfus (Deuxième mémoire avec des expertises d'ecritures)* (Paris: Stock, 1897), p. 49.

29 The phrase is quoted from *Le "Livre" de Mallarmé* at the beginning of Derrida's reading of Mallarmé, "La Double Séance," in *La Dissémination* (Paris: Seuil. 1912), p. 202.

30 Homage here to C. Ozick's rhetorical question, in an essay on literature and "tribalism" (in *Art and Ardor* [New York: Knopf, 1983], p. 168): "Why have our various Diasporas spilled out no Jewish Dante, or Shakespeare, or Tolstoy, or Yeats?" To which we would append, in this context: no Jewish Mallarmé . . .

31 "Mémoire de M. Painlevé," reproduced in Leblois, *L'Affaire Dreyfus*, p. 129.

6 IPHIGENIA 38: DECONSTRUCTION, HISTORY, AND THE CASE OF *L'ARRÊT DE MORT*

1 H. Bloom, P. de Man, J. Derrida, G. Hartman, J. H. Miller, *Deconstruction and Criticism* (New York: Seabury Press, 1979).

2 "The Triumph of Life," in *The Selected Poetry and Prose of Shelley*, ed. H. Bloom (New York: Meridian, 1966), p. 363.

3 *Ibid.*, "Introduction," p. x.

4 P. de Man, in his remarkable analysis of Shelley's poem *(Deconstruc-*

tion and Criticism, p. 42), summarizes – before challenging – the standard interpretation of the Shelley-Rousseau encounter: "Rousseau lacked power, but because he can consciously articulate the causes of his weakness in words, the energy is preserved and recovered in the following generation."

5 J. Derrida, "Living On," trans. J. Hulbert in *Deconstruction and Criticism*, pp. 75–176. The essay is accompanied by a running journal at the foot of its pages, studded with notes for the translator into English.

6 For Blanchot's comments on the "impersonality" or anonymity of death, see *L'Espace littéraire* (Paris: Gallimard, 1955), p. 204: "elle est l'inévitable, mais l'inaccessible mort; elle est l'abîme du présent, le temps sans présent avec lequel je n'ai pas de rapport, ce vers quoi je ne puis m'élancer, car en elle *je* ne meurs pas, je suis déchu du pouvoir de mourir, en elle *on* meurt, on ne cesse pas et on n'en finit pas de mourir."

7 Page references in the text refer to *L'Arrêt de mort* (Paris: Gallimard, 1948).

8 This observation, as Derrida acknowledges, was originally made by G. Hartman in his introduction to Lydia Davis' translation of *L'Arrêt de mort* in *The Georgia Review* 30 (1976), p. 379.

9 Derrida, "Living On," pp. 170, 172.

10 Derrida, "La double séance" in *La Dissémination* (Paris: Seuil, 1972), pp. 200–317.

11 The narrator, in Derrida's reading, might well end up with the Faun's lament:

> Mon crime, c'est d'avoir, gai de vaincre ces peurs
> Traîtresses, divisé la touffe échevelée
> De baisers que les dieux gardaient si bien mêlée.

12 Derrida, "Living On," pp. 161–64.

13 In a recent text, culminating in a consideration of the sexual politics implicit in the writings of Levinas ("En ce moment même dans cet ouvrage me voici" in *Textes pour Emmanuel Levinas* [Paris: J.-M. Place, 1980]), Derrida writes at times "as a woman" ("je parle depuis ma place de femme," p. 56). The essay regularly refers to Levinas as E.L., thus toying with the French transliteration of the Hebrew designation for God, only to suggest in conclusion that E.L. might be appropriately misspelled as "Elle." Given the motif of the "Song of Songs" (and its dark Shulamite beauty) to which Derrida makes recurrent allusion, the entire development appears to move toward the punchline of the familiar joke from early in the astronaut era: "I have seen God and She is black."

14 *L'Entretien infini* (Paris: Gallimard, 1969), p. 498.

15 *Ibid.*, p. 504.
16 *Ibid.*, p. 507.
17 "Comment la littérature est-elle possible?" (Paris: José Corti, 1942).
18 J. Paulhan, *Les Fleurs de Tarbes ou la terreur dans les lettres* (Paris: Gallimard, 1941), p. 26.
19 Blanchot, "Comment la littérature est-elle possible?," p. 24.
20 "Blanchot at *Combat:* Of Literature and Terror," in *Legacies: Of Anti-Semitism in France* (Minneapolis: University of Minnesota Press, 1983), pp. 6–22. Concerning the specificity of the (much abused) term "fascist" in this context, see also Z. Sternhell, *Ni droite ni gauche* (Paris: Seuil, 1983), p. 241: "Maurice Blanchot fournit, en fait, la définition parfaite de l'esprit fasciste en montrant qu'il s'agit d'une synthèse entre une gauche qui quitte ses croyances traditionnelles, non pour se rapprocher des croyances capitalistes, mais pour définir les vraies conditions de la lutte contre le capitalisme, et une droite qui néglige les formes traditionnelles du nationalisme non pour se rapprocher de l'internationalisme, mais pour combattre l'internationalisme sous toutes ses formes." Sternhell, a political scientist, refers to Blanchot's "On demande des dissidents," *Combat* 2: 20 (December 1937).
21 "Le terrorisme, méthode de salut publique," in *Combat* 1: 7 (July 1936): "Il est bon, il est beau que ces gens qui croient avoir tout pouvoir, qui usent à leur gré de la justice, des lois, qui semblent vraiment maîtres du beau sang français éprouvent soudain leurs faiblesses et soient rappelés par la peur à la raison."
22 "Après le coup de force germanique," in *Combat* 1: 4 (April 1936).
23 *Ibid.*: "On n'a rien vu d'aussi perfide que cette propagande d'honneur national faites par des étrangers suspects dans les bureaux du quai d'Orsay pour précipiter les jeunes Français, au nom de Moscou ou au nom d'Israël, dans un conflit immédiat ..."
24 L. Rebatet, *Les Mémoires d'un fasciste, 1: Les Décombres* (Paris: Pauvert, 1976), p. 108. Rebatet offers an impressive account of the paralysis of the right at the time of Munich under the heading: "Au sein de l'Inaction française," pp. 115–37.
25 Derrida, "Living On," p. 155.
26 *Ibid.*, p. 131.
27 *Le Très-Haut* (Paris: Gallimard, 1948), p. 59: "je me rappelais que Louise ne parlait d'elle qu'en l'appelant la reine."
28 P. Klossowski, "Sur Maurice Blanchot," in *Un si funeste désir* (Paris: Gallimard, 1963), p. 171: "Henri Sorge? Ne faudrait-il pas prononcer ce *nom* dans la langue du *Saint Empire* de la Métaphysique et traduire: *Heinrich Sorge?* Plutôt: *die Sorge* comme on l'entend à l'Université de Freiburg? Une *"cura,"* cura pura? Un pur souci – qui se

camoufle sous le *nom* de Henri? Un pur souci: voilà ce qu'est l'existence: le *Dasein* de Henri ..."
29 M. Heidegger, *Being and Time*, trans. J. Macquarrie and E. Robinson (New York: Harper & Row, 1962), pp. 225–73.
30 Laffont-Bompiani, *Dictionnaire des oeuvres* (Paris: Laffont, 1957), VI, p. 512. The same paragraph appears in M. Foucault, "La pensée du dehors," *Critique* 229 (June 1966), pp. 536–37. For the Orestes-Sorge connection, see, in particular, the visit to the tomb in *Le Très-Haut*, pp. 73–74: "Et maintenant, je l'ai juré: là où il y a eu une mort injuste, il va y avoir une mort juste ..."
31 "La Folie du jour" (Montpellier: Fata Morgana, 1973), p. 33.
32 Derrida, "Living On," p. 105.
33 In his eloquent discussion of *Sorge* in *Martin Heidegger* (New York: Viking, 1978), p. 100, G. Steiner comments that Sartre's Orestes, in *Les Mouches*, was plainly imagined within the medium of Heidegger's thoughts on the "uncanny" (*unheimlich*) and "homelessness" (*das Nichtzuhause-sein*). Blanchot's Orestes, Sorge, is then something of a corrective to Sartre's reading of Heidegger. Blanchot's reservations about *Les Mouches* appear in "Le Mythe d'Oreste" in *Faux pas* (Paris: Gallimard, 1943), pp. 72–78. For a remarkable (anti-Sartrean) reading of *Les Mouches*, see D. Hollier, "I've Done My Act: An Exercise in Gravity," in *Representations* 4 (1983), pp. 88–100.
34 Foucault, "La Pensée du dehors," p. 539: "Il y a des récits qui sont voués, comme *L'arrêt de mort*, au regard d'Orphée ..."
35 *Iphigenia at Aulis*, in Euripides, *Ten Plays*, trans. M. Hadas and J. McLean (New York: Bantam, 1960), pp. 323, 343.
36 See Rebatet, *Les Mémoires*, p. 105.
37 See Blanchot, "La Guerre pour rien," in *Combat* 1: 3 (March 1936) and Rebatet, *Les Mémoires*, "Pour l'amour des Tchèques," pp. 67–85.
38 *Iphigenia at Aulis*, p. 318.
39 *Ibid.*
40 *Ibid.*, p. 336.
41 *Ibid.*, p. 342.
42 Jean Racine, *Iphigénie* (Paris: Larousse, 1970), p. 90.
43 *Iphigenia at Aulis*, p. 351.
44 *Ibid.*, p. 354.
45 Blanchot, "La Fin du 6 février," in *Combat*, 1: 2 (February 1936): "Cette date, à la fois douloureuse et grande, n'est plus qu'un symbole. Il est temps, dans l'ordre de la révolte, de penser à autre chose qu'à de pieuses commémorations." On the events of 6 February 1934, see S. Bernstein, *Le 6 février 1934* (Paris: Gallimard-Julliard, 1975) and E. Weber, *Action Française: Royalism and Reaction in*

Twentieth-Century France (Stanford: Stanford University Press, 1962), pp. 319–40. Blanchot's move here, sacrificing an investment in (European) fascism out of fidelity to French nationalism, is the precise obverse of that of the protagonist of Drieu la Rochelle's *Gilles*.

46 Blanchot-Giraudoux? It should be recalled that the first version, long out of print, of *Thomas l'obscur* (1941) was perceived to be written under the joint inspiration of Giraudoux and Kafka. The link has been made by C.-E. Magny *(Précieux Giraudoux;* Paris: Seuil, 1945) and J. Starobinski *("Thomas l'obscur,* chapitre premier," in *Critique* 229 [June 1966], p. 509). See as well "Blanchot ein Epigone Giraudoux und Kafkas," in R. Stillers, *Maurice Blanchot: Thomas l'obscur* (Frankfurt: Peter Lang, 1979), pp. 16–17. For Starobinski, the transition to Blanchot's maturity, from the first to the second versions of *Thomas l'obscur,* is concomitant with the casting off of the idealist "temptation" or "inflection" represented by Giraudoux. Note, moreover, that if the second version, on Blanchot's authority, has been interpreted by Hartman and others as a transposition of the Orpheus myth, the first Greek myth invoked – at length – in the first version of *Thomas l'obscur* is Iphigenia (p. 50): "C'était vers elle [Anne]que le sacrificateur [Thomas] se dirigeait. Il avait définitivement aiguillé, sur cette jeune Iphigénie accablée une seconde fois par le calme de la nature où ne soufflait aucun vent, la colère des dieux." The four-age excursus on Iphigenia, reminiscent in its idealizations of Giraudoux, ends (p. 54): "Farouche, muette comme jamais femme ne l'a été, imposant silence à ses pas et à tout son corps, elle était prête à livrer une ombre anonyme et glacée, simple sosie, biche substituée à la dernière minute à Iphigénie, et c'est sur une jeune fille sans enfance, sans histoire, privée à un point inimaginable de souvenirs et d'amitié, plus lisse et nue qu'au premier jour, que Thomas avança timidement la main." In the second version of *Thomas l'obscur,* Blanchot writes both Iphigenia and Giraudoux out of his text. On Blanchot's early investment in Giraudoux's style, see his column in *Journal des débats* (9 December 1941), uncollected elsewhere, "L'Homme pressé": "... chez M. Giraudoux la métaphore, après avoir commencé par un rapprochement en apparence arbitraire, se développe lentement, solennellement, tirant de cet arbitraire des conséquences qui semblent étrangement justes, étendant son empire par une dialectique qui avec une nécessité inéluctable conduit ensemble son double mouvement d'absurdité et de vraisemblance, pour finir, ayant tendu l'esprit par une angoisse sans cesse croissante, dans une dernière image où le paradoxe et l'évidence s'ajustent avec une perfection insoutenable.

47 *Iphigenia among the Taurians,* in Euripides, *Ten Plays,* p. 258.

48 *Ibid.*, p. 257.

49 See Derrida, "Living On," pp. 142–43: "There is no absolute guarantee of the unity of the two *récits*, and even less of the continuity from one to the other, or even that the narrator who says 'I' in each is the same."

50 E. Levinas, "Exercises sur 'La Folie du jour,' " in *Sur Maurice Blanchot* (Montpellier: Fata Morgana, 1975), p. 60. See also my *Legacies*, pp. 16–22.

51 See G. Préli, *La Force du dehors: Extériorité, limite et non-pouvoir à partir de Maurice Blanchot* (Paris: Recherches, 1977), p. 105.

52 Reprinted in *Gramma* 3/4 (1976), p. 34.

53 See Derrida, "Living On," p. 109.

54 *Ibid.*, p. 115: "Such is the arrhythmic pulsation of the title before it scatters itself like sand. The *arrêt* arrests *itself*..."

55. P. Ariès, *Un historien du dimanche* (Paris: Seuil, 1980), p. 184.

56 On the meshing of leftist (Sorelian) and rightist (Maurrassian) strands, first in the Cercle Proudhon of 1913, then in *Combat*, see my *Legacies*, pp. 6–8.

57 "Orphée scripteur: Blanchot, Rilke, Derrida," in *Poétique* 20 (1974).

58 The "writing machine" was extrapolated from a superimposition of Rilke's text of 1919 about a primitive phonograph ("Ur-Geräusch") and the *Sonnets to Orpheus*.

59 See, in addition to "Living On," Derrida, "Pas," in *Gramma 3/4* (1976), and "La Loi du genre," in *Glyph* 7 (1980). Both texts have since been incorporated in *Parages* (Paris: Galilée, 1986).

7 WRITING AND DEFERENCE: THE POLITICS OF LITERARY
ADULATION

This chapter was originally delivered as an address to the colloquium on "The Politics of Literary Adulation" at West Chester University (West Chester, Pennsylvania) in April 1985.

1 J. Rousseau, *L'Essai sur l'origine des langues*, ed. C. Porset, (Bordeaux: Ducros, 1970), p. 29.

2 J. Derrida, *De la grammatologie* (Paris: Minuit, 1967), p. 327: "Ce mouvement de baguette..."

3 *Of Grammatology*, trans. G. Spivak (Baltimore: Johns Hopkins University), p. 234. Rousseau's French reads: "Que celle qui traçait avec tant de plaisir l'ombre de son amant lui disait de choses! Quels sons eût-elle employés pour rendre ce mouvement de baguette?"

4 "Living On" in Bloom, de Man, Derrida, Hartman, Miller, *Deconstruction and Criticism* (New York: Seabury, 1979), p. 146: "There is a key in the *récit*: a 'Yale' key. Like all keys, it locks and unlocks, opens

and closes …" For a critical discussion of Derrida's analysis of *L'Arrêt de mort*, see chapter 6, "Iphigenia 38: deconstruction, history, and the case of *L'Arrêt de mort*."

5 "The University in the Eyes of Its Pupils," trans. C. Porter and E. P. Morris, in *Diacritics* (Fall, 1983), pp. 3–20: "More precisely, I shall be transcribing in a different code … the dramatic, exemplary nature of the topology and politics of this university, in terms of its views and its site: the topolitics of the Cornellian point of view" (p. 4).

6 Derrida, *Otobiographies: L'enseignement de Nietzsche et la politique du nom propre* (Paris: Galilée, 1984), p. 82.

7 *Ibid.*, p. 81.

8 M. Serres, "L'Antéchrist: une chimie des sensations et des idées" in *Hermès* IV: *La distribution* (Paris: Seuil, 1977), p. 180.

9 *Ibid.*, p. 173: "Toutes les idées qui vont suivre m'ont été données gracieusement par un douanier imbécile et grossier qui veillait, un matin, au *pier* quatre-vingt-douze, au débarqué d'un paquebot touchant à Manhattan. Il veillait, sur un tas d'ordures, a la propreté des Etats-Unis. Et demandait d'une voix dure, si je transportais du *fromage*. Qu'il soit remercié ici; grâce à lui, j'ai compris enfin quelque chose de l'*Antéchrist*, où, comme on ne le sait pas encore, il ne s'agit que de *corruption*."

10 Derrida, *De la grammatologie*, p. 14: "L'avenir ne peut s'anticiper que dans la forme du danger absolu. Il est ce qui rompt absolument avec la normalité constituée et ne peut donc s'annoncer, *se présenter*, que sous l'espèce de la monstruosité."

11 Derrida, *Otobiographies*, p. 93.

12 Derrida, *De la grammatologie*, p. 140; Ezra Pound, *Jefferson and/or Mussolini* (New York: Liveright, 1936), p. 12.

13 See note 4.

14 Derrida, *De la grammatologie*, "L'écriture et l'exploitation de l'homme par l'homme," pp. 173–202.

15 *Ibid.*, pp. 194–95. Derrida refers to "îlots de résistance" and mocks the "résistants."

16 J. Bersani comments specifically on Paulhan's importance for Blanchot in the proceedings of the Cerisy Colloquium on *Jean Paulhan le souterrain*, ed. J. Bersani (Paris: 10/18 1976), p. 145.

17 For a discussion of Blanchot's "Comment la littérature est-elle possible?" (Paris: Corti, 1942), see my "Blanchot at *Combat*: Of Literature and Terror", in *MLN* (French issue, 1980).

18 Editions de Minuit, 1953.

19 See Derrida, *Positions* (Paris: Minuit, 1972), p. 74: "Partout où s'imposaient les valeurs de propriété, de sens propre, de proximité à soi, d'étymologie, etc., à propos du corps, de la conscience, du langage,

de l'écriture, etc., j'ai essayé d'analyser le désir et les présupposés métaphysiques qui s'y trouvaient à l'oeuvre... 'La mythologie blanche' systématise la critique de l'étymologisme dans la philosophie et dans la rhétorique."

20 Paulhan, *La Preuve par l'étymologie*, p. 53.

21 *Ibid.*, pp. 81–82.

22 *Ibid.*, p. 20.

23 *Über den Gegensinn der Urworte*, reprinted in Karl Abel, *Sprachwissentschaftliche Abhandlungen* (Leipzig, 1885), pp. 311–67.

24 Quoted by Etiemble, "Jean Paulhan et le 'Gegensinn der Urworte,'" in Bersani, ed., *Jean Paulhan le souterrain*, p. 324. Freud's review of Abel's text is available in English (trans. M. N. Searl) in Freud, *On Creativity and the Unconscious* (New York: Harper & Row, 1958), pp. 55–62.

25 Quoted in Etiemble, "Jean Paulhan", p. 332.

26 *Ibid.*, p. 326.

27 M. Blanchot, *L'Amitié*, (Paris: Gallimard, 1971), p. 180.

28 Etiemble, "Jean Paulhan", p. 332.

29 "Paulhan le mystique," panel discussion in Bersani, ed., *Jean Paulhan le souterrain*, p. 372.

30 *Ibid.*, p. 374.

31 J. Derrida, "La Double Séance," in *La Dissémination* (Paris: Seuil, 1972), pp. 199–318.

32 *De la paille et du grain*, in Paulhan, *Oeuvres complètes* (Paris: Cercle du Livre Précieux, 1970), p. 316.

33 *Ibid.*, p. 353.

34 *Ibid.*

35 *Ibid.*, p. 380.

36 *Ibid.*, p. 329.

37 *Ibid.*, p. 353.

38 *Ibid.*

39 *Ibid.*

40 C. Péguy, *Notre jeunesse*, in *Oeuvres en prose: 1909–1914* (Paris: Gallimard, 1961), p. 587.

41 W. Benjamin, "On Some Motifs in Baudelaire," in *Illuminations*, trans. H. Zohn (New York: Schocken, 1969), p. 187.

42 *Lettre aux directeurs de la Résistance* (Paris: Pauvert, 1951), pp. 30–31.

43 Paulhan, *De la paille et du grain*, p. 329.

44 Reproduced as an appendix to P. Bourdieu, *Homo Academicus* (Paris: Minuit, 1984), p. 281.

45 G. Heller, *Un Allemand à Paris, 1940–1944* (Paris: Seuil, 1981).

46 *Ibid.*, p. 44.

47 *Ibid.*, p. 144.

48 *Ibid.*, p. 33.
49 *Ibid.*, p. 193.
50 *Ibid.*, p. 108.
51 Paulhan, *Les Incertitudes du langage* (Paris: Gallimard, 1970), pp. 154–55.
52 Heller, *Un Allemand à Paris*, p. 99.
53 *Ibid.*, p. 118.
54 *Ibid.*
55 *Ibid.*, p. 120.
56 Derrida, *"Qual quelle*: les sources de Valéry," in *Marges de la philosophie* (Paris: Minuit, 1973).

8 PERSPECTIVES: ON PAUL DE MAN AND *LE SOIR*

1 Emmanuel Levinas, "Jacques Derrida/Tout autrement," in *Noms propres* (Montpellier: Fata Morgana, 1976), p. 66. Levinas' essay originally appeared in an issue of *L'Arc* (54, 1973) dedicated to Derrida.
2 Concerning the havoc wreaked on psychological understanding *per se* by Hitler's *Blitzkrieg*, see, for example, de Man's article of 23 December 1941: "There was thus at no phase of the present conflict that settling into suffering ... which gave the 1914 war its quite peculiar psychological aspect." Similar remarks on the "shock" of sudden defeat can be found on 30 April 1942.
3 Paul de Man, *Allegories of Reading* (New Haven: Yale University Press, 1979), p. 63.
4 Geoffrey Hartman, "Blindness and Insight," in *The New Republic*, 7 March 1988, p. 31.
5 On the Belgian anti-Jewish decrees, see Raul Hilberg, *The Destruction of the European Jews* (New York: New Viewpoints, 1973), p. 384.
6 The Riom trial of Léon Blum, which was going disastrously for the Collaborators, began on 19 February 1942, and was still in session when de Man's article appeared. See Jean Lacouture, *Léon Blum* (Paris: Seuil, 1977), pp. 469–81.
7 On *Das innere Reich*, see Victor Farias, *Heidegger et le nazisme* (Paris: Verdier, 1987), pp. 250–51.
8 The sequence is well discussed in J. Recanati, *Profils juifs de Marcel Proust* (Paris: Buchet/Chastel, 1979), pp. 54–56.
9 See my *A Structural Study of Autobiography* (Ithaca: Cornell, 1974), pp. 200–64, and chapter 4, "Literature and Collaboration: Benoist-Méchin's return to Proust."
10 For a provocative reading of anti-Semitism as fundamentally a mode of estheticism, see Philippe Lacoue-Labarthe, *La Fiction du politique* (Paris: Christian Bourgois, 1987), pp. 92–113.

11 Marcel Proust, "Léon Daudet," in *Contre Sainte-Beuve* (Paris: Gallimard, 1954), pp. 439–40.

12 On 17–18 May 1942, for example, in *Het Vlaamsche Land*, "Contemporary Trends in French Literature," de Man wrote of Gide, Valéry, Claudel, and Proust as "the major figures, the leaders of the entire European world." In *Le Soir* itself, on 9 June 1942, Proust and Joyce are listed together as major innovators.

13 Paul de Man, "The Return to Philology," in *The Resistance to Theory* (Minneapolis: University of Minnesota Press, 1986), p. 22. The article originally appeared in *Times Literary Supplement*, 10 December 1982.

14 *Ibid.*, p. 25.

15 *Ibid.*, p. 26.

16 Geoffrey Hartman, "Blindness and Insight", p. 31.

17 Miller is thus quoted in Jon Wiener, "Deconstructing de Man," in *The Nation*, 9 January 1988, p. 23.

18 Christopher Norris, "Paul de Man's Past," in *London Review of Books*, 4 February 1988, p. 7.

19 Through a bizarre irony, deconstruction, at its most politically repugnant, has resorted to pairing off its "left-wing" and "right-wing" adversaries as equally deluded. I refer to Hillis Miller's vitriolic – and silly – presidential address to the MLA in 1986, well analyzed by Walter Kendrick in "De Man That Got Away," *The Village Voice, Voice Literary Supplement*, April 1988, p. 7.

20 The most extensive available compilation on Heidegger's Nazism is Farias, *Heidegger et le nazisme*. Of Lacoue-Labarthe's rather hostile critique of the book, the most important sentence appears to me to be: "as far as its documentary complexity is concerned, Farias cannot be reproached: the facts cited are, to my knowledge, incontestable." In *La Fiction du politique*, p. 180.

21 *Parages* and *De l'esprit* were published in Paris by Editions Galilée, *Mémoires* in New York by Columbia University Press.

22 For a discussion of Blanchot's role among fascist intellectuals of his generation, see my *Legacies: Of Anti-Semitism in France* (Minneapolis: University of Minnesota Press, 1983), chapter 1, as well as Zeev Sternhell, *Ni droite ni gauche: l'idéologie fasciste en France* (Paris: Seuil, 1982), pp. 241–42.

23 See chapter 6, "Iphigenia 38: deconstruction, history, and the case of *L'Arrêt de mort*." Derrida's analysis of *L'Arrêt de mort*, "Living On," first appeared in translation by James Hulbert in the collective volume *Deconstruction and Criticism* (New York: Seabury Press, 1979), pp. 75–176.

24 Jacques Derrida, *Mémoires: For Paul de Man* (New York: Columbia University Press, 1986), p. 19.

25 *Ibid.*, p. 21. It is perhaps worthwhile in this context to quote the fundamental affirmation of the proto-Nazi "Kridwiss circle" in Thomas Mann's "Nietzsche novel," *Doctor Faustus*, trans. H. T. Lowe-Porter (New York: Random House, 1948), p. 371: "It is coming, it is coming, and when it is here it will find us on the crest of the moment. It is interesting, it is even good, simply by virtue of being what is inevitably going to be, and to recognize it is sufficient of an achievement and satisfaction."

26 Jacques Derrida, *De l'esprit: Heidegger et la question* (Paris: Galilée, 1987), p. 66.

27 Quoted in *ibid.*, p. 95.

28 "Writing and Deference: The Politics of Literary Adulation," in *Representations* 15, pp. 1–14.

29 David Lehman, "Deconstructing de Man's Life," in *Newsweek*, 15 February 1988, p. 64.

30 See, for instance, Ann Smock's comments (along with my response) in *Representations* 18 (Spring, 1987), pp. 158–64. By virtue of having published my article, the editors of *Representations* themselves were consigned by Hillis Miller, in his 1986 presidential address to the MLA, to the benighted ranks of the "left-wing" adversaries of deconstruction.

31 That "deconstruction" or dispersion may already be at work in a moving page of Derrida's *Schibboleth: pour Paul Celan* (Paris: Galilee, 1986), p. 83: "il y a certes aujourd'hui la date de cet holocauste que nous savons, l'enfer de notre mémoire; mais il y a un holocauste pour chaque date ... Chaque heure compte son holocauste ..."

32 See de Man, "An Interview" (with Stefano Rosso) in *The Resistance to Theory*, p. 117, and Derrida, "In Memoriam," in *The Lesson of Paul de Man, Yale French Studies* 69, p. 14.

33 Paul de Man, "The Rhetoric of Blindness: Jacques Derrida's Reading of Rousseau," in *Blindness and Insight: Essays in the Rhetoric of Contemporary Criticism* (New York: Oxford University Press, 1971), pp. 131, 133.

34 Benno Weiser Varon, "Waldheim – A Post Mortem," in *Midstream*, November 1986, p. 18.

35 See Heinz Wismann and Katharina von Bulow, *Devant l'histoire: les documents de la controverse sur la singularité de l'extermination des Juifs par le régime nazi* (Paris: Editions du Cerf, 1988).

9 PROSOPOPEIA REVISITED

1 J. Derrida, "Like the Sound of the Sea Deep within a Shell: Paul de Man's War," in *Critical Inquiry* 14 (Spring 1988), pp. 590–652.

2 H. de Montherlant, *Le Solstice de juin* (Paris: Gallimard, 1976), p. 189.
3 Paul de Man, *The Resistance to Theory* (Minneapolis: University of Minnesota Press, 1968).
4 De Man's essay on Riffaterre also contains a curious misreading of Hegel. Riffaterre, in a striking analysis of the first page of *Glas*, unravels Derrida's bravura condensation of the *bel aujourd'hui* of Mallarmé's swan sonnet with the Now (and Here) of Hegel's chapter on Sense-Certainty in *The Phenomenology of Mind*. De Man quotes a fragment of Riffaterre's demonstration: "Hegel ... has no difficulty showing that *here* and *now* become false and misleading at the moment we write them down" (*The Resistance to Theory*, p. 41). His corrective follows: "This, as the saying goes, is hardly what Hegel said or meant to say ..." For language, we are told, "appears for the first time [later on] in the figure of a speaking consciousness" (p. 42). But it is sufficient to consult the text of *The Phenomenology* to see that Riffaterre was right. Hegel (in the Baillie translation [The Phenomenology of Mind, trans. J.B. Baillie (New York: Harper & Row, 1967)], p. 151): "To sense the truth of this certainty of sense, a simple experiment is all we need: write that truth down ... If we look again at the truth we have written down, look at it *now, at this noon-time*, we shall have to say it has turned stale and become out of date." Why the blooper? One has the sense that to the extent that Riffaterre was relegated by some to the status of *mere* technician of reading, de Man was eager to see in that apparently humble status something of major (i.e., deconstructive) significance. But to the extent that Riffaterre strayed out of "mere literature" – to such exalted precincts as Hegel and Derrida – it became imperative (even at the cost of the careless misreading just mentioned) to return him to his status as "mere" technician.

10   THE PARANOID STYLE IN FRENCH PROSE: LACAN WITH
LÉON BLOY

1 P. Drieu la Rochelle, *Sur les écrivains*, ed. F. Grover (Paris: Gallimard, 1964), p. 240. It was in Drieu's apartment that Lacan wrote his thesis on paranoia. On Lacan's relations with Drieu, see E. Roudinesco, *La Bataille de cent ans: Histoire de la psychanalyse en France*, vol. II (Paris: Seuil, 1986), p. 125, and D. Desanti, *Drieu la Rochelle ou le séducteur mystifié* (Paris: Flammarion, 1978), pp. 400, 419, 426–27.
2 J. Lacan, *Le Séminaire*, vol. XI (Paris: Seuil, 1973), pp. 172–73. I have discussed the more surprising implications of Lacan's reference to Bloy in "The Suture of an Allusion: Lacan with Léon Bloy," chapter

11 of *Legacies: Of Anti-Semitism in France* (Minneapolis, University of Minnesota Press, 1983), pp. 23–33.

3 M. Foucault, *Histoire de la sexualité*, vol. 1 (Paris: Gallimard, 1976), p. 198.

4 For a discussion of Céline's anti-Semitic writings – in terms of a "rage against the Symbolic" – coherent with the construct elaborated in this paper, see J. Kristeva, *Pouvoirs de l'horreur: Essai sur l'abjection* (Paris: Seuil, 1980), p. 209.

5 The tale first appeared in *Gil Blas* on 2 February 1894 and was anthologized as part of Bloy's *Histoires désobligeantes* (Paris: Dentu) in 1894. Citations in the text are from vol. VI of *Oeuvres de Léon Bloy*, ed. J. Bolléry and J. Petit (Paris: Mercure de France, 1967), pp. 308–12.

6 For a discussion of the inherent resistance of New Testament parables to *any* interpretation, see F. Kermode's analysis of the discordance between Mark and Matthew on the purpose of parables in "Hoti's Business: Why are Narratives Obscure?," chapter II of *The Genesis of Secrecy: On the Interpretation of Narrative* (Cambridge, Mass.: Harvard University Press, 1979), pp. 23–37.

7 In "Baudelaire with Freud: Theory and Pain," *Diacritics* 4: 1 (1974), I presented what is in many respects a Lacanian reading of *Le Spleen de Paris*. The present reading of Bloy – as indebted to Baudelaire and anticipatory of Lacan – is, then, at some level a genealogical critique of the residual metalinguistic assumptions of that earlier text.

8 Lacan, *Télévision* (Paris: Seuil, 1974), p. 28: "Venons-en donc au psychanalyste ... C'est qu'on ne saurait mieux le situer objectivement que de ce qui dans le passé s'est appelé: être un saint."

9 *Legacies: Of Anti-Semitism in France*, pp. 23–33.

10 Bloy, *Le Désespéré* (Paris: Mercure de France, 1964), p. 137.

11 Bloy, "L'Eunuque," in *Belluaires et porchers* (Paris: Pauvert, 1965), p. 153.

12 Bloy, *Le Désespéré*, p. 54.

13 Page references in the text are to the 1964 Mercure de France edition of *Le Désespéré*.

14 J. Derrida, *Glas* (Paris: Galilée, 1974), p. 52.

15 J. Lacan, *Ecrits* (Paris: Seuil, 1966), p. 403.

16 Among the characteristics of Caïn's enterprise that seem most anticipatory of Lacan's work (the irreducible "specularity" of human vision; the metaphysical "sexuality" of events [p. 199]; the definitive humbling of the ego), none seems as pregnant as this characterization of Caïn's prose style: "Ce style en débâcle et *innavigable* qui avait toujours l'air de tomber d'une alpe, roulait n'importe quoi dans sa fureur" (p. 130). Any reader who has paused to admire the elephant on the cover of the first volume of *Le Séminaire: Les écrits techniques de*

Freud (Paris: Seuil, 1975) will appreciate the force of Bloy's *n'importe quoi.*

17 *Oeuvres de Bloy*, vol. VI, p. 362.

18 *Belluaires et porchers*, p. 23: "Il y a deux sortes de triomphants: les Belluaires et les Porchers. Les uns sont faits pour dompter les monstres, les autres pour pâturer les bestiaux."

19 See M.-J. Lory, *Léon Bloy et son époque (1870–1914)* (Paris: Desclée de Brouwer, 1944), pp. 94–96.

20 *Léon Bloy devant les cochons* (Paris: Chamuel, 1894).

21 S. Freud, "Psychoanalytical Notes upon an Autobiographical Account of a Case of Paranoia," in *Three Case Histories* (New York: Collier, 1968), p. 115.

22 S. Freud, "From the History of an Infantile Neurosis," in *Standard Edition*, vol. XVII, p. 85.

23 Lacan, "Du traitement possible de la psychose," in *Ecrits*, p. 558.

24 Lacan, "Réponse au commentaire de Jean Hyppolite," in *Ecrits*, p. 388.

25 In the process, the Jewish intruder of "Propos digestifs," Catulle Mendès, turns into the persecutory host of *Le Désespéré*. As paranoia, indeed, might demand ... Does that anti-Semitic motif find any resonance in Lacan's *Ecrits?* Consider the twin readings to which the myth of Acteon is available in "La Chose freudienne." On the one hand, all psychoanalysts are called on to play Acteon: given the radical nature of the – "castratory" – truth (nude Diana) he discovers, the psychoanalyst (Acteon) is called on to bear witness to the violation of the integrity of his ego by his "own" unconscious drives (dogs). On the other hand, the text is so consistently concerned with the mangling of Freud's insights by his followers that *they* appear to be so many hounds guilty of destroying the integrity of Freud's (or Acteon's) message. Now those disloyal followers are referred to as a "diaspora" of "emigrants" and – in the Rome discourse – as a group so intent on assimilation to their new host country, the United States, that they managed to convert psychoanalysis into an ideology of adaptation (pp. 402, 245). The villains of this scenario, that is, are less Americans than Jews migrated to America. Freud-Acteon, on the other hand, is said to be inspired by "un souci proprement chrétien de l'authenticité du mouvement de l'âme" (p. 407). As for Diana in her bath, given the fact that Truth, before appearing twice as Diana, is presented as a torch-bearing nude, we are hard put not to read the (torch-bearing, "bathing") Statue of Liberty, past which Freud and Jung sail on their way to Clark University, as the first instance of the "Diana series" in "La Chose freudienne." But that would be of a piece with the allegorization of the Jewish immigrant

analysts as Diana's hounds: they are indeed the dogs of Liberty. The two readings of the Acteon myth, then, correspond to the "analytic" ("prefigurative") and "paranoid" ("disfigurative") strands we have isolated in Bloy. The latter version, moreover, corresponds to Christian typology's interpretation of the Acteon myth: the hounds as Jews; Acteon as Christ; Diana as the Trinity. (That reading is recorded in an essay by one of Bloy's more prominent contemporaries, Rémy de Gourmont, *La Culture des idées* [Paris: 10/18, 1983], p. 168). How anomalous is the incipient anti-Jewishness of the second interpretation of the myth? Roudinesco is unambiguous in affirming Lacan's freedom from the French chauvinism – and racism – that "marked the first wave of the introduction of psychoanalysis" in France (Roudinesco, *La Bataille de cent ans*, p. 138). Yet she does so after relating the brokered entry of Lacan to the ranks of the training analysts of the Société Psychanalytique de Paris. In 1938, he was the *protégé* of Edouard Pichon, leading French analyst, eccentric grammarian of the French language, and committed partisan of the royalist movement Action Française. Pichon agreed to support the election of Heinz Hartmann, in flight from Hitler, to the Parisian Society in exchange for support – otherwise not forthcoming – for the candidacy of Lacan. Hartmann would later be a leader of the "diaspora" of "immigrant analysts"; Pichon's work – on French grammar – would later supply Lacan with the term "forclusion," his translation for Freud's *Verwerfung*, interpreted as *the* defense mechanism specific to psychosis. There was thus at the inception of Lacan's career as an analyst a conflict between immigrant Jew and French nationalist that it would not be surprising to see revived during the numerous crises marking the remainder of his career.

26 Lacan, *Le Séminaire*, vol. i, p. 264.
27 *Ibid.*
28 The best history of that development is Roudinesco, *La Bataille de cent ans*. I have translated a number of the relevant documents in *October* 40 (1987).
29 As though Lacan had all along been whistling the same tune as his contemporary, Sartre: "Some of these days, you're gonna miss me, honey." For an analysis of the ramifications of those lyrics through Sartre's work, see D. Hollier, *The Politics of Prose: Essay on Sartre*, trans. J. Mehlman (Minneapolis: University of Minnesota Press, 1987).
30 Lacan, "Letter of Dissolution," 5 January 1980.
31 Bloy, *Belluaires et porchers* (Paris: Mercure de France, 1964), p. 15.
32 Lacan, *Le Séminaire*, vol. i, p. 269.
33 Lacan, *Le Séminaire*, vol. xx, p. 70.

II THE HOLOCAUST COMEDIES OF "EMILE AJAR"

1 Concerning Romain Gary's years in Los Angeles, see his *La Nuit sera calme* (Paris: Gallimard, 1974), pp. 238–88.

2 See Jean-Marie Catonné, *Romain Gary/Emile Ajar* (Paris: Belfond, 1990), p. 102. In addition, a journalist, rummaging through police files, discovered the existence of a Lebanese terrorist named "Hamil Raja," who was temporarily suspected of being Ajar. For details of the Gary/Ajar saga, Catonné's intelligent and imaginative book, on which I have drawn in this paragraph, is the best guide.

3 Pavlowitch, who has written his own version of the Ajar affair, *L'Homme que l'on croyait* (Paris: Fayard, 1981), was in fact the son of Gary's cousin Dinah, but was frequently referred to by Gary as his nephew.

4 See Catonné, *Romain Gary*, p. 103.

5 Paris: Gallimard, 1981.

6 *Ibid.*, p. 18.

7 *Ibid.*, p. 43.

8 *Gros-Câlin* (Paris: Mercure de France, 1974), p. 212.

9 *La Nuit sera calme*, p. 198.

10 *L'Angoisse du roi Salomon* (Paris: Mercure de France, 1979), p. 348.

11 The pseudo-psychiatric memoir *Pseudo* appears to be in part indebted to Louis Wolfson, whose *Le Schizo et les langues* (Paris: Gallimard, 1970) had recently been prefaced by Gilles Deleuze. Concerning Wolfson, see my "Portnoy in Paris," in *Diacritics* 2: 4 (1972).

12 *Vie et mort d'Emile Ajar*, p. 36.

13 Jorge Luis Borges, "Pierre Menard, Author of *Don Quixote*," in *Ficciones* (New York: Grove Weidenfeld, 1962), pp. 45–55. For a discussion of French intertexts of the Borges fable, see chapter 5, " 'Pierre Menard, author of *Don Quixote*' again."

14 *Vie et mort d'Emile Ajar*, p. 14.

15 *La Promesse de l'aube* (Paris: Gallimard, 1960), p. 551.

16 *Ibid.*, p. 296.

17 *Ibid.*, p. 297.

18 *Ibid.*, p. 48.

19 *Ibid.*, p. 346.

20 *Gros-Câlin*, p. 85.

21 *Ibid.*, p. 66.

22 *Ibid.*, p. 36.

23 Thus, when the python temporarily disappears, Cousin wonders if it is not a result of the "emotion" aroused by Cousin's would-be fiancée, who has announced her intention to pay him a first visit. *Gros-Câlin*, p. 148.

24 *Ibid.*, p. 51.
25 *Ibid.*, p. 208.
26 *Ibid.*, p. 15.
27 *La Promesse de l'aube*, p. 245.
28 *Ibid.*, p. 246
29 *Ibid.*, p. 248.
30 *Gros-Câlin*, p. 181. See also *Pseudo* (Paris: Mercure de France, 1976), p. 16: "J'ai alors demandé au bon docteur si je n'avais pas été conduit à devenir un python parce que les Juifs avaient été propagés depuis deux mille ans comme usuriers et boas étrangleurs, et il m'a répondu que c'était parfaitement possible, j'étais capable de tout pour faire de la littérature, y compris de moi-même."
31 *La Vie devant soi* (Paris: Mercure de France, 1975), p. 29.
32 *Ibid.*, p. 79.
33 *Ibid.*, p. 76.
34 *La Promesse de l'aube*, p. 21.
35 *La Vie devant soi*, p. 133.
36 *Ibid.*, p. 137.
37 *Ibid.*, p. 188.
38 *Ibid.*, p. 200.
39 The nodality of the King Solomon motif for our author during his Ajar years is further sustained by an examination of Gary's play of 1979, *La Bonne Moitié*. Adapted from his early novel *Le Grand Vestiaire* (1948), it plays with the Solomonic motif of cutting a human being in two. Vanderputte, like Madame Rosa, is an ailing benefactor, running a clandestine "orphanage." A member of the anti-Nazi Resistance, he takes care of children of the Germans' victims once the War is over. In mid-play we discover that he *also* spent half the war *collaborating* with the Gestapo. Whence the impossible Solomonic imperative: "Il faut le couper en deux, décorer une moitié et fusiller le reste" (Paris: Gallimard, 1979), p. 81.
40 *L'Angoisse du roi Salomon*, p. 333.
41 It may be added that whereas Aline is a contemporary of Jeannot's and erotically available to him, Nadine, her counterpart in the earlier novel, is no more than a (married) adult companion and guide for Momo.
42 *La Promesse de l'aube*, p. 189.
43 *Ibid.*, p. 185.
44 *Au-delà de cette limite votre ticket n'est plus valable*, p. 138.
45 See Pavlowitch, *L'Homme que l'on croyait*, p. 74.
46 *L'Angoisse du roi Salomon*, p. 95.
47 See Jeffrey Mehlman, *Legacies: Of Anti-Semitism in France* (Minneapolis: University of Minnesota Press, 1983), p. 61.

48 *La Danse de Gengis Cohn* (Paris: Gallimard, 1967), p. 272.

49 One risk of the allegorical amnesty implemented by the completion of the Ajar project is apparent in Michel Tournier's essay "Emile Ajar ou la vie derrière soi" (in *Le Vol du vampire: Notes de lecture* [Paris: Mercure de France, 1981]). To speak of the author's philo-Semitism, as Tournier does, as "une certaine sémitophilie," is to suggest (through contamination by the more common term *hémophilie*) a pathological condition. Speaking of Ajar's interest in the Occupation period, Tournier continues: "Madame Rosa et le roi Salomon sont pour Ajar les témoins irremplaçables d'une tragédie douteuse, baignant dans une lumière glauque, mais qui avait paradoxalement le pouvoir de révéler les êtres dans leur vérité" (p. 339). To affix the epithet "dubious [*douteuse*]" to the Jewish tragedy of the generation of Madame Rosa and Salomon is to align oneself with the "revisionist" mystifications of Robert Faurisson. Although Gary/Ajar in no way shared such a tendency, it is clear that the final Ajar novel, with its allegorical amnesty, is available to such a misreading.

12 *POUR SAINTE-BEUVE*: MAURICE BLANCHOT, 10 MARCH 1942

1 The relevant portion of the letter is excerpted in my *Legacies: Of Anti-Semitism in France* (Minneapolis: University of Minnesota Press, 1983), p. 117.

2 See chapter 6.

3 Philippe Ariès, *Un historien du dimanche* (Paris: Seuil, 1980), p. 184.

4 Pascal Fouché, *L'Edition française sous l'Occupation, 1940–1944* (Paris: Bibliothèque de la Littérature française de l'Université de Paris 7, 1987) vol. II, p. 80.

5 Pierre Hebey, *La NRF des années sombres: 1940–1941* (Paris: Gallimard, 1992), p. 136. In Drieu's recently published *Journal* of the years 1939–45 (Paris: Gallimard, 1992, p. 290), we find the author, on 2 March 1942, a week prior to the appearance of the text of Blanchot's which will occupy us, writing: "il me faut un secrétaire à la revue qui me débarrasse du plus gros travail."

6 Pierre Andreu and Frederic Grover, *Drieu la Rochelle* (Paris: Hachette, 1979), p. 489.

7 See chapter 7 for a discussion of the paradoxes of Paulhan's own insertion into the Resistance.

8 Jean Paulhan, *Choix de lettres*, II (1937–1945) (Paris: Gallimard, 1992), p. 280.

9 *Ibid.*, p. 280.

10 For a discussion of Paul de Man's writings during the war, see chapter 9.

11 Maxime Leroy, *La Politique de Sainte-Beuve* (Paris: Gallimard, 1941).
12 Paul Guth, *Histoire de la littérature française* (Paris: Fayard, 1967), vol. II, p. 344.
13 "Compte rendu de la réception de Falloux à l'Académie française," cited in Guth, *Histoire*, p. 345.
14 C.-A. Sainte-Beuve, *Causeries du lundi*, vol. VI (Paris: Garnier, 1853), p. 327.
15 *Ibid.*, p. 336.
16 *Ibid.*, p. 328.
17 *Ibid.*, p. 335.
18 See Roger L. Williams, *The World of Napoleon III: 1851–1870* (New York: Collier, 1957), p. 127: Sainte-Beuve "laughed loudest about the censorship which deprived the Orleanists of publicity."
19 "Les Regrets," p. 335.
20 *Ibid.*, p. 329.
21 *Ibid.*, p. 337: "Cette réfutation, qui s'est fait attendre, prouverait seule combien l'article a touché juste."
22 Cited in Guth, *Histoire*, p. 346.
23 *Ibid.*, p. 347.
24 *Ibid.*, p. 348.
25 *Ibid.* Williams (*The World of Napoleon III*) quotes a letter of Flaubert's to George Sand on how Sainte-Beuve's loyalty to the regime had been bought, p. 130: "when [the princess] has given you an income of thirty thousand francs a year [the Senate], you owe her a certain consideration."
26 Hannah Arendt, *The Origins of Totalitarianism* (New York: Harcourt Brace Jovanovich, 1951), pp. 89–120.
27 Republished in Charles Maurras, *Oeuvres capitales: Essais politiques* (Paris: Flammarion, 1954), pp. 63–97.
28 *Ibid.*, p. 84.
29 *Ibid.*, p. 83.
30 See passage from Zeev Sternhell, *Ni droite ni gauche: L'idéologie fasciste en France* (Paris: Seuil, 1983) quoted in chapter 6, note 20.
31 Maurras, *Oeuvres capitales*, p. 63.
32 Paul Morand, for example, would write an essay in praise of Vichy's recovery of France's provinces and the withering away of her artificially instituted departments. From his *Chronique de l'homme maigre* (Paris: Grasset, 1941), p. 39: "Nous allons donc perdre nos départements et retrouver nos provinces. Moment depuis si longtemps attendu ..."
33 Maurras, *Oeuvres capitales*, p. 71.
34 *Ibid.*, p. 75.
35 *Ibid.*, p. 77.

36 *Ibid.*
37 *Ibid.*, p. 78.
38 *Ibid.*, p. 81.
39 *Ibid.*
40 *Ibid.*
41 In a review of Leroy's book in the April 1942 issue of the *NRF*, Ramon Fernandez could write (p. 485): Sainte-Beuve "a prévu une justice et une morale sur des bases nouvelles ... une justice et une morale enfin comme on les voit aujourd'hui promises ou ébauchées autour de nous."
42 Leroy, *La Politique de Sainte-Beuve*, p. 8.
43 *Ibid.*, p. 95.
44 *Ibid.*, p. 15.
45 *Ibid.*, p. 218.
46 By 1833, shortly after the July revolution, Sainte-Beuve had attained a level of disillusionment anticipatory of Marx's prose on the Second Empire. He wrote (cited in Leroy, *La Politique de Sainte-Beuve*, p. 129) of "l'écume vraiment immonde" bubbling to the top of French society: "les corrompus de dix régimes coalisés avec les roués d'hier, les parvenus acharnés, les intrus encore tout suants, les avocats-ministres tombés dans l'obésité."
47 Leroy, *La Politique de Sainte-Beuve*, p. 194.
48 Nothing is more telling in this regard than Leroy's delight in the lesson in proletarian materialism Sainte-Beuve felt called on to deliver to Tocqueville in 1848. See *Ibid.*, p. 177.
49 *Ibid.*, p. 273.
50 *Ibid.*, p. 212. Walter Benjamin, in his *Passagen-Werk* (Frankfurt: Suhrkamp, 1983, vol. II, pp. 725–26) quotes tellingly from Michel Chevalier's *Fin du choléra par un coup d'état, Religion Saint-Simonienne*: "Il faut un coup d'état, un coup d'état industriel."
51 Proudhon, however, as Benjamin observed in his *Passagen-Werk* (p. 738), was a "vehement adversary" of what he called "la pourriture saint-simonienne." Sternhell (*Ni droite ni gauche*, p. 199) notes that it was the neo-Socialist strand of French fascism (B. Montagnon) that issued appeals to "le vieux socialisme français de Saint-Simon et de Proudhon."
52 Leroy, *La Politique de Sainte-Beuve*, p. 212.
53 For a discussion of the Cercle Proudhon, see Zeev Sternhell, *La Droite révolutionnaire, 1885–1914: Les origines françaises du fascisme* (Paris: Seuil, 1978), pp. 391–400.
54 Leroy, *La Politique de Sainte-Beuve*, p. 273.
55 Isaiah Berlin, "Joseph de Maistre and the Origins of Fascism," in *The Crooked Timber of Humanity: Chapters in the History of Ideas* (New

York: Vintage, 1992), p. 170. Berlin refers to Sainte-Beuve as providing the "best account" of de Maistre.

56 Cited in Leroy, *La Politique de Sainte-Beuve*, p. 67.

57 See Williams, *The World of Napoleon III*, p. 127.

58 Leroy, *La Politique de Sainte-Beuve*, p. 73.

59 *Ibid.*, p. 74.

60 Benjamin, *Passagen-Werk*, p. 709.

61 *Ibid.*, p. 718.

62 See Maurice Blanchot, "Penser l'Apocalypse," in *Le Nouvel Observateur*, 22–28 January 1988, p. 43: Lacoue-Labarthe's book is said to confront the reader with "des questions essentielles." The volume was dedicated to Blanchot.

63 Philippe Lacoue-Labarthe, *La Fiction du politique: Heidegger, l'art, et la politique* (Paris: Bourgois, 1987), p. 97.

64 Gaetan Sanvoisin, "La Médaille de Richelieu," in *Journal des débats*, 4 March 1942. The comment takes on a certain drollery when one recalls de Gaulle's pre-War task as Pétain's ghostwriter for the book Pétain hoped would secure him his place in the Académie Française. See my "De Gaulle With and Against Pétain: The Theme of the Traitor and the Hero" (forthcoming).

65 Marcel Bastier, "Le Discours de M. Pierre Pucheu," in *Journal des débats*, 10 March 1942.

66 Leroy, *La Politique de Sainte-Beuve*, p. 205.

67 Irving Babbitt, *Masters of Modern French Criticism* (Boston: Houghton Mifflin Company, 1912), p. 106.

68 Thus Blanchot, plainly in retreat from his political past, in the article under discussion, refers to "le peu de profit que tous les vrais littérateurs et les esprits critiques ont à se mêler à des groupes politiques toujours plus ou moins intolérants."

69 Leroy, *La Politique de Sainte-Beuve*, p. 273.

70 Henri Brémond, *Le Roman et l'histoire d'une conversion: Ulrich Guttinguer et Sainte-Beuve d'après des correspondances inédites* (Paris: Plon, 1925).

71 *Ibid.*, p. 117.

72 See Jacques Chouillet, *La Formation des idées esthétiques de Diderot* (Paris: Armand Colin, 1973), p. 501: "Iphigénie est de toute évidence le prototype de soeur Suzanne. La religieuse, comme la fille d'Agamemnon, incarne la victime qu'on porte aux pieds des autels, elle est l'image du sacrifice humain."

73 J. M. Thompson, *Leaders of the French Revolution* (Oxford: Blackwell, 1968), p. 3.

74 Sainte-Beuve, *Causeries du lundi* (Paris: Garnier, 1852), vol. v, p. 174.

75 Maurice Blanchot, *La Folie du jour* (Paris: Fata Morgana, 1973), p. 33.

13 FLOWERS OF EVIL: PAUL MORAND, THE COLLABORATION, AND
   LITERARY HISTORY

1 Marcel Proust, Preface to *Tendres stocks* (Paris: Gallimard, 1921), p. 11.

2 *Ibid.*, p. 12.

3 *Les Plaisirs et les jours* (Paris: Gallimard, 1971).

4 *Fancy Goods* (New York: New Directions, 1984).

5 Quoted in B. Vercier and J. Lecarme, *La Littérature française depuis 1968* (Paris: Bordas, 1982), p. 24.

6 J.-P. Sartre, *What Is Literature?*, trans. B. Frechtman (Cambridge, Mass.: Harvard University Press, 1988), p. 161.

7 P. Hebey, *La Nouvelle Revue française des années sombres* (Paris: Gallimard, 1992), p. 394.

8 Morand's final wartime assignment was as ambassador to Berne. See J. Assouline, *Une éminence grise: Jean Jardin* (Paris: Gallimard, 1986), pp. 189–98.

9 J. Brenner, *Histoire de la littérature française: de 1940 à nos jours* (Paris: Fayard, 1978), p. 86: "Après la Seconde Guerre mondiale, il allait préférer les voyages dans le temps aux voyages dans l'espace."

10 Sartre, *What is Literature?*, p. 188.

11 H. Rousso, *The Vichy Syndrome: History and Memory in France since 1944*, trans. A. Goldhammer (Cambridge: Harvard University Press, 1991), p. 66.

12 *Ibid.*, p. 67.

13 J. Bersani, M. Autrand, J. Lecarme, B. Vercier, *La Littérature française depuis 1945* (Paris: Bordas, 1970); and B. Vercier, J. Lecarme, *La Littérature française depuis 1968*.

14 P. Sollers, "Preface" in Morand, *New York* (Paris: Flammarion, 1981), p. 7.

15 *L'Europe galante* (Paris: Grasset, 1925); *Le Flagellant de Séville* (Paris: Fayard, 1951); *France-la-doulce* (Paris: Gallimard, 1934).

16 P. Morand, *Nouvelles complètes*, vol. 1, ed. Michel Collomb (Paris: Gallimard, 1992), p. 987.

17 A. de Musset, *Lorenzaccio* (Paris: Classiques Larousse, 1971), p. 36.

18 *Ibid.*, p. 45.

19 *Ibid.*, p. 122.

20 *Ibid.*, p. 123.

21 *Ibid.*, p. 110.

22 Sartre, *Un théâtre de situations*, ed. M. Contat and M. Rybalka (Paris: Gallimard, 1973), p. 225.

23 Musset, *Lorenzaccio*, p. 28. One should not, however, underestimate the inefficiency of the censors. G. and J.-R. Ragache, *La Vie quoti-*

dienne des écrivains et des artistes sous l'occupation, 1940–1944 (Paris: Hachette, 1988), report a provincial tour of the play during the War by the Compagnie du Regain. It is hard to imagine that act I, scene II went uncensored.

24 *Ibid.*, pp. 84, 93.
25 Morand, "1958, Choses prévues" (*Candide*, May 1928).
26 Morand, "Lorenzaccio," in *L'Europe galante* (Paris: Grasset, 1925), p. 79.
27 Morand, *Nouvelles complètes*, Edition de la Pléiade, p. 987.
28 "Lorenzaccio," p. 86.
29 G. Wright, *France in Modern Times* (Chicago: Rand McNally, 1960), p. 308.
30 "Lorenzaccio," p. 88.
31 *Ibid.*, p. 94.
32 Morand, *Nouvelles complètes*, Edition de la Pléiade, p. 988.
33 Quoted in M. Burrus, *Paul Morand: Voyageur du XXe siècle* (Paris: Séguier, 1986), p. 139.
34 Morand, "Le Festin de pierre," in *Nouvelle Revue française*, December 1940, pp. 73, 75.
35 See in particular chapter 23 of *La Chartreuse*, in which Mosca exults in giving orders to fire on the people and kill three thousand men "if necessary . . ."
36 *Monplaisir . . . en littérature* (Paris: Gallimard, 1967), p. 104
37 Stendhal, *La Chartreuse de Parme* (Paris: Garnier, 1961), p. 391.
38 Fabrizio, like Oedipus, is in flight from his (apparent) father, and undergoes a violent encounter with Robert, his actual father, at Waterloo.
39 I. Howe, "Stendhal: The Politics of Survival," in V. Brombert, *Stendhal: Twentieth Century Views* (Englewood Cliffs: Prentice Hall, 1962), p. 90.
40 Stendhal, *La Chartreuse de Parme*, p. 304.
41 Quoted in H. Levin, *The Gates of Horn: Five French Realists* (New York: Oxford University Press, 1963), p. 91.
42 M. Foucault, *Surveiller et punir: naissance de la prison* (Paris: Gallimard, 1975).
43 Morand, *Le Flagellant de Séville* (Paris: Fayard, 1951), p. 61.
44 See I. Howe, "Stendhal: The Politics of Survival," p. 91.
45 *Le Flagellant*, p. 262.
46 *Monplaisir . . . en littérature*, p. 105.
47 *Le Flagellant*, p. 311.
48 J. Miller, *The Passion of Michel Foucault* (New York: Simon and Schuster, 1993).
49 *Le Flagellant*, p. 20.

50 *Ibid.*, p. 22.
51 *Ibid.*, p. 34.
52 Morand, "Stendhal chez Marie-Louise," in *Monplaisir ... en histoire* (Paris: Gallimard, 1969), p. 91.
53 Morand, *Fouquet ou le soleil offusqué* (Paris: Gallimard, 1961), p. 65.
54 Céline, *D'un château l'autre* (Paris: Gallimard, 1957), p. 106.
55 W. Benjamin, "Theses on the Philosophy of History," in *Illuminations* (New York: Schocken, 1968), pp. 253–64.
56 *Ibid.*, p. 23.
57 *Ibid.*, p. 261.
58 For a discussion of the purges among the intelligentsia, see P. Assouline, *L'Epuration des intellectuels: 1944–1945* (Brussels: Complexe, 1991).
59 *Le Flagellant*, p. 383.
60 *Ibid.*
61 Paris: Gallimard, 1934.
62 For a discussion of the Jewish cult of Napoleon and the messianic expectations he bore, see F. Kobler, *Napoleon and the Jews* (New York: Schocken, 1975).
63 For a reading of the anti-Semitic resonances of Gide's *sotie*, see my *Legacies: Of Anti-Semitism in France* (Minneapolis: University of Minnesota Press, 1983), chapter IV.
64 *France-la-doulce*, p. 73.
65 *Ibid.*, p. 51.
66 *Ibid.*
67 *Ibid.*, p. 86.
68 *Ibid.*, p. 9.
69 *Ibid.*, p. 122.
70 *Ibid.*, p. 138.
71 *Ibid.*, p. 210.
72 *Ibid.*, p. 216.
73 See Burrus, *Paul Morand*, p. 126.
74 For a discussion of the anti-Semitism of *Pleins pouvoirs*, see my *Legacies*, chapter III.
75 Quoted in G. Guitard-Auviste, *Paul Morand* (Paris: Hachette, 1981), p. 183.

Index

Cambridge Studies in French

General editor: Malcolm Bowie (*All Souls College, Oxford*)
Editorial Board: R. Howard Bloch (*University of California, Berkeley*),
Terence Cave (*St John's College, Oxford*), Ross Chambers (*University of Michigan*), Antoine Compagnon (*Columbia University*), Peter France (*University of Edinburgh*), Christie McDonald (*Harvard University*), Toril Moi (*Duke University*), Naomi Schor (*Harvard University*)

Also in the series (* denotes titles now out of print)